the word's body

word's body

AN INCARNATIONAL

AESTHETIC

OF INTERPRETATION

Alla Bozarth-Campbell

THE UNIVERSITY OF ALABAMA PRESS
UNIVERSITY, ALABAMA

Library of Congress Cataloging in Publication Data

Bozarth-Campbell, Alla, 1947–
   The word's body.

   Bibliography: p.
   Includes index.
   1. Hermeneutics.   2. Aesthetics.   I. Title.
BD241.B67   121   79–111
ISBN 0-8173-0009-0

contents

This book is dedicated to my grandmother, Alice Delphine Williams, from whom I inherited my love for the sensual word, and to my mother, Alvina Heckel, who gave me many worlds through her many languages.

acknowledgments

The author wishes to thank the publishers of Harcourt Brace Jovanovich, Inc., for kind permission to quote from T. S. Eliot, *The Complete Poems and Plays,* copyright © 1952 by Harcourt, Brace and Company.

Deep gratitude is due to those persons whose generous gifts of time, energy, and presence have made this book possible. My thanks go to Elizabeth Kedney Campbell for her gracious support and help in gathering materials, and to Cornelia Van Esso for preparing the typescript.

Profound thanks are here extended to the two scholars and teachers who are also gifted performers of the word, and whose exceptionally perceptive textbooks have served as the sustaining inspiration for this book. It has been my personal great good fortune to experience the art of interpretation through these persons as an increasingly stimulating, challenging, and, above all, *love-able* vocation. To Professor Wallace A. Bacon and Professor Leland H. Roloff, for their wisdom, vision, and courage, and for integrity of intellect, heart, and will—my deepest thanks.

Finally I wish to thank the one person whose encouragement, insight, and self-giving labor of love helped me to bring this work to fruition—my friend, colleague, and spouse, Phil Bozarth-Campbell.

author's note

Readers may notice that the textual language of this book carefully avoids conventional male gender bias. As a woman and a scholar committed to authenticity in words, I have attempted to use language which is as accurate—that is, inclusive of the human condition—as is possible. However, I believe that I do not have a right to tamper with other authors' language, so for the most part I have left unchanged male gender bias or anachronistic God-language when quoting other sources. This consideration leaves me with the somewhat uncomfortable tension of two kinds of integrity: a fidelity to language and a fidelity to other writers' use of language. In expressing my dilemma at the beginning I hope to share with you the intent and, to an extent, the genuine twofold concern, of my position in these times of social and linguistic transition.

the
word's
body

one

INTRODUCTION:
TOWARD AN INCARNATIONAL AESTHETIC OF INTERPRETATION

The scope of this book is binary. First, in the broadest sense the whole process of the interpretation of literature as a psychophysical act becomes the subject of exploration. Second, the narrowing of this act into a specific art form—that of the performance of literature which includes the work itself, the interpreter, and an audience—becomes the aesthetic model for the development of an extended metaphor. The purpose of the metaphor is to provide a clearer understanding of the whole aesthetic process of the interpretation and performance of literature.

The two focal points of this same process, in my mind, are always connected, though I speak of them separately as general and specific, or broad and narrow, aspects of the one function of human being meeting literary being. Certainly, all literature exists only within the human body, mind, and feeling spirit, for as the primary metaphor of this book indicates, the *word* exists only as it comes alive in our flesh. This exploration begins, then, with the position of *meeting between* a human person and a work of literature that results in the speaking and hearing and final embodiment of the word within human flesh, blood, and psyche. The meeting and ensuing process may be through either an individual's private (I do not say *silent*) reading of a piece of literature or a public enactment by one or more persons in the presence of one or more persons.

Whether interpretation is private or public, as I have described these, the human act of interpreting literature always involves *performance*. To my way of thinking and as a direct result of my own experience, the written word only becomes *real* when it is physically spoken and heard within the human body and by the human ear. Even the private reader engages in a physical act of taking in the words from the external page, of actually inviting them into the body through the eyes, after which the aural functions of the brain immediately come into play. We have medical evidence of this phenomenon, for patients following certain kinds of throat surgery are told to refrain from any type of reading, since even during supposedly "silent" reading the throat muscles move along with those of the eye, perhaps in atavistic memory of the time when words were only uttered and never plastered in print, or perhaps in response to the simple need of the human organism to translate language from sight to sound.

I begin this study by stating my belief that the good private reader is as much a performing artist as is a public interpreter. Both are interpreting the word—mediating it through their own bodies and total selves—and both are experiencing both the word's and their own forms yielding to one another, meeting each other through the act of *per*formance: *form coming through.*

Whether interpretation of literature—with its simultaneous embodiment in performance—is private or public, it is a human art having as its goal the communion between poem and interpreter. I use the word "poem" to mean any imaginative work of literature. (Likewise, I shall be calling the maker of any such work "poet" throughout this book unless I specify that either word is to be taken in its narrower sense.) In interpretation the poem becomes truly lived experience and is finally presented to the world in a transformed state. Again, this world may be the private world of a single reader alone in her or his chair, or it may be the public world of stage, church, auditorium, electronic media, or artist's chamber. In the latter case we are talking about an event that includes poem, interpreter, and audience in the shared experience of communion—communion of the living word. (In private reading the interpreter is also the audience.)

To avoid confusion as much as possible in this unfolding search for an aesthetic of performance, having stated my belief in the equal validity of private and public interpretation, from now on I shall use interpretation/performance in the narrower sense of a public event unless otherwise defined in a concrete instance. This deliberate limitation is in order to sharpen our focus on interpretation as a *model* for an aesthetic of performance as a public, social art form that creates and enhances human community.

The ideal performance, the performance toward which every serious interpreter strives, is seen here as both a creative process and a transforming event. It is the purpose of this book to explore the nature of both the process and the final event of the performance of literature in terms of the concept of incarnation.

The study will proceed by means of a sustained metaphor in which the art of interpretation is yoked with the act of incarnation in its theological sense.

The metaphor seems highly appropriate as an approach to interpretation, for interpretation is itself a metaphor. It is the coming together of poem as a real being and interpreter as a real being in order to create a *new* being, in which the integrity of each is still preserved, and this new being is what is presented and *present* in the act of interpretation. This unique meeting with its resultant new being is the primary metaphor of interpretation.

It is the act of interpretation as a phenomenon with which this study is concerned—phenomenon in its etymological sense as that which is capable of being, and allows itself to be, brought to light—that which shows itself.[1] Richard E. Palmer explains that

> phenomenology means letting things become manifest as what they are, without forcing our own categories on them. It means a reversal of direction from that one is accustomed to: it is not we who point to things; rather, things show themselves to us. This is not to suggest some primitive animism but the recognition that the very essense of true understanding is that of being led by the power of the thing to manifest itself. . . . Phenomenology is a means of being led by the phenomenon through a way of access genuinely belonging to it.[2]

While this study makes no claims to be "phenomenological" in its approach, it is with the phenomenon of interpretation (as Palmer describes that word) that the study is concerned. The importance of the last sentence in the passage quoted cannot be overemphasized.

What is needed is to approach the phenomenon of interpretation "through a way of access genuinely belonging to it." Seeking a way of access belonging to interpretation means discovering the observable characteristics of its processes and entering into a dialogue with them— questioning, listening, and responding to them. By entering into relationship with its subject matter this study hopes to encounter what is actually happening in the interpretive process and event. Through dialogue the phenomenon of interpretation may come to reveal what was hidden in itself, to show its own processes of rendering what was invisible and inaudible in literature both visible and audible in a dynamic presence. The art of interpretation begins as a dialogue between poem and interpreter, and this dialogue is a *speaking* relationship. Speaking is at the center of interpretation and is one "way of access genuinely belonging to it." At the center of speech is *word.* In the context of the metaphor of incarnation, *in the beginning is the Word,* the *Logos,* the power that allows both speaker and hearer to be seized by what is manifest through it, the power that allows the sharing of world and that creates world as well.

Logos is the center and touchstone of the chosen metaphor. In Christian doctrine and New Testament theology *Logos* is the name for Christ, the creative Word of God the Creator. It is through the *Logos* that all things came to be in the beginning, and through the *Logos* and the *Spirit* that life comes to being in time and that living beings enter into meaningful relationships with one another. The attributes of creativity and related-

ness apply to *Logos* with reference to Christ and with reference to interpretation. For this reason the yoking of a theological and an aesthetic
perspective may significantly illuminate the act and art of interpretation.

The precedent for such yoking is to be found in both theological and
aesthetic traditions. One of the most obvious as well as significant instances of interchange between theological traditions and art is the relationship of Greek religious philosophy and drama to Christian theology
and liturgy. Greek artistic talent and religious genius were combined in
the miraculous spectacle of Greek drama. It was in its drama rather than
its philosophy that the Greek mind struggled for meaning in the deepest
and bitterest events of human life. Jaroslav Pelikan says, "It is strange that
early Christianity, with its profound sense of tragedy and redemption,
should have paid so little attention to Greek tragedy and so much to late
Greco-Roman philosophy. Greek tragedy embodied the best that Greece
was able to discover about the paradox of human life in its relation to the
ultimate under which it is lived."[3]

Greece entrusted the stewardship of life's mysteries to its poets rather
than to its philosophers and thus established a strong cultural pattern of
close identification between religion and the arts. This pattern was to
remain in Western culture long after the art forms that had provided its
basis had fallen into neglect. In the Christian era Greek drama was
instrumental in the development of devotional and liturgical forms in the
same way that Greek philosophy influenced the formulation of theological dogma. The Greek identification between the holy and the beautiful
persisted in the Church, a connection evidenced not only by medieval
mysticism but by the religious concern for artistic forms that dominated
the Romanesque and Gothic periods.

Pelikan describes the holy as transcending the ethical, metaphysical,
and aesthetic categories, but he also holds that the aesthetic has come near
to "domesticating" the holy since earliest Christian times. He attributes
the closeness between artistic feeling and religious devotion to a unifying
emotional factor. The spiritual quest for a union with God aroused an
emotional intensity that transcended rational knowledge and opened the
individual to aesthetic experience. Pelikan's conclusion is that aes-
theticism appears whenever religious faith is put into an emotional
framework and when emotions are particularly refined. Arguing that
neither moral nor intellectual categories have the same personal and
compelling qualities that accompany religious and aesthetic feelings, Pelikan observed Kant's transference of religion from an intellectual to a
moral sphere, which is contrasted by the German poet Schiller's placement of religious consciousness among the emotions rather than in the
moral will. It was Schleiermacher who achieved the synthesis of emotional
and aesthetic sensitivity in religious experience. He protested against the
intellectualism of orthodoxy and the moralism of Kant by defining reli-

gion as the "feeling of utter dependence." His ideal was, always, emotion controlled by form.

For Schleiermacher the holy and the beautiful unlike the intellectual and moral orders, touched the same basic area of the human psyche, the center of human life. The qualification "What no eye has seen, nor ear heard" could apply to both the holy and the beautiful, since both professed to reveal a basic mystery of human existence not accessible by any other means, and in so doing, both claimed the loyalty of the human heart. The artist or poet could cast the ordinary affairs of life in a new light, revealing their inner significance and illuminating their value, endowing the physical world with what could be called a *sacramental meaningfulness,* which was more than it intrinsically possessed but which it acquired through the creative "word" spoken to it. The holy and the beautiful have in common the fact that they are revelatory of the true nature of things not otherwise accessible. As both claim to communicate a mystery, so both use similar means. Religion and art both use material forms to express the more-than-material realities within them. This expression is the function of the symbol: to reveal as much of the mystery of reality as human beings could or should understand.

In ancient Greece there was a determining response expected from both the poet and religious prophet who were recipients of inspiration. Their apparent ecstasy, frenzy, or similar unlikeness to themselves was a sign that they were truly agents of the gods, speaking, not their own voice or will, but that of the divine powers. This response is relevant to the present study because the underlying dynamic of this idea was the realization that both worship of the holy and experience of the aesthetic involved the complete surrender of rational processes, as well as volitional ones, to the overwhelming power of an Other—the creating force that showed itself and spoke from within. The place of the rational intellect and the will is of importance in the study of interpretation as a revelatory and transforming phenomenon, and this role will be discussed in greater detail in following chapters.

Pelikan believes that neither intellectual nor moral concerns have the immediate demand of a total existential commitment as do experiences of the holy and the beautiful. Both art and religion are essentially symbolic, both "reveal by concealing,"[4] and both communicate the unimaginable to the imagination without reducing it. In both art and religion this process is climaxed in incarnation, the full embodiment of spirit in form. Herein we see both the underlying relationship between the Christian view of embodiment of the eternal and creative mysteries in the Person of Christ and the process of incarnation of the inner creative word in art. For Pelikan the desire to know the life within requires absolute commitment to the holy and the beautiful by searching and listening to something outside for a unifying principle of meaning.

Rudolf Otto not only finds a significant relationship between religious and aesthetic feeling but goes so far as to indicate that one may convert into or emerge out of the other.[5] Otto makes a distinction between replacement of one feeling by the other and transmutation of one into the other. In other words, religious feeling may be replaced by aesthetic feeling. The experience of the *numinous* may lead to an experience of the sublime. In the relationship of the holy to the sublime there is more than mere association of feelings. For Otto the sublime is the authentic scheme of the holy, "the intimate interpenetration of the non-rational with the rational elements of the religous consciousness."[6] Otto's idea of the holy can be rationally described to a point, but then it begins to overflow such description and take on pararational characteristics, which defy strictly verbal description. (*Pararational* is used in this book to mean that which includes and exceeds the characteristics of the rational discursive intellect. It does not mean antirational or irrational.)

The rational can be grasped by our power of conceptualizing. The nonrational is for Otto a purely felt experience with no specifically defined object. It is not within the realm of the conceptual. Thus for him the numinous is nonrational and cannot be taught but must be awakened from the spirit. In the arts, says Otto, the most effective means of representing the numinous in human experience is through the sublime (in the Kantian sense).[7] The sublime and the magical have a related effect in primitive Western and Oriental art. Even so, for Otto there is only an indirect passage from the sublime to the numinous. Indirect as it may be, it is a passage, and the numinous may stimulate or spill over into the sublime in art easily enough to draw our attention. There are more direct methods of relating the numinous and the sublime in art, and these will be illustrated more explicitly in chapter three. They are darkness and silence, the *via negativa* in mystical doctrine, which have the effect in art of opening a space for a presence to reveal itself. That this is significant for the creative process of interpretation will be shown later.

The two illustrations of a precedent for the relating of religious and aesthetic experience show that both Pelikan and Otto are chiefly interested in the feeling aspect of both types of experience. It is the feeling aspect of interpretation, and the importance of the incarnating process in interpretation to this feeling aspect, with which this study is concerned. This study does not take an antirational position but seeks to build upon the rational and conceptual approaches to literature and interpretation by adding the dimension of the bodily and the pararational. Only such fullness of approach can finally meet interpretation in the largeness of its own reality.

Because this study concerns interpretation theory, it seems fitting to cite the two interpretation textbooks that adhere to and illustrate a theory of

literature and interpretation compatible with the position herein expli-
cated, and to follow the inspiration of these texts throughout the study:
The Art of Interpretation by Wallace A. Bacon[8] and *The Perception and
Evocation of Literature* by Leland H. Roloff.[9] *The Art of Interpretation* begins
with the question "How does a literary work feel when it speaks?"[10] This
question in itself allows the literary work the status of subject to be met,
rather than object to be mastered. The felt experience of the poem takes
place in the context of a lived relationship with the interpreter and finally
in communion with an audience. Throughout the text runs the motivat-
ing conviction that interpretation is "an act and an art of performance not
apart from but including cognitive study and analysis" as well as a "commitment to the whole physical process of interpretation."[11] *The Perception
and Evocation of Literature* takes the position of "the study of literature
through the performing self." It begins with the belief that the body
"thinks," that physiological and psychological processes are at-one in the
act of the perception and evocation of literature; and it is committed to the
fact that feelings emerge from within and attach values to the subject
matter perceived, that intuitions participate in perception by elaborating
possibilities, and that thinking clarifies and differentiates the various
phases and aspects of the process of the encounter with literature.[12] The
senses and the spirit of the whole person are engaged in a total response to
the literary work. In a sense the poem and the interpreter realize each
other. Each is brought to its fullest state of being, and is actualized in the
becoming process of interpretation.

Both Roloff's and Bacon's texts agree with the premise that interpretation is an incarnational experience. The language of both texts is expressive of the spiritual and physical engagement required of the interpreter in
the encounter with the poem, and both texts stress the interplay of the
other rational, conceptual, and intuitive processes in the total dialogue
with the poem. The language of both texts is essentially *incarnational;* it
calls for a creative relationship between poem and interpreter that culminates in embodiment and communion. In this study these two texts will
constitute the spine along which the primary metaphor will travel, to
explore the central column of the structure as the physical neural network
explores, in dynamic ascent and descent, the spine of the human body.
One cannot deeply consider the nature of incarnation, in or out of a
metaphoric context, without always keeping in view the central image of
the body. All other images will move toward the body. In this study the
primary metaphor will gravitate around Bacon's and Roloff's texts in
order to reach a more clearly defined incarnational aesthetic of interpretation. The pairs of analogies used throughout the text will constitute the
"ganglia" that extend from and incline toward the main structure of the
body. All of this metaphoric network is to indicate that the study is moving

in a structural motion toward a definition of the complex system that is the
union of spirit and word in the expressive body of the interpreter: interpretation itself.

Metaphor and Interpretation

Although the purpose of this study has been described, it may be
defined more succinctly here as being a structured exploration of interpretation as an incarnational process and event, which includes the
literary work as the primary subject, the interpreter in relationship to it in
the creative process of embodiment, and the dimension of performance
in the context of an audience as the transforming moment of communion.
The purpose of the exploration is to give support on behalf of the poem as
a subject in its own right, as potential voice that deserves to be heard and
answered, rather than dominated, used, and controlled as an object of the
interpreter's manipulation. This view of the poem immediately defines
the role of the interpreter as one who comes to meet the poem and enter
into dialogue with it in order to become the incarnation of its reality,
rather than one who takes the poem and imposes upon it in order to use it
for ends other than its actual incarnation. Given this view, the role of the
audience in the interpretation event is no longer that of mere spectator
but includes the dynamic of participation in *communion* with the *new being*
of poem-interpreter, become as one and constituting a living *presence*,
which comes to meet the audience.

Since the study itself takes this view of the poem, something of a general
attitude of dialogue extends to the act of meeting interpretation as an art.
As the interpreter should not violate the poem by imposing personal
opinions and intentions on it, a study should not violate interpretation by
imposing unrelated and manipulative concepts on it from without. What
is needed is to enter into dialogue with the process of interpretation
"through a way of access genuinely belonging to it."

There are two justifications for the claim that this "way of access" is the
metaphor and that the process of interpretation in light of an incarnational perspective may best be revealed in the dynamic context of a
sustained metaphor. The first reason lies in the fact that a metaphor is, not
a closed and absolutist way of looking at something, but a particular
perspective that is by nature both fixed and not fixed, a kind of blurring
for the sake of deeper clarity, a lens with open boundaries. By its nature
the metaphor is a figure that allows simultaneous narrowing and enlargement of vision. This figurative nature is why it is appropriate as a way
of meeting the process of interpretation, which, as has been said, is a
metaphor in its own right. Because the total physical process of interpretation cannot be described in language that is purely abstract, analytical, and

conceptual, simply because these categories do not mutually contain one another, it is necessary to add to the language of the outer observation of form a language expressive of the inner workings of relatedness.

This quality of interiority has been seriously overlooked in most interpretation texts, and when mentioned, it is given undue attention save in the two works that have been mentioned. Interpretation involves both rational and pararational processes in terms of analyzing, defining, and questioning the literary work, and of assimilating oneself with it, opening one's existence to it as one being opens itself to penetration and transformation by another. These two approaches to literature and to interpretation are to be seen, not as antitheses, but as interpenetrating attitudes and acts, twinning, so to speak, the outer and inner aspects of the total process. The metaphor also has this characteristic of functioning in two ways, from two directions, or in two contrapuntal but harmonious patterns of motion. It has the effect of dislocating perspective, so that the outer is seen as if from the inside, and what is inner is rendered visible, is seen for the first time as if from the outside.

Interpretation was described earlier as a phenomenon, that which allows itself to be brought to light, that which reveals itself. Walter J. Ong says of the metaphor that it "creates the impression of extraordinary unity or condensation, and it accounts for the brilliance, the glow of resplendent intelligibility which we sense . . . and which Quintilian long ago referred to as 'light.' "[13] Unity of condensation, intelligibility of light—these are the characteristics of metaphor, properties that seem to qualify it as having the power to evoke like properties in a given phenomenon. Just as in the metaphor of interpretation the poem and interpreter are as one but also separate, each depending on the other for full actualization in performance, but each preserving its intrinsic integrity as a being, so in the primary metaphor of this study interpretation and incarnation are unified in a perspective that sees each term as a corporate agent expressive of a given process, deriving the value of agency from its separate and unique function.

In his essay "Metaphor and the Twinned Vision" Ong observes that the metaphor implies predication. To say "that rat" or "that dog" in reference to a person implies "that person who *is* a rat" or "that person who *is* a dog." Consequently, we feel the impact of the two terms as practically one. It is because of their implied separateness in the joining of two word-images into a single image that we experience the full shock of power in the metaphor. In speaking of a performance, to say "that incarnation" is more powerful than to say "that interpretation which is incarnational" or "is an incarnation." According to Ong this power is not because of the assumption of one word-image under another, but, more subtly, because of the implied separateness of the two terms that are felt as one. Even though they are expressed as one or the other, explicitly or implicitly, the parts of a metaphor are generally separate terms that can only be joined on condition of the possibility of similarity. The impression of unity is not illusory, because in order to function there must be some likeness (no matter how elusive) affecting conscious or unconscious responses between the implied halves of a metaphor. But the impression of unity often does not rest on much more than illusion, for the similarity that is present is often of a curious kind, "since the same term which unites the two concepts must also keep them distinct."[14] In the experience of the metaphor the impact of the unity expressed is the immediate result of the separation implied, and herein lies the value of the metaphor as a dislocating and, hence, revelatory figure. The mind grasps the twinning of likeness and unlikeness in a single vision, so the experience cannot accurately be defined as binary. "Hence metaphor is a kind of economical or condensed judgement."[15]

The second justification for the central placement of metaphor in a study of interpretation lies in the nature of the particular metaphor in view: that is, the specific yoking of the theological and aesthetic viewpoints as centrally concerned with the felt experience of the human being in a religious or artistic situation. It is true that such yoking suggests not only a joining of descriptive terms from the two viewpoints—such as the doctrinally technical terms *hypostasis, logos,* and incarnation with the aesthetic terms assimilation, speech, and embodiment—but also a yoking of hermeneutic approaches in the consideration of the literary work itself. Is this concept, then, simply to be one more comparison, one more likening of interpretation to something else which it is not? The answer is No.

A common complaint in the discipline of interpretation today is that the field lacks a comprehensive and systematic aesthetic of its own and that it is constantly being defined in terms of other disciplines rather than in terms of itself. Interpretation in this study is not assumed to be *like* anything. It is not *like* acting, not *like* literary criticism, not *like* philosophy or theology, though it may contain elements of all of these. It is simply itself. This study is arguing, not that interpretation is like theology, but that the metaphoric language that has traditionally illuminated the formulation of theology may in a different manner serve to illuminate the reality of interpretation, may enable it to show itself in the light.

The language of theology in the first place is not a language peculiar to it. Theological terminology is also primarily metaphoric, because the subject matter of theology cannot be communicated by any verbal means other than metaphor. The subject matter of theology is essentially unspeakable, far more so than the subject matter even of art, which includes interpretation. But the central paradox of Christian faith is that the *Unspeakable speaks* to humanity in the personal presence of the Incarnate Word, Jesus Christ. The joining of the human and divine in the person of Christ, the living Word experienced (felt, seen, and heard) in an actual body, constitutes a mystery of incarnation in which two natures are perceived in one being without being confused, in order to illuminate from two counterbalanced angles the truth of existence. The Incarnation is the historical paradox par excellence. Theologians through the ages have described the meaning of the Incarnate Word with imagery and metaphor (Irenaeus, for instance, who spoke of the Word and Spirit as the two Hands of God), for metaphor is the primary figure of paradox, a use of language that, when authentic, always expresses more than could be expressed by any other means. Metaphor is the linguistic tool of symbolism: the best means for expressing the inexpressible through creating verbal relationship between two different things in order to express what could be expressed in no other way. Metaphor has always been the main linguistic tool of theology.

In her fascinating book *The Mind of the Maker* Dorothy L. Sayers discusses the analogical, metaphoric nature of theological language:

> All language about God must, as St. Thomas Aquinas pointed out, necessarily be analogical. We need not be surprised at this, still less suppose that because it is analogical it is therefore valueless or without any relation to truth. The fact is, that all language about everything is analogical; we think in a series of metaphors. We can explain nothing in terms of itself, but only in terms of other things.[16]

For Sayers all language expresses experience and the relationship of one experience to another: everything can only be equated with something else. Nothing, then, can be discussed in isolation, for this would lead to an endless, and finally meaningless, gyre of babble, and would be the opposite of what authentic language proves itself to be.

Sayers has created an interesting schema of analogies herself, not from the viewpoint of a Christian artist so much as from that of an artist aware of the possibility for insight in the juxtaposition of two perspectives. This insight is possible because this kind of joining lets something be seen *as* something else and thus opens it at a place never before touched. In Christ the divine shows itself as human, the human is seen as divine, but each remains also only itself in substantial relationship with the other. Consequently, a whole world of belief is opened to those who open themselves to the living metaphor who presents himself before them. The interpreter is also a living metaphor, and this may be seen in fresh perspective in juxtaposition with the theological metaphor. Paul Valéry explains that "metaphor is what happens when one looks in a certain way."[17]

Sayers begins her analogical schema from the standpoint of the imagination. Unlike the material world, whose components are fixed, the world of imagination increases

> by a continuous and irreversible process, without any destruction or rearrangement of what went before. This represents the nearest approach we

experience to "creation out of nothing," and we conceive of the act of absolute creation as being an act analogous to that of the creative artist. Thus Berdyaev is able to say: "God created the world by imagination."[18]

She goes on to note that poets have often described truths according to their own modes of expression that coincide exactly with theologians' truths, but just because of the difference in the two modes of expression we fail to recognize the value of the relationship, or even that a relationship exists. By the same token, artists do not realize that the phrases of the creeds are descriptions of the creative mind *as such*, and so they fail to receive valuable insight about their own processes. Sayers accuses the theologians of limiting the application of their phrases to the divine Maker and of failing to seek insight from the human artists to see what light they can throw on them from their own immediate apprehension of truth.[19]

Her own analogy is for the writer, whose work has a kind of trinitarian aspect. The creative writer's Idea is juxtaposed with God the Creator as creative Source, the Energy or Activity is placed with God the Savior as Creative Expression, and the Creative Power is aligned with the Holy Spirit, proceeding from the Idea and Energy together and flowing back to the writer to make her or him, as it were, the audience of her or his own work. From the point of view of the reader Sayers believes this trinity functions as an indivisible whole. It is by the Creative Power that the Idea and Activity of the work are communicated to the reader. Through it the reader perceives the book as both a process in time and an eternal presence or wholeness, and this perception creates an inner dynamic or tension in the reader that is transferred to the book itself. Sayers, speaking as a creative writer, finds a source of insight for her own processes in the thought of St. Hilary that "Eternity is in the [Creator], form in the Image and use in the Gift" and that "these three are one, each equally in itself the whole work, whereof none can exist without the other." If a writer were asked which of these she or he identified with "the real book," Sayers responds that it would be impossible to tell, since these aspects are essentially joined.[20]

I agree with Sayers that the Christian metaphors of the creativity of God can also apply to the creativity of the human artist.[21] In the language of theology the artist can recognize a description of and relation to her or his own creative experience. An incarnational view of the artistic process attempts to explore that recognition from any angle that may illuminate it. For Sayers the most likely means for such an exploration is the metaphor.[22]

Finally, to inquire into the interpretation process as lived experience, in the words of critic George Whalley: "one needs, not only to use language delicately and precisely, but to use language as the artist uses it; each single metaphor must be exactly rendered, for if the relation can already be explained in unmetaphorical terms there is no need for the metaphor."[23]

The exploration of this book will move along the path illuminated by the primary metaphor of incarnation, as has been said, but within this primary metaphor of interpretation as incarnation many peripheral[24] but essential metaphors will be used to express, in as precise language as possible, the illuminating relationship between specific terms or moments of interpretation and coincidental terms or moments of theological significance. By a process of sustained pairing of complementaries the study will try to enter into dialogical relationship with the interpretation process. These paired complementaries, which will be explained shortly, may be thought of as forming a double helix ascending and descending, but always encircling, the aesthetic position that is the spine of the study.

The Art of Interpretation: Creation, Incarnation, Transformation

It has been suggested that interpretation is a process involving the *creation* of a new being by bringing two separate beings together in an *incarnation* and that this process leads to an event which constitutes a *transformation* of all who participate in it, including, to an extent, the literary work itself. Now it is possible to examine each of these aspects of interpretation systematically in terms of the metamorphosis of interpretation from process to event. The three following chapters will attempt to do just that.

Chapter two will begin with the literary work as it presents itself to the interpreter. In his essay "A Dialectic of Aural and Objective Correlatives" Walter Ong maintains that "of all the forms of language literature has in a sense most interiority because, more than other forms of expression, it exists within the medium of words themselves and does not seek to escape from this medium."[25] Ong's conviction of the dialogic nature of the poem as spoken language is shared by this study. He views the literary work, not as an object, but as an invitation to dialogue. For Ong all speech, including the spoken poem, is an invitation to enter into its ambience and meet it from within, rather than merely to observe it from the outside. The speaking-poem evokes the hearer to enter into its own life.[26]

In a similar attitude Palmer pleads, "The text must be allowed to speak, the reader being open to it in its own right as a subject rather than as an object."[27] Thus viewed, the poem is a speaking-subject unto itself, uttering expressions that emanate from the human psyche. All works of art, in this sense, partake of interiority, but for Ong literary art does so in a special way, because both its inner and outer form are constituted by words, the primary material of utterance. For Ong each literary work is an advance over what has gone before it and is a promise of future extension, precisely because it is not an object but a "word," something spoken, "a moment in an age-old exchange of talk."[28] He brings in the temporal dimension (which will be of central importance in chapter four) when he says that a literary work should be thought of and spoken to as a moment in a dialogue. Such an attitude engenders a sensitivity to its "open," or unbounded, historical richness and to its unlikeness to any "object" as a discrete object. The form of literature and the form of criticism are interwoven because each is a language-pattern. Ong sees an intimate and intrinsic connection between literature and criticism because each is "part of the total dialogue in which all literature exists."[29]

In chapter two interpretation will be briefly explored in relationship to hermeneutic theories from Schleiermacher to the present, with special emphasis on the movement from positivistic approaches to literature (Harnack), to modern existential approaches (Ebeling, Fuchs), and, finally, to the recent open-ended tendencies toward an "erotics of interpretation" (Sontag, Harder, and Stevenson). The discussion will be concerned primarily with the poem as presential subject, that is, the poem as *word,* and will seek to elucidate the presence of the *word* within words that gives the poem its power of being.

In relationship or dialogue with the interpreter's bodily presence placed at its disposal the poem as word receives a human voice and achieves its entelechy, while at the same time it gives its potential speech over to a human subject. In Merleau-Ponty's phenomenology of language, "The word is understood only insofar as the hearer is ready to pronounce it; conversely, the subject who speaks is in a way transported in the one who listens."[30] This idea raises the question as to whether or not the literary work must become an aural presence in order to be realized. For the purposes of this study the literary work remains potential being until it is given opportunity to speak itself, and this can only happen when it is heard by a human ear, whether through the silent but nevertheless bodily dialogue with the inner ear or through the overt and holistic participation of the entire human psychophysical being in some manner of performance. Interpretation falls into the latter category, since the concern here is with the *art of oral interpretation.*

Chapter three will begin at the point where this entelechy is set into motion. The poem as potential speaking-subject remains voiceless until it is taken into a body and allowed to resonate from within. The gesture of the human body can release the word from its own interior. Through a complex process of dialogue, self-emptying assimilation and fullness, the interpreter enters into a mutually transforming relationship with the poem that results in the incarnation of the word. In terms of the theological metaphor, "the Word was made flesh." The process of incarnating involves the self-actualization of both poem and interpreter. Self-actualization for the interpreter is possible through a way that involves self-renunciation. The technical word for this process in Christian theology is *kenosis,* or self-emptying, and its purpose is to lay aside the demands of the self-centered ego in order to open a way to the deeper self and the subsequent filling of this true self. This filling is called *plerosis,* and with *kenosis* constitutes one of many complementary pairs in the incarnational process.

According to the psychologist Abraham H. Maslow "self-actualization means experiencing fully, vividly, selflessly, with full concentration and total absorption. It means experiencing without the self-consciousness of the adolescent. At this moment of experiencing, the person is wholly and fully human."[31] Cary Nelson believes that when the reader enters the world or "universe" of the poem, she or he experiences it in a way similar to its author's experience of it in the making: "I view verbal form as an author's projection of a self-generative space that transcends or escapes historical time. The writer's need to create is gradually transferred to the reader, both sharing a desire to enact the work."[32] As Bacon describes R. S. Crane's view of Aristotle, "the degree of excellence of a poem is the degree to which it *actualizes,* 'within the necessary limits of its matter,' what it is by nature capable of actualizing."[33]

According to Nelson the critic enters the literary work as a space in which she or he discovers a new energy and discerns its operation on the mind and body. Author and critic move toward simultaneity in the space of the poem, or in its energy field, so to speak. For our purposes this view is relevant only insofar as author and interpreter are both centered on the locus of the poem. Nelson sees literature "as a unique process in which the self of the reader is transformed by an external verbal structure. Yet the reader never passively submits to the radical inwardness of an author's vision. Reading is both ecstatic and painful, for we are both hunter and hunted."[34] Reading offers the reader a total and instantaneous vision, not an imaginary world entirely available to rational explication, but an entire universe, in part ambiguous, yet wholly present. "The reader enjoys for a time the sense that his own life is a form moving toward completion."[35] While identification with the verbal space of the literature never frees us absolutely from historical realities, it does allow us freedom from the impulse toward historical assimilation. We also take this universe into ourselves, and this realization is most important: the reader takes the reality of the poem into her or his own body where it is dispersed and assimilated. Image and word become apprehended as one; revelation and resonance occur simultaneously as poetic integration fills the space of consciousness—the human body.

The creative process of both poet and interpreter is centered in the realization of the poem. In a sense the poet is also interested in the embodiment or incarnation of the poem, because the very process of its coming to being through and beyond the poet is a bodily dialogue. The poet is interpreter insofar as the work that is coming to be is held out as a subject expressing itself, articulating its own being, and is helped in any way possible. The interpreter is a kind of poet, because she or he is a participant in the process of making something genuinely new. This making, as has been suggested, is the outcome of the joining of two beings in a single presentational event. It is at this point that the incarnational aspect of interpretation is also seen as transformation. The transforming power of interpretation is larger than that of literature alone, for it is a different experience complicated and hopefully enhanced, "filled out," by the interaction of the interpreter with the poem. In interpretation the poem and the interpreter seem to give themselves over to each other and so change each other. This alteration occurs by means of a process which Bacon calls "matching":

> It is to the process of matching—of bringing his own life form for the moment into congruence with the life form of the poem—that the interpreter first and foremost devotes his attention. The process of matching is also a process of maturation; one grows by giving in to the otherness of the life of the text, by extending oneself, by reaching out, by loving.[36]

This reaching out, this committed loving, is an "exercising of the spirit in the act of understanding," and it tends toward communion. Once again in terms of the theological metaphor, "[the Word] lived among us."

Chapter four will begin at the moment when the members of the triadic relation of poem, interpreter, and audience enter into communion. This moment presupposes that the interpreter and poem *are* in communion and that the communion is large enough to fill the space in which the audience is present, thus to encircle the audience, take it up into its life, and so transform it, just as poem and interpreter are transformed. For Bacon this process begins with "the tensive life of literature," expands into a relationship with the interpreter, and finally culminates in "the relationship between these two lives and the life of the audience. . . ." This complexity of relationship creates growth in all of its parts: poem, interpreter, and audience each grows and becomes more itself through the others. Each becomes larger and more meaningful than itself by itself, for "growth of the self depends on one's willingness to look beyond the self." The first thing is to *look*. If the looking is appropriate, open, and unself-centered, it will lead to growth and change, to a transformation of the self by way of inner enlargement.

The neo-Thomist philosopher, Jacques Maritain, speaks of the poet in a way that may be more appropriate to the interpreter. He says to the poet,

> you do not have the *notion* of things, but the experience of them in you and of yourself in them. They do not become eternal in you, it is rather you who

become visible in them. You are not here in order to sacrifice them but in order to suffer them, while they draw from you a sign of themselves and of you. . . .

Things are not just what they are; they pass unceasingly beyond themselves, and give more than they have, because they are traversed from every direction by the influx of Existence in pure act, and they love that Existence more than themselves.[37]

The three following chapters will explore in greater detail the complex aspects of interpretation. To place them in a metaphor, first comes the creative word, coinciding with the Word united with God the Creator from the beginning; then the word becomes enfleshed and receives a human voice in the interpreter, coinciding with the entelechy of God the Savior; and finally the embodied spirit, the agency of communion, speaks itself into the human condition by addressing the audience, coinciding with God the Spirit Who converts by breathing over human souls and changes lives.

This beginning looks toward an incarnational aesthetic of interpretation. After exploring the premises of such an aesthetic, it is hoped that the final chapter will be an affirmation of what has been set out here.

two

IN THE BEGINNING
IS THE WORD

Interpretation As the Embodiment of Literature

The interpreter's reason for being lies in the literary work, specifically in "the primary need of a work of literature to be experienced."[1] It is not enough for the literary work to be analyzed, for often the process of analysis stops with an intellectualization of the poem, and hence a weakening of it. The relationship between poem and interpreter is organic. The relationship begins with the overall *feel* of the literature, rather than with any of its parts in isolation. Literary analysis and performing technique serve the larger activity of the interpreter's experience and assimilation of the literary work.[2] Roloff responds to the question "What is the oral study of literature?" "It is, at its most fundamental, somatic thinking—that is, thinking, intuiting, and feeling about literature with the body. Somatic thinking transmutes intellectual, critical responses to literature into intuitive and 'knowing' responses of all the body: the voice, the musculature, the senses."[3]

As *poiēsis,* literature is an act that gives itself over to observation and is thus perceived as a work of art whose function is to unite humanity with itself. The work of art is conceived of as a creative process, an act working in human life.[4] The work of art as *poiēsis* spills over into interpretation, for its creation can only be perceived in a form available to the senses: interpretation renders the work of *poiēsis* visible and audible in the resonating body of the interpreter. Interpretation is a presentational form, concerned with the perception of forms through utterance and behavior. It is a process that directly affects the senses. The oral experience of literature is sensory experience.[5] In his article "The Dangerous Shores: From Elocution to Interpretation"[6] Bacon says that three things are involved in the interpretation process: the text ("the interpreter's excuse for being"), audibility, and aliveness.[7] These last two are yielded by the body of the interpreter.[8] For both Roloff and Bacon interpretation is a spiritual and incarnational dimension of literature, breathing life into it and giving it body, and thus evoking from it its own utterance of life.[9]

The unique function of the oral interpreter is to create a presence, and to create it so fully that it can contain and involve an audience.[10] This function distinguishes the oral interpreter from the silent reader.[11] The oral interpreter is an active participant in the perception of the poem, not merely a passive body of flesh onto which the poem is written.[12] It is not the poem acting on the interpreter *alone* or the interpreter acting on the poem *alone* that constitutes the interpretation process, but the dialogic yielding of their interaction. In "The Dangerous Shores" Bacon states that the possibility of dichotomy exists in interpretation as the "dangerous shores" of text on the one hand and delivery on the other. The art of interpretation is always balanced, dynamically poised between these two constituents. Balance consists in the union of logic and emotion, reason and passion, and so on, which is to be determined, not by the idiosyncratic performer, but solely by the "determining character of the text."[13] This union implies participation in the life of the text—participation that follows from understanding. The art of interpretation, according to this position, is "an art of enactment, of embodiment, of becoming. The poem is active, the reader active; the art of interpretation aims at establishing in oral performance a congruence between these two sets of acts."[14]

The joining of the two acts of interpreter and poem has the effect of integrating the various aspects of the poem, a process made possible by a simultaneous and accurate perception of multiple qualities through sight, sound, and feeling; from this process emerges the wholeness of the literary work.[15] The understanding of the literary text constitutes knowledge, which in turn results in a full reading of the poem. Knowledge is possible only through entering the structure of the text as fully as possible and listening to all that one finds in its wholeness and particularity. Everything that happens must relate to and be justified by what constitutes the text.[16] Literature probes the human flesh and seeks to revive in human beings a basic awareness of things and events by demanding responses that are alive and spontaneous. It seeks, in fact, to vivify life.[17] A work of literature involves the human body in a real situation and real attitudes toward its own world. *Significant purpose* materializes in interpretation when the body of the poem and the body of the performer are congruent.[18]

For William F. Lynch the relationship between the physical poem and the body of the reader is through the imagination and the play of the word-image. The word provides a direct vision and placement; it creates an immediate inscape. It is a vision and a choice experienced in the flesh.[19] For Lynch imagination contains the prototypes of interpretation. It is primarily analogical in that it insists on interlocking the same and the different, idea and detail, in a single imaginative act. Its patterns flow into images of reality, and it adapts itself to every difference of detail without losing its identity. Lynch traces *analogy* to *ana-logon*, meaning "according to the measure." The literary imagination should grasp human reality according to the measure of its every dimension.[20] For Lynch action and imagination are inseparable. The imaginative work of art is an action, always rooted in the concrete of time and place. This act, he says, is incarnational realism or materialism. He cites *The Spiritual Exercises* of St. Ignatius to illustrate the importance of time and place in the theological imagination. Each of the meditations and exercises in the spiritual guide is concretely presented as a time-place context for the imagination. In the bodily imagination meaningful events resonate simultaneously through several levels of perception.[21]

Paul Campbell notes the place and value of the imagination in the literary experience: "As with all art, the reader is dealing with a combination of the real and the unreal. The feelings that the reader experiences are real feelings. As long as he accepts the fact of real feelings in an unreal context, he will appreciate and respond to literature."[22] What is wanted is *belief* in the world that the literature presents, regardless of its likeness or unlikeness to life. If literature were exactly *like* life, there would be no point in it. Because it is in many respects unlike perceived life, literature is able to create an insight into life. It is a part of life and serves to illuminate it when literature is perceived as separate from life but beside it in a creative relationship.[23] Literature provides the perceptive reader with an opportunity for growth by reaching to a perspective and an experience not her or his own.[24]

Alethea Mattingly describes the interpreter as the "expressive agent" for the literary work.[25] As the interpreter embodies literature, she or he gains knowledge.[26] This knowledge allows the interpreter to "fill out" the poem. "Thus, the *ideal* interpretation may be defined as *the full revelation of whatever experience is inherent in the literature.*"[27] Roloff cites this poetic knowing or realizing as an apprehensive knowledge indicating the inner experience of reverberation felt and described by writers.[28] Style in oral interpretation functions as the embodiment of meaning, which is communicated through an aesthetic form proper to it. Form is the artist's capacity to embody perception, conflict, and action into an integrative experience that maintains a focus on all of its elements and reveals development. Form in interpretation is the artistic communication of literature in a creative activity that holds together its parts in a tensive relationship, thus to allow all of the elements within the work to "echo" for the percipient.[29] For Bacon form is the visible structure of life. It is both the boundary of the poem and its point of contact with the world. "Seen this way, the poem is a body, a life form which means that it is active."[30] The proper form for the poem's presentation to the world is also active and bodily. W. Keith Henning defines interpretation: "As an artistic endeavor, Interpretation is considered a presentative art form in which a literary experience is created and offered to others for their attention, empathetic participation, and contemplation. . . . The Interpreter's medium is his behavior, bound by temporal and spatial design."[31] Henning perceives that it is the interpreter's task to concretize the more general statement of the poem in the unique situation of performance, which is a symbolic event because it both *is* itself and *points beyond* itself. The interpreter personifies, personalizes, or embodies a poem and so becomes the presenter of phenomena as phenomena, providing an experiential rather than a conceptual way of knowing. Experiential knowing constitutes true perceiving.[32] On occasion the presential nature of interpretation penetrates both poem and percipient to a level of life that brings them into full face-to-face relationship with each other. In such a case the interpreter has given authentic bodily entelechy to an authentic poem. "As authentic poem—one born out of an imaginative encounter with the presential aspect of the What Is—demands a subsequent responsiveness from the reader. . . . Fresh, novel associations suggested by the metaphorical elements within the poem require intuitive, insightful responses from the Interpreter-reader."[33]

In Henning's application of Wheelwrightean formula to the interpretation act he perceives that the interpreter's discovery of the poem is a process of responsive-imaginative act. Literature can reveal itself only to the truly and fully responsive percipient. The semantic function of literary art is to arouse and educate the imaginative faculty, and it does so through the Wheelwrightean formula of coalescence and interpenetration, presence and tensiveness, perspective and latency.[34] An authentic work of art enters the auditor by these means and so becomes a reality and a presence directly given to the imagination.[35]

The opening question of *The Art of Interpretation* is "How does a literary work feel when it speaks?"[36] *The Perception and Evocation of Literature* asks "What happens in literature?" and "What happens in performance?"[37] One hears an echo of the dictum of Longinus: the literary work is required to show what the subject matter is and how it can be acquired by the reader.[38] What does art tell us about ourselves? As artists, what have we in common with the gods? Longinus responds, "the conferring of benefits and the telling of truth." The interpretation of literature is a perceptive and creative art that seeks to describe possibilities of human experience and provide an integrative means of human knowing.[39] This art depends entirely on the availability and lability of the human body, but it also transforms the space of the body by overflowing physical boundaries. For Wheelwright this overflow constitutes a direct intuited perception of something beyond the immediate sensuous content of the work.[40] The problems of meeting the work involve a willingness to meet more than at first shows itself, to grow into an unfolding simultaneity or synchronicity with the poem, to become a new being with it, to enter a situation or relationship larger than oneself or the poem.

Thomas Sloan expresses a sensitivity to the *being* aspect of interpretation: "To study Interpretation one must study also, the *being* of a work of art—and how and where the poem exists. Oral Interpretation, like hermeneutics, always poses ontological questions."[41] The *being* of literature is constituted by language.[42] In order to approach the *being* of a work of art, it is necessary to look at it not only as having subject matter but as being a subject. Bacon suggests this attitude when he speaks of interpretation as embodying "the text that is its subject."[43] Some interpretation theorists speak of the literary *object* but describe it in such a way as to give it subjective attributes.[44] Others do not consider the problem at all and express a consistent attitude toward the literary work as object. This difficulty in oral interpretation is shared by hermeneutics in general: whether to treat the literary work as a subject or an object: to allow it to reveal itself through dialogue, or to probe and penetrate it by reaching into and almost "behind" it through analysis, or in some way to combine these attitudes in an approach to literature that does not violate it.

Hermeneutics and Interpretation

Philosophical discussion of the word doubtless precludes that it is prior to life. In theology, however, this assumption is not so. The Eternal Word coexists with God the Creator from the beginning. It calls life into being. It precedes existence, all existence save its life with the Spirit in God. The primacy of the Word is manifest in Christian dogma. This primacy, because of the Incarnation, takes on existential importance in the human situation. Interpretation of the word of God in the Scriptures is a receptivity to the Divine Word within them. Communication of the Word of God through oral reading of the Bible and inspired preaching from the text is equal to the communication of God. The word has a sacramental nature as the outward (uttered) manifestation of the indwelling holy.

Theologians have been concerned with the preservation and communication of the word from the time of Origen to the present day. This tradition has been called hermeneutics, or interpretation.

> *Hermenēia*, interpretation, is constantly being carried out without calling attention to itself, as people seek to understand one another and make themselves understood. Only when such normal communication breaks down due to some serious impediment to understanding . . . is attention drawn to the understanding process itself in such a way as to call forth reflection upon the *theory* of interpretation.[45]

The theory of interpretation emerged as a science at the time of the Reformation. The Latin term *ars interpretandi* was replaced by the more Greek-sounding *hermeneutica,* from which the English term "hermeneutics" is derived. The precedent for this coinage is given by Plato's allusion to the hermeneutical art, "which, in distinction from the critical arts that judge between true and false, belongs to those arts that merely give commands, and this not in one's own name, but, like the prophet and the herald, under another's authority."[46]

Traditionally, hermeneutics has been a method or system for proving or disproving the authenticity of a text—its originality, individuality, and so the author's personality and style. The "hermeneutical circle" projected was the interaction between a given text and its author's personality. Schleiermacher's late concern with the psychology of the author reflected in the text indeed became descriptive of the general outcome of hermeneutics. Interest in the author resulted in the slighting of the text as an integral entity: the subject matter became lost as the goal of interpretation.[47] A dramatic change occurred in the hermeneutical approach to literature at the turn of the century, when philosophical discussion in the field revolved around the distinction between "explaining" and "understanding." Wilhelm Dilthey articulated a new historical hermeneutic that was committed to the distinction between nature and human being. The occurrences of nature are explained, but historic understanding of human knowledge forms another and a unique category. Nature can be *explained,* but we *understand* the life of the soul.

Dilthey relativized traditional hermeneutics by means of the contrast between impersonal explanation and the deeper, more complex nature of understanding. He perceived an inner logic in the history of hermeneutics, and finally he achieved "the analysis of understanding" as the departure point for formulating hermeneutical rules. Dilthey contributed to laying the foundation for a "new" hermeneutic by revealing that understanding is, not the end of hermeneutics, but its very foundation, prior to and more basic than rules of analysis. It is by no means the equivalent of understanding to read textbooks on hermeneutics, or to develop exegetical skills, or even to describe the qualities of exegesis or the exegete. The question prior to hermeneutics and exegesis must be: "How is understanding possible and what means are there for understanding?"[48] The new hermeneutic began to form as a recognition of the inadequacy and superficiality of the old hermeneutics and was characterized by a deepening concern for *understanding.*

Dilthey focused upon literature with the justification "that in language alone does what is inside [us] find its complete, exhaustive and objectively intelligible expression. Hence the art of understanding has its center in the interpretation of the remains of human existence contained in writing."[49] In this instance language is viewed only as the objectification through which one must penetrate to the understanding of the existence hidden and expressing itself through the text.

The hermeneutical debate continued and reached an interesting moment in the discussion between Karl Barth and Adolf von Harnack in 1923. From Harnack's point of view the task of theology was to "establish the content of the gospel," that is, "to get intellectual control of the object."[50] Barth, on the other hand, was convinced that theology's claim to scholarliness consisted in its "being bound to the recollection that its object was *first subject* and must again and again become subject."[51] According to Robinson, Barth was ahead of his time, for he was first to perceive the incongruity between the rigid enforcement of an applied method in contemporary scholarship and the reality of truth in which we live. This incongruity has been a matter of discussion in philosophical hermeneutics for only a short time. For Barth what is at issue is the violence done to the subject matter. Citing St. Paul and Martin Luther, he believes that authentic interpretation consists in "doing justice to the subject matter."[52]

In his work *Wahrheit und Methode* Hans-Georg Gadamer attempts to relate aesthetics to the philosophy of historical understanding.[53] He begins with the dialectic interaction between the "historically operative consciousness" and tradition as relayed through the text. From here he carries hermeneutics one step further into the linguistic phase and pronounces the controversial phrase "Being that can be understood is language."[54] Hermeneutics for Gadamer "is an encounter with Being through language."[55] At this point hermeneutics is placed at the center of philosophical problems, for its raises the question of the relationship of language to being, history, understanding, and existence. Gadamer's theory is controversial because it asserts that human nature and human reality are essentially linguistic.[56] Gadamer and Bultmann, breaking away from the positivistic basis for interpretation and following the highly suggestive lead of Dilthey, describe hermeneutics not as an analytical *method* but as an *encounter with being*. Hermeneutics in a broader sense includes the basic challenge of meeting and being seized by the meaningfulness of a text.[57] The core problem, then, becomes that of achieving a meaningful dialogue with the text as a beginning. Such a dialogue depends on the fullest possible definition of understanding, the most sensitive approach to meaning that can be achieved.

Hermeneutics becomes interdisciplinary out of necessity in realizing this fullness of understanding and meaningfulness. It begins to require both a general phenomenology of understanding and a specific phenomenology of the act and event of interpreting the text in a fully physical and lively sense. The lines of philology and historical hermeneutics cross in the act of grasping the inner and outer content of the literary work as a unity. Truth from the past cannot be grasped without hearing the word that comes to us, uttered and echoed through the ages; for language, once uttered (outered) into the universe, becomes the primary means of transmitting the voiced spirit within and, in a sense, behind it—the source of its meaning, for speaker and hearer alike, across the barriers of time and space.[58]

This source of a hermeneutical theory would extract the spiritual *(geistige)* meaning from the text: human beings have a common participation in *Geist* that gives them an understanding of written texts. In Schleiermacher's early hermeneutical thoughts he conceived of understanding as a re-creative process, in which the interpretation process is a re-enactment or re-cognition of how the text came to be in the first place. For Schleiermacher the reproduction of the creative process was the only valid means of getting at the inner meaning of the text. This reproduction, or *Nachbildung*, was a repetition of the author's original creative process and work. In order to understand the human cultural meaning of the text, the reader needed to undergo the original creative experience as a present event. Creation and interpretation, from this viewpoint, are both rooted in understanding. Understanding ripens as forms are taken in and perceived as if from the inside. Thus, hermeneutics is *the art of hearing,* a view integral to the position of the present study.[59]

The Romantic theorists Schleiermacher and Schlegel believed that hermeneutics assumed elements of intuition and understanding of style, not by any rules of method, but according to the comprehending nature of re-creative art—re-experiencing the mental processes of the author. Emphasis on the experience of the author is replaced, for our purposes, by emphasis on the experience of the poem itself, as will be shown later. Schleiermacher perceived the paradox of interpretation: if one wishes to understand a person, one comes to do so from that person's speech; yet in order to understand what is spoken, one must have an understanding of the person, at least so as to be able to draw upon a common culture.[60] Here Schleiermacher understood interpretation as a linguistic rather than a psychological matter. When he later assumed the psychologistic view, the process of understanding was transferred from the manifestation of voice through the language of the text to an interest in the text as a catalogue of inner psychic processes given over to the "empirical exigencies" of conceptual form.[61] Gadamer criticized Schleiermacher in this phase for "bad metaphysics." To view art (as Schleiermacher's later psychologistic approach does) as the creation of fantasy and delight without also discerning in it the truth of lived experience is not "to do justice to the subject matter."

Palmer describes modern hermeneutics as an original creative perception of world. Since for Palmer the task of hermeneutics is that of innovating and expressing perspectives not yet in existence, what is needed is more than historical or scientific syntheses. What is needed, as much as these, is a new understanding of interpretation itself, one that allows for the depth of what I shall call the hermeneutic encounter and for the genuine ontology of the word itself: the ability of the word (never to be divided from the human voice) *to create being* from its own voiced being.[62]

Biblical, legal, and strictly literary disciplines have adapted hermeneutic theory to their own ends. Hermeneutics as a core discipline could serve as a foundation for all the *Geisteswissenschaften*—all the disciplines focused on understanding human art, actions, and writing. The philosopher Martin Heidegger sees hermeneutics as the matrix of philosophy: *philosophy itself is interpretation.*[63] For Heidegger the great sign of human existence is expressed in the *Logos* power (speaking power), which is not really a power given to language by its user, but a power which language gives to the speaker.

In his book *Der Satz von Grund* Heidegger called attention to the fact that the Cartesian formulation of the principle of sufficient cause is responsible for the demand on an object to give an account of itself and state its cause to the investigating subject to whom it is answerable. Nature and the observable elements in science and art cease to exist for themselves but are seen as objects having to give account to an investigating subject. This demand amounts to a Cartesian exploitation of the objectified world by an extreme subjectivity and results in the stark subject-object schema that first dominated the natural sciences and then gained prominence in the humanities.[64] For scholars such as Harnack science could only be conceived as the epitome of this objectifying approach to the matter at hand, and theology as a science had only one possibility: to gain intellectual mastery over the object of its investigation. Heidegger believes that the only way for scholarship to free itself from the necessity of gaining control over objects and pinning them down is thus to relativize, and so transcend, the Cartesian mentality. So rooted is Western philosophy in this mentality that its total conversion is necessary before scholarship can practice a relationship to reality that would consist of a dialogue with being. This relationship between scholar and subject would consist of calling up the being of the subject. Scholars and interpreters would have to make a responsible answer to the beings that come to meet them.

In the new hermeneutic (exemplified especially by Fuchs and Ebeling) language is not viewed as an objectification that one must move behind in order to understand. In his work *Unterwegs zur Sprache* Heidegger makes the claim that it is not human beings who "ex-press" themselves in language, but rather language itself that speaks.[65] Thinking in these terms, Helmut Franz warns the interpreter against a more subtle kind of subjectivism that consists in replacing the interpreter as primary subject with the author as primary subject. In this case it is the author, not the exegete, who dominates. The author, as subject, becomes isolated, a mechanical functionary abstractly composing texts, but having neither participation nor impact—only *intention*—in history.[66] I find this view invalid. The work itself moves and has its being in history and culture. The work, not its author's intention, is the important thing.

E. D. Hirsch, Jr., differs in his attitude toward this interpretation of texts as he follows Emilio Betti. Hirsch presents an attitude toward the text and its author that is essentially incompatible to that of the present study.

For Hirsch validity in interpretation consists in mastering the relevant evidence.[67] He states that two distinct moments in interpretation combine the virtues of negative capability and severe discipline. These moments correspond to "the stage of romance" and "the stage of precision," phrases that he borrows from Whitehead.[68] In interpretation the stage of romance is the divinitory moment—unmethodical, intuitive, sympathetic—the initiatory imaginative guess. The stage of precision is the critical moment, which submits the moment of divination to a high intellectual standard by testing it against all relevant and available knowledge.[69] Hirsch rejects the theory of semantic autonomy because for him the banishment of the author denies the connection between meaning and consciousness.

Meaning for Hirsch is the author's conscious meaning, and it is constant and unchanging in the text. The central dictum around which Hirsch builds his case is that *meaning* is intrinsic to the text as its author's self-expression and that the reader brings no *meaning* to the text but finds *significance* in it by relating it to personal data.[70] In response to the argument that the meaning of a text changes with virtually each reading of it, and changes even more markedly with the passage of time and culture, Hirsch would say that the meaning does not change, but its significance for the reader changes because the reader has changed. Meaning experiences are private, and they do not constitute *meaning*. In order to get at the meaning of the text (the author's meaning), the interpreter must "recognize" the author's processes in the work.[71]

For Hirsch meaning is the intention of an author, and the text is simply an intermediary between author and interpreter, who manipulates it from different ends, since it is the interpreter who declares what is to be actualized in interpreting the text, and what purpose this actualization should achieve. For Hirsch the text has no ontological status as such and therefore cannot be expected to yield an ontological definition of itself. It is an object, and to protect the authenticity of the object from the interpreter's whims, the corporate enterprise of interpretation must establish norms proper to the task. Hirsch argues that no presently known normative standard of compelling character exists other than the author's meaning. Hirsch's desire to spare the text the imposition and dominance of the self-seeking interpreter is honorable; however, from the viewpoint of the present study he discredits the text by referring it to its author and denying it the status of a subject or being in its own right.

Hirsch refers to textual judgments as "probability judgements," pointing to a reality that is partly unknown and so only partly known and which, indeed, may never be known with absolute certainty. A probability judgment may be correct with respect to the known evidence but incorrect with respect to the unknown reality. The nature of such a judgment is paradoxical because "no matter how hard we may think about a reality that is inaccessible to direct experience, we cannot know what it is until we do experience it."[72] Hirsch expresses doubt in the possibility of ever truly knowing what is in the text. The art of interpretation is a counter to his narrow conclusion that since the text cannot be *experienced,* it cannot be known in any degree of fullness.

In interpretation the probability judgment can be more than an informed guess, simply because the discipline offers the *opportunity for the unknown to be experienced,* and this opportunity is performance and all the preparation leading up to performance. Interpretation provides test situations for probability judgments each time the interpreter works with the text in a bodily dialogue. What Hirsch describes as "the unknown traits of human beings, human actions, and human meanings"[73] are not, as he says, completely inaccessible, because the interpreter has access to the infinite possibilities for all of these things within her or his own body.

In response to Hirsch's re-cognitive theory of interpretation this background exploration returns to *The Art of Interpretation.* In this guidebook for the oral interpreter's journey into the life of the poem, the text *is* granted its ontological status; poet and interpreter are both seen as concerned with entering as fully as possible into the discrete world of the poem and with creating that world in some manner for others. The text must be born again in the interpreter, truly re-cognized, and known from within—the *text,* not the author's work in the text. The poet's experience and the interpreter's experience of the poem may coincide, but they may also overlap and complement each other in a fuller realization of the poem. It is the poem itself that must be heard and understood: "literature itself aspires, speaks, and the interpreter becomes language in its full and most significant sense."[74]

The interpreter enters the poem and is in the position of the poem in order to allow the audience to hear and see the poem rather than either the poet or the interpreter. The poet and interpreter both may share the same creatively charged state from which the poem arises, and in this sense they work together for the enactment or realization of the poem itself. As a living ontological reality, the poem does have the power to change; it is not a heavy, static object, but a buoyant subject moving with the liveliness of words.[75] The living quality—and the human quality—of the literary work is in its language. A work of art is *not* simply either its author's or interpreter's self-expression. To reduce the expression to the author's self-expression is of more value than to see it as an opportunity for the percipient or interpreter to "be expressive" of self, but it does not yet seem large enough for what experience tells us of the power of a true work of art. It seems more accurate simply to say that the work of art is expressive of its own self, its own discrete being. As the poem expresses itself it acts, feels, and thinks. The interpreter realizes its meaning through coalescence with these three aspects of its self-expression.[76] The interpreter's obligation is to the poem, to maintaining a constant focus of attention on the poem, to listening to what it has to say as it reverberates in the interpreter's body, mind, and spirit. But when poem and interpreter have achieved congruence, both have had to make adjustments; each has been changed by the other to some degree. Thus, every interpretation is a unique, revelatory meeting, and the poem "is born anew—really *anew*, with changes—every time it is read."[77]

The subject matter of which language speaks is primarily being. In this way language is located at the center of human existence. It is a fundamental human tendency to respond to the call of being and to call others to being. From this point of view language is not regarded as merely an objectification of a separately formed self-understanding. Heidegger, Gadamer, and the proponents of the new hermeneutic conceive of human nature as linguistic. It is the human role to speak and respond to the call of being.[78]

This view of human nature requires something more than discursive abstraction. The philosopher Ludwig Wittgenstein presented a notion of meaning coming, not from the makeup of words, but from their context in human situations. This notion was rejected by analytical philosophy, according to Frank Ebersole, because the analysts wanted to get meaning strictly from the word analyzed, which must be constant. What Ebersole says about Wittgenstein may be applied to the problems in interpretation as well. The call for a new approach "must be taken as exploring the possibility of something else in philosophy—something other than analysis—something other than any form of analysis."[79]

Toward an Erotics of Interpretation

In the last two hundred years hermeneutics has evolved, from a post-Enlightenment positivistic approach to the literary work as an object of intellectual mastery, to a modern existential approach to the text as either a subject or something that can be traced to a subject, with which the interpreter can enter into a holistic dialogue. Granted, this last viewpoint has not been universally adopted. Indeed, the resistance of analytical philosophers to this approach has been noted, and this resistance is the topic of attack in Susan Sontag's now famous article "Against Interpretation."[80] What Sontag means by "interpretation" is

a conscious act of the mind which illustrates a certain code, certain "rules" of interpretation. Directed to art, interpretation means plucking a set of elements . . . from the whole work. The task of interpretation is virtually one of translation. The interpreter says, Look, don't you see that X is really—or really means—A? That Y is really B? That Z is really C?[81]

By its insistence upon translating the text from its own voice into a voice foreign to it (the exegete's) literary interpretation implies that something is wrong with the text in the first place, or at least indicates a discrepancy between the meaning in the text and the demands of readers. This kind of interpretation tries to fill in gaps which it judges to exist between the text and its readers, and it amounts to the judgment that for some reason the text is unacceptable or inadequate, yet it cannot be discarded. Sontag concludes that the interpreter who acts in this capacity claims to be disclosing the true meaning of the text but is in reality altering—and violating—it.

The rationale for this approach to the text is the underlying assumption that content is something that is buried under the form of the text and cannot be exhumed except through the expertise of the trained exegete. Sontag criticizes the view that by shredding the inhibiting form of the text one can find the concealed content that, supposedly, is the true text behind the words. For Sontag this dichotomizing approach to the literary work is inexcusable in the present day, yet it is the accepted and normative method for explication. It amounts to an excavation of the text that ultimately destroys the integrity of the work altogether. Sontag writes that these modern theories are aggressive and impious: In Freudian language, they attempt to hold the "manifest content" of the work in analytical skepticism by prodding, pushing, and probing "beneath" it in order to find the "latent content"—the truly meaningful "subtext."

But this subtext is not at all the world that reveals itself through the given language of the text. It is the phenomenon of the text restated by the interpreter, given an exegetical equivalent. To interpret in this manner is to impoverish the text and deplete the world of the poem. Interpretation of this kind is characterized by "an overt contempt for appearances." The justification of the modern method rests in the form-content split in the work of art, which Sontag finds spurious at the least and vicious at the most. Her insight into the problem focuses on a defensive, reductive tendency: "Real art has the capacity to make us nervous. By reducing the work of art to its content and then interpreting *that,* one tames the work of art."[82]

This attitude toward the text reduces it to an article for use, an object to be conveniently arranged in mental schemes or categories.[83] The remedy for this pernicious treatment of literature depends on an end to the fallacious form-content split. Sontag calls for the development of a descriptive vocabulary of form to replace the presently employed prescriptive one. "Equally valuable would be acts of criticism which would supply a really accurate, sharp, loving description of the appearance of a work of art."[84] Such a vocabulary would be able to reveal the sensuous surfaces of art "without mucking about" in them.

Finally, Sontag praises *transparence* as the highest and most liberating quality in art and criticism today. Transparence is a true aesthetic value. It means experiencing the work of art as it really *is*, perceiving the light that is uniquely its own. Interpretation theorists have literally lost their senses, and the one thing needed is sensorial recovery. The senses must not only be reawakened but reeducated, drawn out of their impotence, so that interpreters can learn to hear more, to see more, to feel more. The functions of criticism and oral interpretation coincide in Sontag's pre-scription for interpretation. With respect to the literary text interpreta-tion's task "should be to show *how it is what it is*, even *that it is what it is*, rather than to show what it means."[85] Summarizing her argument, Sontag says, "In place of a hermeneutics we need an erotics of art."

Sontag's call for a new approach to literature is based on a recognition of forms as instances of being. In an unpublished paper Bacon asserts

> that the art of interpretation is concerned primarily and centrally with a form (literary form, if you will) which is alive but asleep, and which is awakened fully only by the sympathetic, responsive reader. If the form is to be fully alive, it must be completely filled, and in literature the form deter-mines both the shape and in part the quality of the life it contains. The reader must re-verberate—be resonant, force-ful, re-flective. Since the reader is himself alive, his own life enters necessarily into the form which is to be awakened.[86]

It is the interpreter's task to undergo a *matching* process with the form of the literary work by submitting her or his own form to the form of the poem, by changing oneself to fit it, fill it, and become it. Form is not to be conceived as merely an external outline or shape on the one hand, or as merely an internal purpose or idea on the other, for to do so is already to separate it from content.[87]

Form is the state of being manifested in the body, expressed in the liberating experience of motion. In interpretation the poem and the human body move toward each other. Their movement and growth together results in the self-actualization of the poem. The form of the poem is released into the body of the reader, and thus the poem comes into its own body. When the poem is set free, feelings, words, worlds are set free. Bacon describes this bodying forth as reverberation: "not hol-lowness resounding within the form, not merely resonance resulting from an establishment of sympathy with the form, and diffused throughout the form, but the repercussions in the life-stuff of the reader as well, a stuff which takes new life from the form which it fills."[88] It is not possible that every interpreter will find a way of access to or a way of matching with every literary form, or that the totality of every interpreter can enter into a form to its profit and enhancement. When this formation does happen, the poem is awakened, not the reader, who is presumably already "awake" during the entire process of meeting and matching with the poem.

Embodiment of the poem is through participation in the awakening life of the poem. The poem expresses and defines the interpreter insofar as the interpreter becomes what the poem expresses.[89] All of the other phases of the interpretation process—critical analysis, descriptive and evaluative criticism, comparative performances, and such—are necessary to the enactment of the poem, but they are not its *essence*. The essence is the reverberation of the poem's life and being within the bodily being of the interpreter. These other elements of interpretation have been explored and executed throughout the history of interpretation. What is yet needed is to learn the process itself; "the way in which life dissolves into life, lives into lives,"[90] as the interpreter learns the art of becoming a poem.

The way toward an erotics of interpretation begins with the forms engaged in the interpretive encounter. An aesthetic of interpretation that involves the principle of *eros* may look to an integrative psychology of *eros* for insight into what an erotics of interpretation means. James Hillman, an analytical psychologist, defines *eros* as a synthesizer.[91] C. G. Jung himself contrasts *Eros* with *Logos* as complementary "feminine" and "masculine" traits of the human psyche: "By Logos I meant discrimination, judgement, insight, and by Eros I meant the capacity to relate."[92]

M. Esther Harding, another analyst, expands upon the concept of *Eros* as the principle of relatedness: "Relatedness, the law of Eros, demands that one's own desires shall not be taken as absolute but shall be adapted to the needs and desires of the other . . . and to the requirements of the situation. This means that one cannot remain in a fixed or taken attitude but must be flexible."[93] *Eros* as a principle of relatedness is not reserved to the area of interpersonal relationships between human beings but also applies to the realm of ideas and objective goals.[94] *Eros* transcends purely personal intentions in gaining a relation to transpersonal values, as *logos* involves the revelation of transpersonal truth. The activation of either *logos* or *eros* means deliverance from ego orientation toward personal power. One must obey forces and values that are beyond the personal self. Harding calls this need to obey a religious attitude.[95] An erotics of oral interpretation would involve this religious attitude toward the text's fullest possible realization along with subordination of the ego toward that end.

Hillman calls *eros* a binder, an intermediary that brings two realms together. *Eros* forms symbols, is indeed the symbol-making urge itself, for a symbol is the primary medium for binding the known with the unknown. Moreover, *eros* is the principle of transformation. Its stirrings toward relation are a striving for expressive being, for the entelechy or realization of relatedness between two beings. It transforms reflection into genuine creativity.[96] This property is of importance to the interpretation process itself and will be explored further in the next chapter.

Hillman also attributes to *eros* all transactions of the libido, which in Jung's view "is synonymous with psychic energy," or the psychological value of psychic processes.[97] Every genuinely imaginative and creative activity involves vivid libidinal participation if it is to have more than slight impact. It involves the imagination and creative faith of "interested love." For Hillman "interest" and what has usually been called "disinterest" blend in a creative way in instances of relatedness that involve the imagination.[98] This facet of creativity describes the imaginative process involved in the act of interpretation.

In the discussion on hermeneutics two ways of approaching the text were described: (1) penetrating behind the text through a subject-object relationship in which the interpreter dominates the text and (2) discovering the real presence of the text as a being in its own right through a subject-subject relationship in which the interpreter listens and responds to the text in dialogue. Many contemporary writers would call these opposing attitudes—dominance/penetration and dialogue/discovery—masculine and feminine ways of approaching the world, or, in this case, the text. I am interested in the description of these differing attitudes, and I shall refer to several authors on the subject, but, while allowing them their opinions, I must first of all state my own disagreement with the labeling of these different approaches as "masculine" or "feminine." For example, Susan Sontag criticizes the overuse of the so-called "masculine" approach to the text, by which she means the tendency to brutalize it into submission to the always dominant interpreter. The humanistic psychology of A. H. Maslow centers on the dichotomy of product versus process in creativity in similar language:

> I believe also that we cannot study creativeness in an ultimate sense until we realize that practically all the definitions which we have been using of creativeness, and most of the examples of creativeness that we use, are essentially male or masculine definitions and male or masculine products. We've left out of consideration almost entirely the creativeness of women by the simple semantic technique of defining only male products as creative and overlooking entirely the creativeness of women. I have learned recently (through my studies of peak experiences) to look to women and to feminine creativeness as a good field of operation for research, because it gets less involved in products, less involved in achievement, more involved with the process itself, with the going-on process rather than the climax in obvious triumph and success.[99]

I certainly agree with Maslow that the art of women must be recognized and valued—indeed, high time! I also think that much of the problem lies in the very language we use. In reality I believe there are no "masculine" or "feminine" qualities that cut irrevocably between the two sexes, that permanently exist in dichotomy, and that can define us simplistically along the narrow limits of gender. We are all the intricate sum of all that has gone before us and of the accidents of our cultural experience. I believe there are human qualities that have become distorted, imbalanced, one-sided in our culture. The more mechanical, dominating tendencies now need to be restrained, and the more spontaneous, receptive qualities need to be experienced and valued anew. The point is the type of quality one is describing, not that generally speaking and for various reasons it may appear to be more obvious in one sex than in the other, and hence be termed "masculine" or "feminine." This language is less and less realistic or helpful as we grow more and more human (accepting of multiplicity and individuality at the same time) in our dealings with ourselves, with one another, and with the varied content of our formal experience, including that of the creative process. Unfortunately it is still convenient to use the labels, since we have as yet found no universal language to describe these characteristics, but it is important to be conscious that even while we use these words for convenience, we have already outgrown their precise purpose and meaning.

In *The Art of Interpretation* emphasis is on "the process of becoming." A literary work "is what it is because it tries to become what it wants to be."[100] The interpreter's task is to cooperate with this process: "It is perhaps not too much to suggest that there is a kind of love relationship between reader and poem, each reaching out to the other. The interpreter must not deny to the body of the poem its right to exist."[101] The becoming process is a unique meeting whose climax is a unique moment. The interpreter is always attaining new perceptions of quality and relationship in the felt experience of the poem's process. The interpreter organizes, selects personal responses that match the poem, and creates a unique moment through a unique relationship with the poem. The realization of this process depends on the interpreter's attitude toward the poem. Unless the interpreter *cares* about the poem, all else will be to no avail.

In *The Perception and Evocation of Literature* Roloff writes that *caring* "suggests the capacity to listen. To perceive and evoke the personae of literature, one must listen to what is said."[102] Certainly any intellectual or critical understanding one has of the poem is essential so long as it is relevant to the life of the poem and can be integrated, however subtly, in the actualization of the poem. One must come to a full intellectual understanding of the poem in order to meet it in its totality, in order to perceive, to *awaken* its potential qualities. But caring—that is, a genuine respect for the poem, a kind of courtesy to it—protects the interpreter from overintellectualization and restores the meeting to its proper domain as a dialogue between personalities. Roloff describes the poem as an "art working," truly forming its own existence out of its components, through engagement with a skilled and perceptive performer. Moreover, Roloff defines interpretation as a *transformational process* in which volition is involved. The interpreter needs to subordinate her or his own will to the will of the poem to become itself.[103] Elsewhere Roloff describes this process as *compresence,* or the presential manifestation of all things working together between poem and interpreter in the existential act of performance.[104] When the interpreter is willing to yield to the necessities of the symbols and values embodied in a poem, associating them with personal sensibilities and perceptions, she or he engages in a self-sustaining process of clarification that reveals the "felt aspect" of the text. The interpreter's aesthetic attitude is a caring commitment to the speaking poem. Thus the act of interpretation becomes the embodiment of experience given a living voice.

As evidenced by the two texts cited in this study, and supported by the greater number of interpretation texts, interpretation is the aesthetic antithesis of all tendencies toward abstraction. It is the embodiment of literature in its human concreteness, not the further removal of literature from lived experience. The primary characteristic of an erotics of interpretation is the replacement of abstractions by specific and material events and things. These specific, material events and things need to be perceived in the present in terms of a personal knowledge of communion between an *I* and a *Thou.* Such communion defines the concrete world of space and time in which human beings live and which in turn defines human life. Interpretation is the evolution of wholeness realized through the interpenetration of concrete beings.[105]

Participation with the literary text demands that one always grow, always become more than what one is. Interpretation as the dialogue and interpenetration between poem and interpreter begins with the concreteness of both poem and interpreter. The poem itself is present to the interpreter in all its possibility for meaning. The poem "is haunted by many presences" and is filled with possibilities for invading and capturing the senses. These possibilities are viable from the moment of confrontation and grow toward the presentational act of performance.[106] Jacques Maritain says that "Poetry is ontology," which "finds its birth in the soul in the mysterious sources of being, and reveals them in some way by its own creative movement."[107] Everything communicates in being, and the literary being abounds in signification, to reveal by its speaking presence more than can be found by analyzing its parts. Interpretation depends on the power of the poem to be itself and of the interpreter to participate in the poem and so direct an audience to the realization of its full presence.

The practice of an erotics of interpretation would abolish the dualisms of mind and body, analysis and performance, acting and interpreting, and the splitting-up tendency in general, which, as Harder and Stevenson say, has "resulted from the highly abstractive activity of a relentlessly masculine [dominating] imagination."[108] The emergence of the so-called "feminine" principle—which in reality is a human principle lived out in an attitude of caring participation, receptive dialogue, and active relatedness—would constitute a revolution in the art of interpretation. It could restore interpretation to its philosophical position as an art dealing with ontological realities in an epistemological and existential ambience of encounter and knowledge, through communion, in the process of performance. Applying Sontag's suggestion to their own field, Harder and Stevenson see the way for an erotics of history by means of a renewed commitment to the process of traditions through language. By entering into a loving relationship with language and events a sense of history as the re-creation of the luminousness of the events themselves can be restored. This restoration is not the type of hermeneutics in its limited sense as penetration behind the appearances of form to reach the real content hidden beneath, but it is a hermeneutics that is also an erotics, for it allows us to experience the past as present, made luminous in the present situation as a still ongoing process of creation.[109] The parallel with interpretation can be discerned immediately since the goal of the interpretation of literature also can be described as making what is absent present.

Maritain writes that a work of art, be it painting or poem, always speaks, and it speaks no longer in terms of logical reason.[110] The purposiveness of art is its intention for the good of the work done. The whole process of an "art working" is toward the realization of itself as an utterance of being. The chief virtue of the poem throughout its coming to be is its refusal to have itself interfered with.[111] Maritain perceives that the poem includes its reader or interpreter in its intention as much as it includes the poet. Neither poet not interpreter can express her or his own substance in unison with the poem's substance unless the work resounds within her or his being. Within the interpreter those things resonating against the fibers of human feelings and realities, and in union with the substance of the interpreter, "in a single awakening . . . rise together out of sleep."[112]

The question Who is speaking? must be put to the text. It has been said that the literature or language speaks itself. Yet it is rather a vague proposition for the interpreter that what must be done is to enter into a dialogue with *language,* a word richly personal in implication (since all language is human in origin), but starkly vacant as an image. The solution which some contemporary interpretation theorists offer is that of the *implied author. The Art of Interpretation* poses the question Who is speaking? as a primary question for the interpreter.[113] If the work is a drama, the question is not so difficult to answer. If it is another literary genre, a difficulty arises. The effect of the work on the person (or being) speaking in the work is of absolute importance for the interpreter, since it is through this voice that the interpreter must enter the work. Bacon responds to the difficulty by describing the nature of the speaking voice in the poem. This voice may be taken as the implicit author within the work as distinct from the actual living author, with whose personal attitudes it may or may not agree.

Dialogue as a receptive and substantial encounter with the poem must be as specific and concrete as possible. One comes to learn what the poem *is* through the self-revelation of its speaker. The speaker may not necessarily be conceived as a physically defined person, whose hair color, height, and clothing style can be described. Such physical literalism might be the opposite of what the interpreter should achieve, for not every literary work has a speaker who is thus a "character." The voice of the text may not belong to a character unless there are definite characters defined by the text, but the voice in the work will always belong to a being or speaking-subject—the incarnate form that gives expression within the text and is entirely (although potentially) present within it. Roloff describes dialogue with this being in terms of mythic enactment, rhetorical presence, and psychological reality.[114]

Don Geiger's dramatistic approach to literature begins with the poet's discovery of the poem. The search for an aspect of reality or a subject of contemplation is the poet's purpose for composition. The poet's task is not so much to find the best way of *saying* what is meant, but to *discover* fully what is meant.[115] Geiger seeks to defend the poem's autonomy, by which he means that the poem yields meaning that cannot be translated into any other form of discourse. Yet the poem is nevertheless accessible to the reader and can be recognized in terms of ordinary experience. What is emphasized by Geiger is the poet as discovering explorer, the poem as revelation. Dramatic theory, which for him both combines and goes beyond aspects of Romantic and contextualist theory, sees the journey into the poem's world as a journey through experience. Hence, the poem is not "dissected" to find its hidden point, but rather the reader comes to see what the speaker in the poem sees and to experience the world of the poem from the perspective of its speaker. Only this participation can bring about an understanding and a sharing of the speaker's values and the realization of the poem itself. Geiger is working toward a doctrine of literature which acknowledges that the speaker in the poem speaks to "a fictively real person about a fictively real object" and that this utterance takes place for no other reason than its taking place. More recently Geiger has said with even greater force that knowing the poem is knowing what it is and that we cannot know it until we have fully experienced it from the inside out.[116] A *real experience,* as something apart from ordinary experiences, is a separate moment of insight that is present in the authentic poem as a manifest embodiment in its construct. The essence of the poem's reality, therefore, depends on its dramatic embodiment.

For Paul Campbell interpretation is the oralizing of literature. It is through what constitutes the text that we discern the speaker of the text: "The *what,* in other words, is the material from which the *who* is created."[117] Campbell suggests combining the dramatistic approach and contextual analysis to create a speaker from the words that are spoken. It may be doing more justice to the text to say that the speaker is *discovered*. The creativity of interpretation is in the interpreter's ability to create a new being out of relationship with the poem's being—not in creating the *poem's* being that already is—and in creating a way of entelechy for the potential voice of the poem. Granted, the entelechy is achieved by means of the material that is in the poem.

The way to an erotics of oral interpretation is through the enactment of the unique experience within the poem. *Eros* means (according to the sources already cited) *relatedness*. Combined with *agape* as disinterested love, it means caring about the text and, in interpretation contexts, making it present, through the gift to it of one's bodily being, to an audience. To interpret means "to bring out the meaning" and "to act as an agent between two parties"[118] by bringing into relationship beings that have not yet found coalescence or communion in just this way.

The systematic theologian Paul Tillich speaks of *eros* and *agape* in terms of faith in a being. For Tillich faith is a matter of *ultimate concern*. The human spiritual function, whether expressed as artistic creation, scientific knowledge, ethical insight, or political-cultural endeavor, is an expression "of an ultimate concern which gives passion and creative *eros*" to all its manifestations, conscious or unconscious.[119] He defines grace as a complete openness to the integrating power of faith in a concrete situation. Tillich dismisses the separation traditionally made between the Greek *eros* type of love and the Christian *agape:*

> *Eros* is described as the desire for self-fulfillment by the other being, *agape* as the will to self-surrender for the sake of the other being. But this alternative does not exist. The so-called "types of love" are actually "qualities of love," lying within each other and driven into conflict only in their distorted forms. No love is real without a unity of *eros* and *agape*. *Agape* without *eros* is obedience to a moral law, without warmth, without longing, without reunion. *Eros* without *agape* is chaotic desire, denying the validity of the claim of the other one to be acknowledged as an independent self. . . . Love as the unity of *eros* and *agape* is an implication of faith.[120]

Eros and *agape* with regard to interpretation would mean that the interpreter enters into a relationship with the text and longs for union with it, but through surrender of self to the text, is committed to the preservation of its integrity and identity as a subject also apart. This type of love involves a blending of what Tillich describes as mystical, ethical, and ontological faith. Mystical faith unites by negation of self and is primarily ascetic. This asceticism could be one phase, not necessarily the end, of the love of the text and belief in its world. Ethical faith transforms by affirmation of self and is predominantly a formative activity, driving toward the transformation of an estranged reality. Ontological and ethical faith both operate from love. Ethical faith drives toward union with the beloved being through *eros* by transformation of both beings into something that is beyond each separately. Ontological faith drives toward acceptance of the beloved being and its transformation into what it potentially is through the dominance of *agape* seeking to transcend separation of being from being. In any case "faith determines the kind of love and the kind of action."[121]

Eros means meeting the text in order to become one with it, and *agape* keeps *eros* in balance and sees that the preservation of the being of the text is realized above all. This dynamic is essentially one of listening, an activity of receiving the word of the text into one's own being. *Logos* is the power that lets both speaker and hearer be seized by what is manifest through it. *Logos* lets something be seen as something else: Christ, the *Logos,* lets God be seen as human (cf. chapter one, Metaphor and Interpretation). *Logos* as phenomenon renders the invisible visible in a structure of being-in-the-world. *Logos* as understanding is not the mere sympathy of the spectator, but participation in the life of the other in relationship through speaking to its being in a living context.

Poetic speaking is sharing of world. Speech is not a reflex, but experience of the subject matter and meaning. Language becomes the power of laying open a space in which the poem can disclose its own world. It is the process by which the human world, moving and shifting in the changing process of human saying, is ever newly created, in which the unsaid is as much expressed as the said and comes to be understood as real. Language does not stand for reality or relationship; it *is* reality and relationship. It does not copy, but actually expresses, a relation to the whole of being and allows it to come to expression. It is not a method of analyzing humanity, but, as Heidegger's later theory expresses, it is an ontology of disclosure, the disclosure of being. Language is both an act and an event of humanity. The phenomenon shows itself in itself as a distinctive way in which something can be encountered. *Logos* as discourse also means to reveal what one is talking about in one's speaking.[122] The function of the *logos* (word) is to let something be seen (image). *Logos* acquires the signification of relationship because it can signify that which becomes visible in relation to something or someone as that to which one addresses oneself and which addresses one.

The theologian John Macquarrie, translator and interpreter of Heidegger, states that to speak of the self (soul) as "substance" is to reify it and reduce it to the level of a static object, whereas the biblical view of the self (soul) is not distinguishable from the vision of the psychosomatic unity of the whole person.[123] The notion of self as form suggests that the self is not given full-blown and ready-made but is to be made in the course of existence and in the context of relationships and, indeed, that authentic selfhood may never be achieved at all. The model for this conception of self is temporality, life primarily as process. In an existence that is fulfilling its potentialities the three dimensions of temporality—past, present, and future—are held together in a unity of balance-in-tension. "This is the 'moment' of which existentialist philosophers from Kierkegaard to Heidegger have written, the authentic present that does not shut out either past or future, but, through its openness to both, forges them into a unity."[124]

It is in this moment of existence that relationship between interpreter and text takes on the properties of vivid presence in the power of performance, when all things come together to effect a quality greater than the sum of them as separate. It is the moment of authentic selfhood for both poem and performer. This moment will be described in detail in chapter four as *kairos,* or the transformational aspect of time. Macquarrie states that this unifying moment of authentic selfhood occurs from a deep sense of the facticity of the situation, and from a commitment and acceptance with regard to the convergence of facticity and possibility as making sense and power of the situation. Macquarrie speaks of a committed existence as being motivated by some *master possibility.* For the interpreter the master possibility would be the realization of the text in full embodiment. Macquarrie is describing a basic attitude of existence: "If anything like unified selfhood is to be reached, the facticity of the situation has to be accepted in its entirety, with no loose ends rejected."[125]

Macquarrie also describes three kinds of thinking that might be helpful for the interpreter to understand. The first level of thinking is what Heidegger calls "calculative" thinking. This kind of thinking is in the subject-object mode. We think about an object as a thing that is over against and outside of us. The purpose of the thought is to find a way of using, handling, manipulating the object in order to incorporate it into our instrumental world. At its height of sophistication it becomes technological thinking, in which the theoretical scientist can be a mere spectator observing elements of utility. The knowledge corresponding to calculative thinking is objective knowledge. Objective knowledge dominates what is known by rising above it and, always to some extent, mastering it. In this kind of knowledge the thinker is active and in control, while the object is, for the most part, passive. The observer's activities are experimenting, deducing, measuring, demonstrating, and showing connections.

The second level of thinking Macquarrie designates "existential" thinking, proper to existential or personal being. It does not aim at use or exploitation, as calculative thinking does, though it may aim at the well-being of either the other in question, the self, others outside the situation, or all of these. It does not own what is thought about as an object but rather recognizes it as another subject. This kind of thinking involves participation, "a thinking into the existence of the other subject," and proceeds on the basis of coparticipation in existence.[126] It can be said that the first, or calculative, level of thinking corresponds with the positivistic approach to hermeneutics exemplified by Harnack, whereas the second, or existential, level of thinking corresponds with what has been called an erotics of interpretation.

A special instance of existential thinking is "repetitive" thinking, that is, going into some experience that has been handed down, so that it is again and again brought into the present and its possibilities are made newly alive. This renewing may happen with a historical event, a document, or any literary text. Macquarrie says that if we are to understand it, we must think *into* it, and so think *with* its agent or speaker.

Macquarrie writes that a consideration of the two modes of thinking— the subject-object and subject-subject modes—leads to the possibility for yet a third kind of thought, one in which the subject/thinker becomes subjected to the being known, becomes in fact *known* as well as knowing. Such a mode is nothing less than transcendent. Heidegger calls this type of thinking "primordial" or "essential" thinking. Rather than the probing character of calculative thinking, it has a meditative character. It rather waits and listens. Heidegger speaks of it as thinking that "answers to the demands of being" (*Was ist Metaphysik?*, pp. 47–49). It is a kind of philosophical thinking, but one that responds to the address of being and "is explicitly compared both to the insights of religion and to those of poetry."[127] Macquarrie says that it is a paradigm for understanding what is meant by revelation and that it shows revelation to be located in the realm of human cognitive experience. A being reveals itself to us from the depths of our own being. Coparticipation in being through the self-communication of particular beings opens onto a realm of expansion. The knowledge that belongs to primordial thinking has a giftlike character, which is, in theological language, revelatory and filled with grace. Macquarrie notes that aesthetic experience touches upon the whole existence and participates in primordial thinking, but he does not identify it with the latter. He acknowledges that it strongly involves the feelings, while it also has a distinctive cognitive aspect. What is known or revealed in aesthetic experience is not something additional to or beyond what is open to universal observation, "but rather the depth of what confronts us, a structure of a *Gestalt* that is noticed in the experience."[128] This awareness also has a giftlike quality, for the being of aesthetic experience, like the numinous, seems to take possession of us. The artist's description of inspiration is not unlike the contemplative's description of revelation.

The significance of these three types of thinking for the interpreter lies in their differing relationship to the thing known. In the first instance the thing known is made an object to be controlled; yet aspects of its approach, such as analysis, comparison, and experimentation, are certainly descriptive of essential phases of the interpretation process. To obviate the external and analytical means of learning the nature of the text would certainly destroy the interpreter's chances for knowing and realizing the text as fully as possible. Knowledge, too, is a necessary part of meeting the text. But the meeting must not stop here. Analysis is only the beginning, indeed, the most superficial way of coming to know the poem. However, if the interpreter bypasses this phase altogether, there is reason to believe that trying to go on to a meeting with the poem on a deeper level would only be futile. Nothing that might help the interpreter fully realize the poem must be avoided.

The second and third levels of thinking in Macquarrie's account of Heidegger are more relevant to the immediate discussion, since they involve an aspect of interpretation that concerns the present study: the in-depth, subject-to-subject meeting between poem and interpreter. In the case of existential thinking the emphasis is still on the one who thinks. The interpreter's attitude is receptive, open to the text as a subject in its own right, but there is as yet nothing here of the power of the subject itself. In primordial thinking, however, the subject (what is met by the person thinking) is given credit for having the power to make itself known and for having a powerful, transforming effect on the person to whom it presents itself. This power of the poem unleashed in dialogue with the interpreter and fully manifest through performance is what this study is concerned to acknowledge. The connection between primordial or essential thinking and aesthetic experience was made, although vaguely, by Heidegger. He suggests, not that they are identical, but that they are related and may overlap.

The case for the relationship of these types of thinking to interpretation is that all three types are involved in the interpretation process as phases increasing in significance as one moves into the next. Further, the meeting probably begins superficially with a calculative textual analysis and the acquisition of technical skills, but these move into the domain of the master possibility and very soon are subsumed under the greater impact of meeting the text on ever-deepening levels. Existential thinking opens the way for the text to enter the receptive, nonmanipulative mind of the interpreter, and this tends to open out onto the transforming effects of primordial thinking in which the interpreter's whole being is captured by the poem. The result of these three phases of encounter is the manifest union of poem and interpreter in the phenomenon of performance. The existential and primordial phases of meeting (or thinking, if one recalls Roloff's insight that the body also *thinks*) make it possible for the poem's being to reveal itself to and through the interpreter's being. Macquarrie writes that being is the condition for something to come into being in its *is-ness*. It is the transcendent quality of letting-be. He is speaking, not of primordial (or eternal) being, but of expressive being, manifest by *logos*.

Being is present and shows itself through *logos,* expressive being itself. *Logos* expresses being fully only in incarnation.

In *The Perception and Evocation of Literature* it is said that the interpreter is first an embodied being accepting the facticity of her or his own bodily existence. The speakers embodied in a literary text are released from print to enter the interpreter's body, where they can be liberated in self-actualizing movement. "The interpreter seeks to know the sounding-body-voice of another." The interpreter cannot totally embody another character, but the interpreter can know *what the other feels like.*[129] Hans-Georg Gadamer says that the hermeneutical task is to bring the word out of the alienation in which it finds itself in the printed text and back into the world of living dialogue.[130] Interpretation seeks to redeem the word from print through embodiment, or incarnation.

Another hermeneutic philosopher, Emil Brunner, notes that the peculiarity of the positivistic approach to the text is not so much that it considers the literary work—a human design—to be an object, but rather that it believes itself capable of grasping humanity in its totality as an object. Brunner claims that its error is epistemological in that it does not realize the limitations of such a view of human life.[131] Would a critic, having a comparable *religious* experience, speak of it in abstract and conceptual terms, or with regard to its structure and pattern, as she or he would speak of a deeply moving *aesthetic* experience of the word emerging from the text into life? Yet such abstraction happens: "The hubris of trying to be the absolute master of a religious experience is apparent; the hubris of trying to be the master in the literary encounter is less apparent but no less real."[132] The literary interpretation should allow the language event to overpower and transform the interpreter—to *seize* the interpreter—so that both what is spoken and what is left unspoken in the text are *heard.*

Again, it must be said that analysis is *part* of the process of interpretation, although it must not be its *end,* and it certainly cannot be what interpretration *is.* Just as one can learn about the human body by dissection, so one can learn about the text by analysis; but these are means to the realization of physical health and integrity on the one hand and the full embodiment of literature on the other.[133] The key to the dynamics of analysis and integration is appropriateness, and this will be discussed in chapter four. The point here is that the work cannot be ultimately encountered at the deepest level as an object to be analyzed and controlled. It is helpful to view the work, not as an object placed at the interpreter's disposal, but as a *thou* who comes to meet the interpreter and addresses her or him through a dialogue that arises in the growing, becoming process of relationship. If a wrong relationship is established (such as that of subject to object), its issue can only be distorted and incomplete meaning.

The meeting between text and interpreter is always a meeting of two horizons, since the interpreter can never come into relationship as an empty space, devoid of experience and meanings of her or his own. Interpretation begins as a dialogue between forms and ends in the creation and presentation of a new form. In a real sense the form *is* the incarnation that is seen and heard in a performance. The poem is not a ghost that borrows a body for its expression; form and expression realize the world that *is* the poem, as poem and performer stand together in an indivisible unity. As Ernst Fuchs says, "Language is not the abbreviation of thinking, but thinking is an abbreviation of language."[134] There is an old saying: "I don't know what I'm thinking until I've said it," which translates for the creative writer, "I don't know what I'm thinking until I've written it." In this case the interpreter does not know what she or he has met until it is both spoken and heard. Fuchs goes on to say that language is a gift through which being is given to us when language "directs us into the dimension of our existence determinative for our life."

It was suggested earlier that the experience of literature and language exceeds the boundaries of reason as we generally think of it. Rudolf Otto's discussion of reason and faith can throw light on what is at issue here. Otto blames orthodox Christianity for not keeping alive nonrational religious elements in the heart of truly religious experience. The value of these elements has not been recognized, and this failure gives a one-sided rationalistic interpretation to the idea of the holy. The present task is to correct this serious error and restore balance and proportion to the religious sensibility. The same task may be placed in the hands of literary critics and interpreters. The first thing is to become aware of activity in other areas of the psyche and then to acknowledge that what is ineffable to an extent—anything that contains elements of mystery not directly accessible by any means of analysis—cannot strictly speaking be taught but can only be evoked, awakened from within. It is not intended that the pararational replace the rational but that there be a permeation between the two ways of knowing, that the pararational (or Otto's "nonrational") can lead to an enhancement and a deepening of the rational approach to the world. For Otto disregard of numinous events impoverishes religion and life generally. For the serious interpreter disregard of the pararational can impoverish the experience of literature. The incorporation of pararational elements can only illuminate the rational mind and facilitate the bodily enactment of the literary work, so long as the end kept in view is always the incarnation of the work to the fullest degree. The interpreter must know the poem, but, as Otto says, to know and to understand conceptually are two different things.[135] In the numinous experience the Wholly Other is not beyond reach but, as Otto describes, has a truth and a reality apart from the experiencing self. This truth and reality make contact with the affective, or pararational, areas of the psyche. Reason must not cloud or bury these areas if contact is to be made. The numinous appears here as an energy, a reality and liveliness, a quality of being, a beyond, an Other.

While the importance of reason is not to be minimized, insofar as any of these elements are manifest in the literary work, something other than discursive reason perceives and responds to them. Otto notes that the numinous cannot be discerned in dogma or even in exhortation unless it is *heard.* "Indeed no element in religion needs so much as this the *viva vox,* transmission by living fellowship and the inspiration of personal contact."[136] But the mere word, even if it is spoken and heard, does not have the power by itself to move the hearer. In addition to the living voice, the spirit in the heart must move both speaker and hearer to an apprehension of the word. This spirit, as Otto says, is the essential thing. When it is present, even the rational terms have the power to arouse the affective side, and the hearer is tuned by both rational and pararational influences to the right tone. Otto cites Schleiermacher, who says that one who reads the written word "in the spirit" lives in the numinous and is open to what is given in the word.

Interpretation, then, is something grounded, not entirely in human consciousness or in human categories, but also in the manifestation of what is encountered, the reality that comes to meet us. Interpretation is in large part being able to see inner realities of experience as manifest in the literary work and to perceive the boundaries of that work from within. Dialogue concerns more than speaking and hearing words. It concerns listening to voices of being to which one is either obedient or disobedient. For Aarne Siirala all of human life is in this respect a word, a response to that which life speaks to us.[137] The response to the speech of life is essential to becoming human. Word and spirit work together to create the texture of life in human existence, to repair the damage caused by the denial of life. Becoming human, for Siirala, is a gift that comes through listening to the giver of life; in theological terms it is being a hearer of God *(auditor dei),* the perfect life-giving Word. From his hermeneutical position hearing is the basis for all human communion.[138] Siirala refers to Luther, who insisted that simply to regard Jesus as a teacher of reality was to deny the divine Word contained in his whole life and the essential influence of that Word upon the community of faithful—persons transformed in communion, in a "we" relationship with one another, coparticipants in life. Siirala sees the bodily living Word as a New Testament phenomenon, the miracle of the visibly enfleshed Word creating an experience of community among persons who mutually experience the power of Christ's presence.

Thus, human life is realized as a dialogue in which every person is a word about life to every other person, and the word itself is a being with autonomous power (though it requires the cooperation of a human voice for the expression of its power). To be a listener to the active word of life implies obedience to that word and to life; it means an active participation in the ongoing process of creation.[139] Thought and soul for Luther were dimensions of human reality that was basically bodily reality. He argued that thinking should never be separated from the rest of human experience, in contrast to his intellectual opponent Erasmus, who had developed a hierarchical division between reason and the body. When a disembodied idea is divorced from the living word, it becomes life-denying. Thinking that tries to absolutize itself dissipates. When such absolutizing occurs, it leads to the fragmentation of human experience and the splitting into dichotomies of sense and thought, soul and body.

Emil Brunner conceives of the goal of encounter as the attainment of the truth of existence. In his work *Truth as Encounter* he places *alētheia* at the center of human dialogue. Etymologically *alētheia* means "nonconcealment," originally "a fact or state of affairs insofar as it is seen, shown, or expressed, and in such seeing, showing, or speech, is fully disclosed or discloses itself as it really is, bearing in mind the possibility that it could also be concealed, misrepresented, distorted, or suppressed. Thus *alētheia* is the full or 'actual' state of affairs."[140] For Brunner *alētheia* emerges out of participation in the life of another. In an authentic philosophy of existence it results when the subject-object antithesis is transcended and the human being is apprehended as a whole. This doctrine of truth comes to persons in dialogue, to give them a place in its coming and make them new. The word is the way in which being communicates with being, subject with subject; it does not convert the subject into an object but stimulates self-activity in the subject revealing itself.[141]

In the encounter with the truth of the literary work (that is, the reality intrinsic to it, its *is-ness*) the interpreter is not so much a knower as one who experiences. The encounter is not so much a conceptual grasping as an event in which a world opens itself up to the interpreter. Because each interpreter stands in a unique horizon, the language event that comes to emerge in the encounter is something truly new, something that could never have existed before. Roloff writes of this encounter in terms of perception and creativity. The performer perceives "potential evocations radiating from the literature" and, through an oral and bodily act, gives flesh and voice to these elements by intending to invoke perception *in others*.[142] Performance is interaction with literature and with others (the seeing and hearing audience) through the interpreter's sensitive perception of and assimilation with evocative qualities in the poem. This interaction is the nature of the interpreter's creativity. The creative act in interpretation is the expression of the inexpressible, the communication of the incommunicable.

From the point of view of an erotics of interpretation the perception of evocative elements in literature is something that can only arise in the context of a dialogue with the *word* or the *speaking voice* within the text.

The nature of this dialogue constitutes a structure of openness characterizing authentic questioning.

Socrates is the great model for authentic questioning in the dialogic quest for *alētheia.* The playful exchanges between question and answer knowing and not knowing, probe the subject matter without violating it but do so in order to come upon an appropriate access to its true nature. Another illustration of this dialogue is given from "The Mustard Seed Garden Manual." In the Chinese painting of a solitary man standing below the moon, moon and man seem ever so subtly to incline toward each other.[143] This posture is one of true dialogue in which both subjects question the true being of each other and work reciprocally to free the true nature of the other. Art as dialogue is not *mimesis,* but a unique creation of word and spirit through the human form. What is expressed is not imitation, but a true image, an icon that both expresses and leads to the reality beyond it through appropriate exchanges. The unimaginable is seen through the image with the inner eye. The word is heard through the image meeting the soul through the eye of the body. The poem constitutes experience as it reveals experience and manifests the truth that is experienced. The art image at the center of dialogue with an audience expresses itself in power and communion. Everything depends upon the question being addressed to the subject in a certain light, for the answer that the subject can yield will have meaning only in terms of the question put to it. In a sense the subject is dependent upon the interpreter for asking the right or the best question that will enable it to break through in self-revelation. The problem for the interpreter is: How to ask the right question? Gadamer describes only one way to find the best question to put to the work: through immersion in the subject itself.[144]

Roloff speaks of dialogic immersion in the subject as a "creative disposition" that characterizes both the engaged performer and the receptive audience. Immersion in the text is immersion in the affective domain of language. It is a willingness to listen to the creative expression of the language itself as the poem unfolds itself to the interpreter and finally to an audience. It is the ability to respond to the ongoing creation of newly perceived relationships between events. The interpreter acts upon the creative dispositions in the language itself, as well as upon her or his own dispositions, and the audience is held in this dynamic and is invited to participate in the poem through it. By coalescing with the creative disposition in the language the interpreter releases a power latent in the poem and manifest in utterance.

In his essay "Word of God and Hermeneutic" Gerhard Ebeling defines existentialist interpretation as interpretation of the literary work with regard to the word event: "existence is existence through word and in word."[145] Both Fuchs and Ebeling insist on the place of the interpreter as being important for receiving the gift of faith as revelation through word.

For Fuchs, language is always the word spoken in a given place and time.[146] In interpretation, faith would be faith in the world that is disclosed through the spoken language of the poem, and revelation would be the disclosure itself through the oralization of the poem's word in performance. The form of life that is literature is a language event that expresses "both individual forms of life . . . and the worlds in which they exist. . . . [W]hile I am in the world in which they live, I believe in them (which is not the same as saying I sympathize with them). By suggesting, by working through indirection, by miraculous creating through metaphor, . . . language *embodies*." And this embodiment of language, of the world presented to us by language, requires "the most intense application of the whole interpreter, head to foot and all the way through!"[147] *The Perception and Evocation of Literature* also speaks to the word-event when it says that "A performance of literature is a behavioral revelation in language and gesture."[148] Human beings speak their world. As we do so, we speak the world that is inside us, and the literary work also functions in this way. Through meaningful dialogue with the poem in the text the interpreter is given the power, in language that fills her or his whole bodily presence, to summon forth experience.

In the beginning is the word. The interpretation process is the coalescence between poem and interpreter. But the word is primary, for it is that which comes to be realized through the interpreter and which gives power to the interpreter. If we think of "faith," not in a doctrinal context, but in the sense of Tillich's "ultimate concern" or as giving ourselves over to belief in something that presents itself, what comes to be in interpretation is faith in the world of the poem revealed through the interpreter.

The creativity of the Word is something that is stressed in Christian theology. For Luther the creative Word is operative in the present condition. The work of creation is a continual process of the Word of God (Heb. 1:3), through whom all living beings are continually being made new (II Cor. 5:17; Gal. 6:15). God as Speaker *par excellence* creates from beginning to end. Faith as openness to the creative action of the Word means the coming to be of what is human. All of life emerges from speech. The creative Word "calls into existence the things that do not exist" (Rom. 4:17) and so brings newness into the world. Through union of Word and Spirit all things come to be. Faith is stretching out toward the Word and obtaining life from it. Spirit and Word (as utterance) are not separate but are in each other as creatively interpenetrating energies. Faith constitutes mutual activity on the part of speaker and hearer. It is a dialogue in power. The interpreter lays aside personal, judgmental values and attitudes in order to take on the values, stance, posture, and physical attitude within the literary work, revealed to the interpreter through language. The poem acts on the interpreter. In the encounter of interpretation two subjects meet each other as an *I* approaching a *Thou*, to realize the being of both in their creative relation. They change each other; they create each other.

Fuchs says that when we interpret a text, the text in turn interprets us. The text interprets itself by what it has to say about human existence. When the word interprets us, language becomes an active showing, or letting-be-seen, and so constitutes a phenomenon in the pure sense.[149] With regard to the biblical text (which is the hermeneutical topic for Fuchs and Ebeling) Ebeling asserts that it is not the text that is to be proclaimed, but the Word of God perceived as an encounter between God (as primary Speaker) and the listener. This encounter involves the text, is indeed dependent on the text, but is finally more than the text. In giving life to the text the interpreter (for Fuchs and Ebeling, the preacher) needs to consider both who is speaking (whose word it is) and who is listening (who forms the "audience"); she or he keeps a kind of double focus or draws an elliptical reality around two foci: one in the text and the other in the world.[150]

What is acting in this language encounter, or word-event, is *logos,* not the abstractive thought-*logos* of the Greeks, but the biblical *logos,* the utterance that communicates the self of the speaker.[151] The word that is united with an act of self-giving is the very essence of the literary text and must be treated as such by the interpreter. As Walter Ong writes, a word is an event in the world of sound that enables the mind to relate actuality to itself.[152] The Hebrew word *dabar* (from which comes the biblical use of *logos*) means both word and event, because it always implies speech, or the act of sounding a meaning, giving words an aura of power when they are spoken. This sounding of *dabar* implies that the spoken word conveys the person speaking as well as the message. Ebeling relates *logos* and *dabar* by pointing out that *logos* connotes coherence, and *dabar* implies that something is showing itself. Thus the combination of these words—and the combination of their respective connotative meanings—expresses the nature of the word-event as a *meaningful* event that involves at least two beings. Word, from this point of view, is not a statement but an invitation to participation and communion.[153] Thus, the biblical *Logos* is not only Christ come bearing the Creator's message but Christ come *as* the Creator's message. The *Logos* described in the Gospel of John is both the message of God and the person who delivers the message.[154]

A word-event is an event because it is rooted in experience. When the word becomes loosed from its roots in experience, it is diminished and is no longer an event. What admits one to the experience of *word?* It is *truly hearing* the word that comes to meet us, and this admits us into the experience of new worlds, even to new being.

If word and spirit are joined in the word-event, something needs to be said about spirit and the interpreter. Paul Tillich says of spiritual power that it can inspire human beings to insights into the depths of being that remain inaccessible to most people. "Without a doubt," he writes, "wherever it works, there is an element, possibly very small, of self-surrender, and an element, however weak, of ecstasy, and an element, perhaps fleeting, of awareness of the mystery of existence."[155] The presence of spirit can awaken one to insight into the way in which the world is to be taken. It can seem to break into consciousness through causing us to recognize what we are, shaking and transforming us. Finally it can reveal the object of ultimate concern to us in any given situation or moment of experience. For Tillich ultimate concern is nearly synonymous with passionate response to a quality of life. And even the most "spiritual" passion is not real without a bodily basis:

> In every act of genuine faith the body participates, because genuine faith is a passionate act. The way in which it participates is manifold. The body can participate both in vital ecstasy and in asceticism leading to spiritual ecstasy. But whether in vital fulfillment or vital restriction, the body participates in the life of faith. The same is true of the unconscious strivings, the so-called instincts of [the human] psyche.[156]

For the interpreter *faith* means something other than "ultimate" concern. Bacon points out that it is perhaps not too much to say that a *love* relationship exists between poem and interpreter, and it may not be too much to say that interpretation does involve faith and that that faith does take the poem as the subject of an ultimate concern in the context of the interpretation process. This process is a becoming process involving word and spirit, and it is realized through the bodily being of the interpreter, to involve both conscious and unconscious dynamics of assimilation. This process of incarnation is explored in the next chapter.

three

THE WORD BECOMES FLESH

In chapter one the course of this study was described as a sustained metaphor yoking interpretation with incarnation, unfolding through the juxtaposition of pairs of complementaries seen in a dialectical relationship of interpenetration and creation, some of which pairs are simply related qualities of the interpretation-incarnation process and some of which have the characteristics of opposition. In the last chapter contrasting approaches to interpretation were placed in relationship and examined in terms of a new attitude toward the *word* of the text: dominance or dialogue, penetration or discovery, forming the contrasting attitudes of hermeneutics (in the restricted sense) on the one hand and an erotics of interpretation on the other. The literary work was shown as a subject in its own right, as potentially living speech, or utterance: the *word* as *logos* (*dabar*).

The poem as a speaking-subject exists in potentiality. It exists as a potential voice until it enters the living field of what Roloff calls *acoustic space,* "the sound of life as it is happening."[1] Acoustic space as the world of experience centered in sound and emanating from the vocal body of a human being is the *seizing of sound* in a lived context. The potential "voice" of the poem is realized or actualized in the entelechy of performance, in the whole process of expressing itself through the living voice of the interpreting body-subject. The process of expressive entelechy is the process of incarnation, of the bodily form of the text joining with and showing itself through the bodily form of the interpreter, who has entered into a relationship of loving receptivity with it.

The process of interpretation as incarnation is a process of meeting and embodying in which the interpreter becomes the poem. This is to say, not that the interpreter becomes individual characters in the sense of imitating or impersonating them, but that the actual embodiment of their essence takes place as the entire text achieves its moment of fullness in performance. The locus, or position, of the interpreter is the locus, not of the poet, but of the poem itself. This process is a complex one and can only be described from the standpoint of several aspects at once. For the purposes of this study these aspects will be explored as pairs of complementaries forming an intricate pattern of interdependent elements.

Making/Acting

There is a sense in which the interpreter is both maker (poet) and actor, for the work of creation involves both of these aspects. In his *Nichomachean Ethics* Aristotle differentiated between making and acting as two separate activities. All art, said Aristotle, is concerned with the matter of the coming-to-be of something that can either be or not be. The task of art is to determine how best to bring something into being. The origin of the being is in the maker and not in the thing itself, for a thing cannot create itself out of nothing. If the human imagination is the source of all artistic making, Aristotle's statement is true. In a sense the art work is autonomous and self-determining, but this subject will be discussed later. For Aristotle the artist is the creative source of the art work, and artistic activity is not acting, but making.[2] It is the view of this study that the interpreter is not a critic but an artist. Interpretation is a unique art, though it has elements in common with both *poiēsis* and acting. Not because it is related to these, but simply because it is an art—and all art, according to Aristotle, is a making—does interpretation have the quality of original creation. *The word becomes flesh* means that the word is *made* flesh, is given the mode-of-being of flesh, and the imaginative activity of the interpreter does the making. But making itself is an act, a highly concrete and explicit act. Making the word to become flesh constitutes the enactment of the word.

In making the word to become flesh the interpreter makes herself or himself into the word, takes the word as poem into her or his body, continues the creation process begun by the poet. Continuing the creation process is different from "re-creating." The interpreter does not "make over" the poem but continues to make the poem into itself, to complete the process of its coming into being, by allowing it to achieve bodily entelechy through her or his own body. The interpreter's artistic activity is not based in a personal need to communicate to others and cannot be defined as "communication." It is essentially related to the need of the "art working" to speak itself and the interpreter's willingness to fulfill this need by making it manifest, even if there is no one in particular to see or hear. Thus Maritain says of artistic activity that it is not so much an activity of knowledge as of creation: it aims at making something according to the internal exigencies and the proper good of that being.[3] Defined thus, the art of interpretation is a creative striving toward being.

The interpreter makes the art of interpretation out of an act of incarnation, and the interpreter enacts this making or creating of new being through the givenness of the poem and the availability of her or his own bodily presence. The making and the acting are seen as one.

The being that comes to be itself, whose entelechy is realized, is not any particular aspect of the poem, such as its author, narrator, or characters. It is just the poem itself in all of its *is-ness*. Bacon differentiates between actor and interpreter by describing the actor's relationship with the writer and audience as lyrical: "the actor reading Keats' letter is Keats, insofar as he is able to be Keats." The interpreter's relationship with writer and audience is dramatic: "the interpreter reading Keats' letter tries to disappear into the life of the letter itself."[4] While Bacon is speaking of the interpreter's locus as matching the locus of the poem, he finds that it is helpful to see a relationship between locus and mode. The interpreter's task is not to impersonate the outer character of the speaking-subject, but to embody that subject's inner style—or, more fully, to embody the entire poem by manifesting as much of its inner quality as possible. The interpreter's locus is in the *logos* of the text—not only to speak what the text is saying but also to become the inner reality of the poem and to manifest that reality outwardly in bodily utterance.

Logos/Eros

In the last chapter *logos* and *eros* were discussed in terms of a hermeneutical approach to the literary work, which is also an erotics of interpretation. *Logos* and *eros* are of significance here in a different context, as central to the incarnating act of interpretation. In the Johannine Prologue *Logos* and light are identified in the person of Christ: "the Word was the true light that enlightens all . . . and he was coming into the world. He was in the world that had its being through him" (John 1:9–10, *Jerusalem Bible*). Through the living voice both speaker and message are revealed. Word and image are related in the manifestation of the real presence of the living utterance. *Logos* is neither the thing uttered nor the one who speaks, but the two manifest as one in the speaking voice.[5]

Logos also includes the idea of will as a concept of activity that experiences entelechy—the will to being. The self-revelation of the *Logos* takes place in three ways: creation, revelation, incarnation. In interpretation these aspects are seen as one, as the creation process of the poem ends in the incarnation of performance that constitutes the self-revelation of the poem. In *Logos* doctrine the Incarnation is the natural consummation of creation. Irenaeus followed this thinking, as did the medieval Franciscan Duns Scotus, contrary to Aquinas who believed the Incarnation to be simply the remedy for human catastrophe and the direct response of God to save humanity from the wages of sin. For the purpose of the present metaphor, incarnation in relationship to interpretation is best seen as the natural and only logical consummation of creation.[6] *Logos* speculation tended to assume two forms in Greek and Hebrew thought: the Greek concept of *logos* as indwelling thought or reason and the Hebrew notion of *logos (dabar)* as thought expressed in word and act. J. S. Johnston compares these concepts with the Latin distinction between *ratio* and *oratio*.

According to Johnston's study the Stoics were the first to distinguish between the two uses of *logos:* reason and word.

For Philo *logos* blended the Hebrew concept of act and utterance with the Stoic idea of immanence and Platonic transcendentalism. Philo's *logos* was the first-born, the image of God, the personal mediator. On the impersonal side *logos* was the intelligible world created from Idea by giving reality to all subordinate ideas. In relation to the world *logos* is creator. In relation to humanity *logos* is mediator, as between human beings and God, sharing the nature of both. In the Johannine Gospel *Logos* is the vitalizing principle that brings forth life and movement throughout creation and is also the active manifestation of the personal Creator, always moving, always creating and vitalizing, by means of an ongoing quality of relatedness with human life and world. St. Augustine wrote, "If God were to cease from speaking the Word, even for a moment, heaven and earth would vanish away."[7] For Irenaeus what was of importance was not only that God *spoke* to the world in Christ but that human beings *heard* and entered into dialogue with the Word of God. The importance of the Word in Incarnation is that through Word, God enters into relationship with humanity—Word is both spoken and received.[8]

For the Hebrews the spoken word was considered to be a source of power producing what it signified. In speaking the word the speaker revealed herself or himself. In early Christian theology the Word was the natural thing to become flesh, the perfect point of personal encounter between beings (God and humanity). The Word was uttered in the beginning as God's most intimate self-expression, the expression of Being calling to being.[9] The *Logos* existed before the Incarnation but was fulfilled only in the Incarnation as the necessary climax of creation.[10] In the beginning, through this same Word, "God said, 'let there be light'; and there was light" (Gen. 1:3). "By the word of the Lord the heavens were made" (Ps. 33:6). "The forces of nature continue to obey the Word which called them into being."[11] In Hebrew theology human words also participated in creation and had power. Words of curse and blessing had a power thought to be something more than that of producing a psychological effect in the hearer. They were believed to influence events and produce results. Thus the words of the prophets were endued with power, and "true" prophets were distinguished from "false" prophets by the intention of their utterances and what they effected, not by the seeming power or powerlessness of them. This belief in the quasi-autonomy of the word led to the later belief in the personification of the word.[12] St. Paul writes of his personal *logos*: "My speech [*logos*] and my message [*kerygma*] were not implausible words of wisdom, but in demonstration of the Spirit and power" (I Cor. 2:4). *Logos* here is nonverbal; Paul is writing of the utterance of his whole being manifested in his actions.[13]

St. Athanasius also writes that the Incarnation continues the work of creation: *"the renewal of creation has been wrought by the Self-same Word Who made it in the beginning."*[14] The Incarnate Christ is the One in whose image human beings were made as embodied spirit. The presence and love of the creative Word toward human life called that life into being.[15] The Incarnate Christ was a living mystery: "being the Word, so far from being Himself contained by anything, He actually contained all things in Himself." Christ is the Uncontained, existing solely in God, yet existing in a human body and alive; the source of all life in the universe, present everywhere, yet outside the whole, revealing light and life through bodily works and through activity in the world. For Athanasius the Word of God is seen as human power and energy.[16]

The interpreter becomes the incarnation of the poem by bringing her or his energy to it and by joining two life-forms in a presentational act. The word as life and light reverberates in the interpreter. The word "comes into the world" through the interpreter and manifests the world within it "that had its being" through it. The word voiced by the interpreter throws light on itself by means of the clarifying energy of sound. This incarnation depends on the interpreter's "capacity to establish and evoke imaginatively the auditory space within the literature."[17] It is not the printed page that is speaking in performance, but the interpreter alone is the *sound source*. The interpreter becomes the sounding and visual presentation of the literature, an icon, a being filled with sensuous form and structure, an iconic being that is *showing*.[18] This showing is light being cast on the poem's world from within the dynamic union of poem and interpreter. The word *is* the light, and it shows itself to the light, as the interpreter's voice and word-act of her or his whole bodily being illuminate the experience of the poem. The unique phenomenon of performance is a result of the unique perspective on the poem given by the interpreter's own light. The living coalescence between poem and performer is an active participation of the two energy sources in each other in order to accomplish the one thing necessary—the revelation of the poem in the bodily light of the interpreter acting with it.[19]

According to Wittgenstein language is a state in which we act as human persons. Human life is linguistic life. To ask if utterances are "meaningful" and "justified" is finally to ask whether we are "meaningful" and "justified," that is, if the words are authentic utterances to begin with.[20] Words have no meaning in themselves, but meaning is in us, the human users of words. Words spring from human sources, and human beings are defined by the language that emanates from them through the intentional-acting of being.[21] The notion of speech includes a *someone* standing behind the words, intending meaning through them, and the possibility of self-disclosure to the hearer. Utterances are self-involving in belief, performance, and commitment. For Wittgenstein *meaning* is like my approaching someone and announcing myself to someone who is invited to do the same. It is essentially relationship.[22]

John Hospers puts forth an aesthetic theory based on a similar attitude toward meaning—that meaning is not in the work of art but in ourselves and that we can recognize the manifestation of meaning in art as the meaning-act of a human artist. The aesthetic attitude then becomes an affective-receptive attitude in the percipient of art.[23] Likewise, for Hospers no word has meaning of itself until it is given meaning by someone (one could say, until it is uttered in a context or world of meaning). A poem "means" to us what it evokes in us or draws out from us.[24] Following this line of thought, Arthur A. Vogel adds a theological dimension to meaning and, in incarnational terms, relates all meaning to body-meaning: "The source of all meaning is the personal presence of a speaker."[25] Primary experience, which is experience of world, is prior to thought and comes from our relationship to world through our personal embodiment. A human being is more than a bodily location; it is also a personal presence reaching beyond the body. A personal presence is something always left open, never completed, but always overflowing definition and representation. A person is never wholly known but, in the process of always becoming more and more herself or himself, is always transcending and "beyonding" her or his own presence.

There is a dimension of personal being that, although expressed through acts, is always beyond the totality of acts. For Vogel personal presence overflows thought and is applicable to nonhuman beings as well as humans, insofar as nonhuman beings participate in a human world. "If we think about it, we will discover that every experience we have of the world, or of anything within the world, as other—as something that can say something to us—depends upon our prior acceptance of the other as a self-sufficient speaker."[26] As human beings, we are body-words, and speaking is a sacrament that involves our whole being: human beings are linguistic because our "most immediate and intimate existence has the nature of a verbal utterance." Human *being* is interpreted through utterance and formed through utterance. There is a sense in which a human being *is* a word. We are able to use words only because our being is of the nature of words.

Words are extensions of the body; they are meaning in matter, a location of presence, embodied presence. Meaning is in words as we are in our bodies, and it is only because we are our bodies that we can "be" our words—or, as it is usually put, mean what we say. We can stand behind our words because our presence overflows them and is more than they can contain, but we choose to stand behind them with our infinite presence because we are also in them.[27]

Georges Gusdorf articulates a phenomenology of speaking as a form of bodily gesture expressing time (the convergence of past and future in the *now* moment of utterance) and space (the speaker's place in the world).[28] Not speech, but the speaking human being in a context of human reality is what constitutes meaning and reveals experience. For Gusdorf speaking implies a nondualistic attitude toward world: the person as lived experience, speaking as a way of being-in-the-world and stretching out toward others, bodily insertion in the world (as a lived body, neither machine nor ghost), and the actual phenomenon of the lived world. Speaking itself is neither being nor nonbeing but is the engagement of persons in others. Reflection on language should begin only with human reality as self-affirmation and self-definition, a way of being a presence in and to the world. Speaking as a human reality is always language in action, language showing what-is, language as a verbal image. Speech is always a process and relation.[29]

As God called the world into being from nothing through the Word, so human beings call world into more and more being as the natural continuation of the creation process. Speaking (as language in action) is something that can only happen *between*. It expresses the relational nature of human life and signifies dependence on others through encounter. Speech distortions (or inauthentic speaking) appear in one of two extremes: the alienated, highly personal, noncommunicative language of the schizophrenic that excommunicates the rest of the world, or the generalized, nonpersonal, nonexpressive, superficial language that implies a loss of selfhood and relatedness and is basically de-energized. Both of these language perversions indicate a dis-eased one-sidedness in which the profound sense of self dominates and excludes on the one hand through extreme "density" of speech, or the superficial ego as non-self dominates on the other and fails in self-communication or expression through a "thinning" of speech.

Gusdorf's speaking theory takes communion as the goal toward which speaking strives, when it is both authentic self-expression and communication. The consummation of authentic speaking would be permanent, transforming communion, through which values are discovered and the self emerges from solitude through conscious being-with another. This emergence amounts to an enlargement of the whole person made possible through openness to the *Other* met as a *Thou*. Finally, true communion is overcoming the hyphen between *I* and *Thou* and transforming that relationship into a "We." The "We" relation does not mean loss of self, for "I still reach out as I to the Other." For Gusdorf the "We" relation means mutual recognition and hospitality.

Speaking as expression is another aspect of language, one in which speaker as actor creates landscapes through bodily presence. Expression becomes a movement beyond the self that gives voice to the real. Invocation and evocation are fused when speaking becomes *the ultimate call of consciousness.* Authentic speaking as expression is an act of living that comes from listening to the world and yielding an original response to it. Thus, authentic expression is appropriate, honest, and responsible according to the perspective of the speaker.[30] Speaking as expression tending toward communion is called a holy action by Gusdorf, the realization or enactment of a personal eschatology. Speech as a sacrament is the outering of the inner self, which results in communion between beings.

Again, speaking is brought into the realm of sound, or the sounding space of the body. In his study of the history of language Noah Jonathon Jacobs sums up the biblical view of language and its implications for a Christian sacramental theory of language: "All we know is that the first feeble sounds which broke forth from Adam have come down to us from ear to ear, the open gateway to the soul, and that the fatal sequence of that inexhaustible voice reverberating down the ages is the bond of solidarity which unites us in one continuous humanity."[31]

The linguistic philosopher Ernst Cassirer implies the identification of language with bodily reverberation in his discussion of the relation of speech to myth. The metaphorical and indirect modes of description to which language resorts lead naturally to the origins of myth, which Max Müller believes to emerge from speech.[32] Cassirer suggests that there is present in primitive myth and religion a kind of sense and reason and that they are by no means entirely incoherent: "but their coherence depends much more upon unity of feeling than upon logical rules."[33] Cassirer also calls for a view of language that does not objectify it. The semantic function of language is centered in the principle of a dynamic *logos*: "Language must be looked upon as an *energeia* rather than as an *ergon.*"[34]

Though it is impossible to trace the origins of language, we can trace attitudes toward language found in other cultures that can illuminate the place of language in the human community in various periods. Relevant to the interests of this study is the place of language in Hebrew culture and its influence upon Christian ethos. In the Hebrew tradition words were essentially names insofar as their evocative power was concerned. By invoking the name of God one called forth God's presence; this is why it was forbidden to utter the holy name YHWH. A celestial power was attributed to a name, and these powers were invoked by utterance to answer the call of the speaker. In describing the superstitious aspect of Jewish religion Joshua Trachtenberg writes that a universal characteristic was the conviction that a person's name was the essence of her or his being. One Hebrew text says that a person's name *is* the person, and another that the name is the person's soul.[35] Thus the essential character of persons and also of things is contained in their names. To know a name is to have access to its bearer's being. The name was believed to hold an autonomous potency. To speak a name was to gain power over its bearer, not because a name could coerce the being to whom it belonged, but because the word itself was invested with power that transferred to anyone who uttered it.[36]

In his anthropological study of literature Wayne Shumaker notes a similarity in thinking patterns between primitive expression and the act of literary composition.[37] Pararational psychic patterns seem to emerge during literary creativity that reveal deeply implicit biological and racial tendencies to indicate that the artist is somehow in touch with her or his own physical structures and the vast storehouse of the racial and cultural past, both of which reassert themselves in the powerful act of literary creativity. The artist is potentially a whole person in whom discursive thought and affective response to perceptions are reintegrated through a creative process of language.

Otto Rank, also relating primitive expressive attitudes to the power of language, says that primitive peoples place singing in an inferior role to dancing and instrumental music, possibly because of a fear of pronouncing the *word* that is still identical with the being it designates.[38] The magical effect of the spoken word may also be salutary, as when it does form the basis of songs and hymns of praise, which Rank believes to be the oldest forms of prayer and the original forms of the art of poetry. Rank also notes that the reintegrative effort to overcome dualism in aesthetics is related to the same tendency in religion and erotic love: "The artistic solution to dualism appears to be somewhere between these two."[39] The intention of the artist transcends and combines the collective religious quest for union and integration and the individual erotic quest that replaces God with the beloved. In the language arts this aesthetic integration is achieved through union with the inner being of what is expressed.[40]

Speech is the sign of human power precisely because it reveals that a person is not her or his own master. Gerhard Ebeling says that this lesson is a primary one taught us by the two questions What empowers us to use word? and What is the power of the word?[41] These questions force us to recognize that we participate in word in the form of answerability—we have neither the first word nor the last, but our word arises as a response to what-is and has the characteristic not only of a call to being but of a response to that call. We depend on finding the right or best word to speak out our situation, and therein lies our freedom. Thus, responsible speaking comes from the silence of listening. Ambiguity in speech is the result of the unfinished nature of language. Words are not labels for finished products but are the materials of a process that implies an ongoing inner and responsive movement from the speaker through the word to the world. Words may both evoke the presence of what they name and allow that presence to become audible in the world.

Speech, for Ebeling, does not close off areas of interest or enforce uniformity of meaning, but is linguistically creative in that it opens up new dimensions of meaning and world as it creates them. Speech becomes

responsible participation in the word-event. The word is its own illumination, for what is hidden within it must be identified with what is spoken
into the context and thereby brought to light. The spoken word can
illuminate the entire word context.[42] Understanding is not understanding
of the word but *through* the word. A situation in which the verbal utterance
is made is an obscure situation that is illumined by the verbal utterance.[43]
Logos then becomes another *aspect,* a possible *way of seeing.*[44] Here Ebeling
emphasizes the fact that a word must take place *between two beings,* that it
brings the two together, and that it shows something by showing itself in
relationship. "Where word happens rightly, existence is illuminated," and
that always means an existence with others.[45]

In *The Perception and Evocation of Literature* the literary work is said to
create specific worlds from specific namings. In the context of this spec-
ificity the word opens up both within and without, as it were, to embody
both a literal meaning and an inner symbolic power. Roloff calls the
speaking symbol in this context "an idea-word-utterance" and says that it
reveals world in three ways: "(1) it sets up a sound, (2) it condenses
perception, and (3) it symbolizes experience."[46] Roloff calls the specific
world created by the literary work through the symbol power of language
the "metaworld" of authentic poetic experience. The metaworld is a new
and inner world that always involves the perceiver.[47] This world—when
powerfully revealed through a perceptive and evocative performer—lives
with the perceiver always. *The Art of Interpretation* also views the word as
constitutive and creative, indeed as self-illuminating in the sense in which
Ebeling speaks of it: "Poems name and define feelings and provide new
contexts for them. They give us words for feelings, and, in a sense,
knowing the word for it makes a thing intelligible."[48]

Cassirer says that language does not describe life but that it creates life.
The *form* of language is the counterpart world of emotion and sensation.[49]
Language emerges through a speaking-self, and the speaking-self can
only be an incarnate self. Cassirer traces the identification or integration
between the sense of self, soul and body, and certain languages, and
illustrates the essential place of the body in the phenomenon of the
speaking-self:

In Coptic "self" is rendered by the noun "body," to which possessive suffixes
are attached. Likewise in the Indonesian languages, the reflexive object is
designated by a word which can mean "person," "spirit," or "body." Finally
this usage extends even to the Indo-Germanic languages; in Vedic and
classical Sanskrit for example, the self and the I are rendered sometimes by
the word for soul *(ātmán)* sometimes by the word for body *(tanu).* All this
makes it plain that where the intuition of the self, the soul, the person, first
appears in language, it clings to the body.[50]

Hebrew also manifests this tendency of exchangeability between aspects as coequal expressions of the self. The personal reflexive pronoun is rendered by the words "soul," "person," "face," "flesh," and "heart."

In the early Christian church words for the *Logos*-Christ also reflected the centrality of the body. Words such as *sarkothenta*—"enfleshed"—were used of God incarnate.[51] Jesus has been more recently described by the term *Logos ensarkos*—"the Word enfleshed." Elsewhere the term "incarnate" is said to mean "embodied, or more strictly 'made to be in flesh,' . . . 'coming to be in flesh.' "[52] Origen wrote that "the diversity of the world cannot exist apart from bodies." Bodily nature admits of various changes to such a degree that it can experience every kind of transformation.[53] No being in the universe can live apart from the body, for only the Trinity can experience life without a body, and since the Ascension of Christ a human body may be said even to participate in that life.[54] Finally, Origen says that the Word of God is "in one flesh."[55]

The human body, however, has been deposed from its primordial place of personal integrity, and despite the ethos of incarnational Christianity, Western culture has not yet recovered from the philosophical schism of personal being into body and soul, feeling and thought, spirit and senses. The result of this loss of the sense of body as personal being has been twofold, taking the form of Manichean mortification of the purportedly "evil" flesh on the one hand and of libertinism on the other, which indulges the flesh in excesses only pointing to its supposed irremedial separation from the soul. Either extreme reflects the dualism that has infected our culture since the time of Zoroaster's influence in the morally split religious consciousness of Persia. Christian theology has tried to combat dualistic tendencies by referring to the effects of the Incarnation, in whose light the human body and all material creation are shown in their original integrity. Incarnational theology has not always been successful in countering dualism, however, even in the Church. Mistrust of the body and of the integrity of humanity as bodily, spiritual being is still reflected in instances of psychological dis-ease and moral disorder. Even the arts, which are symbols of incarnation and whose existence depends on the incarnation of the art work, have tended to reflect a dualism in which spirit has been expressed as something "over against" and "more noble" than the body.

The art of interpretation may have suffered the ill effects of this kind of thinking more than other art forms because of an unfortunate philosophical position used to develop an aesthetic of interpretation as an art separate from acting. Even in recent years interpretation students have been told by instructors to inhibit bodily expression of the literary work in performance, because physical movement implied that the interpreter was "acting" rather than interpreting. Some instructors have gone so far as to suggest to their students that movement from the waist up, if it was not explicit but toned-down or "suggestive" movement, qualified as interpretation, but if the performer moved the lower part of the body, she or he was no longer "just" interpreting but was dangerously near to "acting"! Such advice not only is aesthetically unsound but is artistically harmful and, from an incarnational standpoint, wrong. Academic emphasis on intellectual comprehension of the literary work may have been of value in directing the potential interpreter to valid methods of critical analysis, but it has done the art work and the interpreter an injustice in denying the value—and necessity—of a holistic response to an encounter with literature. As Bacon and Breen point out in *Literature as Experience,* the artificial "antitheses of mind and body, thought and action are disastrous." They cite Alfred North Whitehead with regard to the reasoning behind teaching students to read aloud: "I lay it down as an educational axiom that in teaching you will come to grief as soon as you forget that your pupils have bodies."[56]

Theorists today are seeking a more balanced and holistic approach to interpretation, an approach in which the engagement of the whole person with the literary work is primary. In the past a tendency to overintellectualization has been responsible for imbalance and a resulting lifelessness in the art of interpretation. What Thomas Merton says of parallel trends in theology applies to interpretation as well: "What is important is not liberation from the body but liberation from the mind. We are not entangled in our own body but entangled in our own mind."[57] The source of division is not incompatibility between body and spirit, but an overemphasis on the analytical capacities of the rational mind and its tendency to divide without putting back together whatever happens to be the object of its analysis. The remedy for this overemphasis is not to eliminate the place of rational analysis in the encounter with the literary work, but to restore it to a perspective that views poetry and the word as bodily creations and incarnational expressions that cannot be comprehended in their *is-ness* only by logical dissection.

Literary theorists have recently made bold statements in defense of this position. Stanley Burnshaw maintains, "Poetry begins with the body and ends with the body."[58] The poetic process is a life-sustaining activity deriving from a continuous dialogue between body and situation. Creativity involves a relaxation of the ego-functions and a "creative regression" to the openness of unconscious gesture. The poet, says Burnshaw, is above all else a person committed to keeping alive both inner and outer worlds and to bringing those worlds into the interchange of dialogue. Burnshaw examines poetry and poetic process as a fusion of voluntary and involuntary, conscious and unconscious dynamics, originating in bodily being and nondualistic in nature. Poetry is considered as somatic and affective activity. All poetic rhythms, sounds, and images echo movement within

the poet's body. The poem is an *internal metaphor* of the body, and "the
entire human organism always participates in any reaction."[59] For poet
and interpreter creation is the process of taking in the world and releasing
it transformed. This transformation takes place through a process of
assimilation and coalescence between inner and outer worlds and is made
possible through the poet's or interpreter's love of the world to be made.

Creation is an intimate union of meaning and act, which incarnates
realities in the human situation and transforms thought-images into lived
experience.[60] Leicester Bradner writes: "It is only when an idea becomes
flesh and blood and dwells in our imagination that we truly behold its
glory and that it takes possession of us for better or worse. In poetry,
drama, and fiction, as in religion, there is no salvation in abstract proposi-
tions."[61]

This entire process of incarnating is a process of *eros* for the word.
Maritain writes of the similarity between the "I" of poetry and the "I" of
the saint: both speak from a "substantial depth of the living and loving
subjectivity, . . . a subject-act, . . . a subject which gives."[62] The interpreter
enacts spirit in the flesh through a creative energy of love for the poem.
The interpreter's "I" is the same as the poet's "I," for the interpreter and
poet are both artists and speak themselves into their work as artists. The
creator seeks, then, never to subdue the work to herself or himself, but
just the opposite—to become subdued to the work. The more truly creative the artist is, the more she or he will want the art work to develop
according to its own nature.

According to Dorothy Sayers, "Love-in-Energy" and "Love-in-Power"
are related as artist and art work, for the work of love "demands the
co-operation of the creature, responding according to the law of its
nature."[63] Sayers quotes a passage from St. Augustine, *On the Trinity*,
which is applicable here:

> We behold, then, by the sight of the mind, in that eternal truth from which
> all things temporal are made, the form according to which we are, and
> according to which we do anything by true and right reason, either in
> ourselves, or in things corporeal; and we have the true knowledge of things,
> thence conceived, as it were as a word within us, and by speaking we beget it
> from within; nor by being born does it depart from us. And when we speak
> to others, we apply to the word, remaining with us, the ministry of the voice
> or of some bodily sign, that by some kind of sensible remembrance some
> similar thing may be wrought also in the mind of [the one] that hears,—
> similar, I say, to that which does not depart from the mind of [the one] that
> speaks. . . . And this word is conceived by love, either of the creature or of
> the Creator, that is, either of changeable nature or of unchangeable truth.[64]

St. Augustine was speaking of a love for the creature created by an
entirely loving Creator—the Divine Word being for him the Source of all

words—and so rightly indicated that love of the creature passes on to love
for the Creator. In the case of the interpreter's relationship with the
literary text, love of the creature is an end in itself and determines all other
motives and inclinations. Love of the creature may overflow into love of
those to whom the creature is given, so that the moment of performance
becomes a conscious or preconscious act or intention of good will—the
love called *agape*—toward the audience, to bring the audience into the
energy field of the interpretation event and so make communion possible.
But the interpreter's *eros* is for the *word* within the literary work and
includes a self-giving love for all that the work is. All artists participate in
this love of the work according to Maritain. The interpreter's love for the
word is like the poet's, for both artists are committed in different ways to
realizing and embodying the art-utterance of the poem. The writer's
commitment to fictional characters in the following passage from Maritain can be converted into the interpreter's attitude toward the being of
the whole poem:

> *Amor extasim faciens:* it is by love, not by an obscure collusion, that the
> novelist is in his characters. He does not paint them well, . . . does not know
> them unless, living in them, he judges them, not to "intervene" from without
> and twist their destiny, but, on the contrary, to follow their destiny from
> within, and make it true.[65]

Stanislavski's most frequently and insistently given advice to his students was "Love the art in yourself and not yourself in the art."[66] A true
love for the art involves searching oneself and finding the means to relate
to the work, not altering the work to suit oneself. Actors and interpreters
who "charm and seduce audiences" by their ability to reveal themselves
through the work, rather than the work through themselves, are not true
artists for Stanislavski, but egotists whose aim is not to love, but to exploit,
the art work. Such persons really love themselves in the art more than the
art in themselves. There is no creation in this attitude, no inner exchange
of energy, but only exploitation.[67]

Reality is the chief goal of the artist, reality as a universe of feeling, and
this reality is connected with values found through loving encounter.[68]
George Whalley believes that to find reality through an encounter with
the art work is also to become real. The nature of the energy exchange
between *logos* and *eros* in the art process is centered in the fulfillment of
reality as it communicates itself to loving participants:

> The fullest and deepest reality is achieved through love. This is clearly the
> case for love of persons; but it applies also to the "inorganic" world. Only
> when a thing is grasped in the closest conceivable relationship—the relation-
> ship of love—do we begin to know that we are penetrating into the inner
> nature of that thing. Only in love can we give ourselves out fully enough to

lose ourselves and so make real both the world and ourselves. It is the function of the artist with his capacity for loving things, to see things "as they really are." . . . [T]he artist can discover . . . reality only by making a work of art. By embodying in physical material his feeling of reality, by incarnating his feeling for reality, the artist discovers and realizes both himself and the world.[69]

Loving union with the word is consummated in revelation, the illumination of world: "the Word was the true light that enlightens all" (John 1:9; JB). The relationship of the interpreter to the light is twofold. The interpreter embodies the light (as word) and is a witness to the light, as is said of John the Baptist, the forerunner and proclaimer of the Word: "a witness to speak for the light" (John 1:8, JB). Because the interpreter does not cease to be a person, but for the moment of interpretation is shown as a being transformed into the word of the poem (the revelation of a long process preparing for that moment), the interpreter can be described metaphorically as *both* incarnation and witness. Insofar as the interpreter *is* the poem, she or he is shown as the incarnation of the word; insofar as the interpreter *shows* the poem, she or he is a witness speaking for it. It is important to include this last aspect in the metaphor, because it recalls the perspective that poem and interpreter are ultimately separate beings, and though they are seen as one in performance, they are ultimately two, whose function in relationship is to illuminate a world, explicitly given within the poem, and implicitly present and recognized from within the interpreter. The coming together of the two may be described as an intersubjective relationship.

Intersubjectivity/Hypostasis

The symbol of the Incarnate Word has been described as having the effect of overcoming the opposition between the self and the not-self, between subject and object. The Incarnate Word is seen as a principle of unity "presupposed in all the differences of things, and in all our divided consciousness of them."[70] Yet the Incarnate Word causes beings, not to be absorbed into each other, but, just the opposite, to enter into open relationship with each other despite their intrinsic separateness.

In chapter two the word within the poem was described as a speaking-subject. The interpreter, then, meets the word-poem not as an object, but as a subject showing itself through presence. Martin Buber distinguishes between true beings and objects in noting that objects have their life only in the past, but an authentic being is always lived in the present and is encountered in the present situation.[71] For Buber *I-Thou* is the primary word, establishing the world of relation. Love and spirit emerge *between I* and *Thou* and are not energies that cling to the *Thou* as a "content," for that would be to reduce the *Thou* to an object. Spirit is not in the *I* or in the *Thou,* but between *I* and *Thou.* [72]

When Buber first went to Vienna as an eighteen-year-old student, he encountered the theatre for the first time and there received the inspiration for his later philosophy of dialogue. Buber *heard* the players *speak* the German language and bring it to life. He experienced the power of the words not as mere printed signs, but as the sounds which they actually were, and he saw how a dramatic creation was made from these soundings. He perceived the spokenness of speech as the illumination of human existence. This revelation became a way that would lead him directly to *I and Thou,* for here was the reality of human speech as an event. Thus, Buber discovered the life of dialogue through the spokenness of speech. [73] For Buber dialogue never dissolves into fusion, for what is essential in true dialogue is *seeing the other* or *experiencing the other side.* [74] The *Thou* for Buber must always be *Other,* not merely the projection of the image of the *I* onto the *Thou* as a solipsistic identification.

The *I* and *Thou* relation is an event that arises between two beings who yet remain separate. It is not a fusion, but a true dialogue. Buber taught that each thing or being has two natures: one passive, comparable, appropriable, and dissectible; the other active, incomparable, inappropriable, and irreducible. This latter nature engages in the *I-Thou* encounter. The dialogue between the "inexpressible circle of things and the experiencing powers of our senses" is not just a matter of vocalization and response; "it is the incarnate spirit." [75] The primary word *I-It* involves the first nature described, and this word can never be spoken with the whole being. The primary word *I-Thou* can *only* be spoken with the whole being. *I-Thou* is the word of relation and togetherness, within which each of the members remains integral and separate. The two beings are essentially different, each one unique, and this uniqueness is what is discovered and celebrated in the relationship. Buber also likens the work of art to the meeting between *I* and *Thou,* for the work of art expresses neither lifeless objectivity nor personal subjectivity but is a "witness of the relation between the human substance and the substance of things." [76] Another being can only become a *Thou* by being made present, by becoming a presence. To make another being present means imagining the inner processes of the other: making vivid the other's thoughts, feelings, wishes, and desires. In making present something of the other's character the other is made present in a concrete way. To an extent, the one imagining feels, wishes, and thinks what the other feels, wishes, and thinks. The other is felt and known from within. The *I* and the *Thou* are joined in a common situation, are made present to each other, and acknowledge each other as selves.

Drama, as a species of poetry, is regarded by Buber to be "the formation of the *word* as something that moves *between* beings, the mystery of word and answer." When the word is also a *Thou,* a special form of dialogue emerges which is the incarnation, not just of spirit, but of the word itself. This special dialogue is the interpreter's relationship to the literary work. For this dialogue to be real, the interpreter is not merely a passive recipient of the word of the text but actively engages in a mutual questioning and response with it. If the thought of one's own appearance in the dialogue, or the effectiveness of what one has to say (through gesture, intonation, and such) to the poem, outweighs the commitment to the speaking-poem, then the interpreter works not as a creator, but as a destroyer. *I and Thou* as a primal experience always takes as its goal the recognition and preservation of the integrity of the other and works to affirm this through the interplay of understanding and misunderstanding, openness and closedness, which always constitutes genuine dialogue.

Maurice Merleau-Ponty's phenomenology of perception and existence is pertinent to this discussion of relatedness, for it is ultimately a phenomenology of incarnation, of open unity between life-world and the body-subject's self-awareness as both perceiving and perceived.[77] This dual direction of perception is the body's fundamental approach to world, and it is experientially prior to reflection and conceptualization. Incarnate consciousness is the body-subject's primary mode of existence. For Merleau-Ponty perception rather than dialogue marks the vital relationship between human being and world. Corporeal perception is our original and fundamental mode of becoming a presence in the world. The perceiver and the perceived tend to become indistinguishable, so that it may be difficult or impossible to tell who is seen and who is seeing. Painters often say that what they perceive also looks at them. They are expressing a prepersonal consciousness that is the essence of life in the flesh and is the way in which the body is present to itself. This double nature of perception is the body teaching itself to know the simultaneous presence of multiple perspectives, because the body is present to itself in two ways—as perceived in self-awareness and as perceiving actor—powerfully linked in "compresence."[78]

For Merleau-Ponty language varies and amplifies intercorporeal communication, as it speaks thoughts from a body-subject to a body-subject, causes the other to speak and to become what she or he *is* but never could have been alone. Thus, we do not have speech, but speech has us.[79] We are formed by, we become by, means of our speech. Speech as a gesture moves beyond thought, beyond self, to fill and create a *beyond,* toward which the body-subject is always being moved by the meaning that is the total movement of speech.[80] Thus, the evocation of being lies in "A certain manner of being flesh."[81] The body-subject knows itself only in encounter with the world and through other body-subjects. Merleau-Ponty says that at the heart of the subject the ontological world as well as the ontological body is discovered; the knowing subject is the ontological body-subject taking in, in a comprehensive view, the world.[82]

Gabriel Marcel's philosophy of presence is more personal than Merleau-Ponty's phenomenology of perception. For Marcel presence can be achieved only by relinquishing the role of spectator and participating in a situation as one truly engaged and available to it and open to the possibility for communion. Marcel asserts that one who would think and feel as a whole person must think and feel as an actor, not as a mere spectator in the world.[83] To the degree that we can recognize mystery (as a truth of existence that contains us and that does not give itself over to analysis), the interpenetration between mind and body, self and world, person and person (interpreter and text), will be seen as deepening our participation in relationships that illuminate their participants and clarify their situations. Primary reflection is what Marcel calls the divisive, rationalistic tendency of thinking, which may reduce life, love, or faith to experiences that are too dim or general to be understood. When this reduction happens, secondary reflection must arise to "assert the rights of participation over observation, encounter over objectification, concrete existence over abstraction."[84] Participation is experience that takes place at a preconceptual level and is creative. Creation for Marcel is never a production but always means an active receptivity to presences that are met as other selves, or subjects. Thus, all creative reality is intersubjective—not merely objective or subjective but an actually lived dialogue and mutual *disponibilité* (availability, disposability) between beings present to each other.[85]

Marcel's philosophy of presence also had its origins (and later, expression) in drama. The philosophical validity of the drama best illustrates intersubjectivity by letting the subject speak in a situation of being with other subjects. The dramatic act is the best example of participation. In it beings are illumined. For Marcel being is light, an *illumining,* and being finding itself as a presence is also *illumined.*[86] The virtue of dramatic art consists in the fact that participation (its very nature) cannot occur unless the ego-centric spirit is exorcized. Authentic creation in drama absolutely depends on this exorcism, for preoccupation with self is always a barrier between self and others. If the barrier is overthrown in dramatic creation, a paradox arises, in that the actor in an authentic relationship with the dramatic work rediscovers her or his own personal experience: the actor's experience enters communication with the experiences of others. But this experience can only happen when the actor is freed from the demands of the ego. "The fact is," says Marcel, "that we can understand ourselves by starting from the other, or from others, and only by starting from them."[87]

Poetry is also significant in Marcel's philosophy of presence, for the poem's being is a word-being, and "it is in the nature of the word, as such, to evoke a presence."[88] When language dies or the word is vitiated for some reason, poetry functions to restore power and vitality to it. The word is essentially a physical gesture, for without the body it cannot exist. The body speaks and evokes reality, not as an instrument, but as the only personal way of being in the world. Poetry, like all art, depends on personal involvement. For Marcel this amounts to saying that it has its source in a vocation in the true sense of the word—in the sense that poetry is a summons to which being responds. Spirit and word are manifested together in an intersubjectivity that transcends collectivism and individualism. Marcel views poetry as a kind of prophecy, as one voice speaking for another or many others in an intersubjectivity that is universal.[89]

Poetry is the highest form of dialogue, for it opens out onto the world of presence and relatedness by speaking its being into the world. The actor's or interpreter's work in coalescing with the poem passes over from a subjective act into an intersubjective significance, not as a possession, but as an ongoing task.[90] The interpreter *speaks* the poem; the poem cannot speak itself except through her or him. Insofar as the interpreter sustains the words of the literary work by her or his own being, the interpreter truly speaks in one voice with the poem. This act presupposes an openness between poem and interpreter. Marcel relates this activity to the phenomenon of being: "One could say that intersubjectivity is the fact of being together in light."[91] It constitutes *being in a situation* together, which, for interpretation, becomes the situation of performance preceded by all the rehearsal situations leading up to it.

Another pertinent concept presented by Marcel is the idea of *ingathering,* "A state in which one is drawing nearer something." It is not an introversion, but more like a "conversion," though not in a religious sense. It involves the distillation of energies and attitudes into a centering of power in relatedness. Marcel points out an internal paradox in ingathering: "to enter into the depths of one's self means here fundamentally to get out of oneself."[92] Ingathering is an act of inner creativity and transformation involving intense responsiveness through a kind of interior hospitality, openness, or active receptivity to another presence. Ingathering as an aspect of intersubjectivity entails intentionality, an orientation of the will to entering a new relationship involving the whole body as a way of existence. This aspect of intersubjectivity means self-exposure to the other, so that both the self and the other become mutually interpenetrable. Hospitality becomes allowing the other to participate in "a certain plenitude"; it is a gift of oneself in a movement from dialectic to love (*eros* and *agape*) made visible in communion.[93] This other-directed hospitality enlarges the self, precisely through making it unself-conscious and outgoing. "Such a transformation can be accomplished only by an inward relaxation in which I abolish the sort of constriction which makes me shrink into myself and which deforms me."[94] It is by this reciprocal and unself-conscious outgoing that we gain access to being and can enter into relationship with the *Thou.* It is a goal to be achieved, not through scientific techniques, but by a responsiveness to the call to transcend the self.

The goal of intersubjectivity is ultimately a union with other selves brought about through permeability and spiritual availability. It is an "affective unity characteristic of incarnate being or existential participation."[95] The nature of incarnate personality is such that to affirm that a being exists is to acknowledge that it can come into contact with one's body, however indirectly.[96] To treat the other as a *Thou* is to treat the other as freedom and to cooperate in helping that freedom to be. It is to acknowledge the mystery of the other as something in which I am involved. It is to recognize the other as a presence, a subject opening itself and inviting me to do the same, for presence is intersubjective. The subject is the magnetic center of presence.[97] While we can attempt to grasp an object, we can only incline ourselves toward a presence. We cannot gather to ourselves and welcome what is merely an object; we can really only take it or leave it. But a presence can, in the final analysis, *only* be invoked or evoked, and the means for evocation is the word. This evocation opens to us what Marcel calls *the presential side* of a being.[98] Objective messages are transmitted; presences enter into communion through manifesting themselves to each other. Insofar as the process of interpretation does involve the transmission of messages and objective analyses, it has not yet reached the threshold of being. That is the very place where presence reveals itself, to refresh and renew those to whom it is shown as a manifestation of wholeness.

Walter Ong writes of the relationship between the *Other* and the *I* in terms of belief. Belief as faith (belief *in*) is higher and deeper than belief as opinion (belief *that*). The former acknowledges the *Other* as a Subject-*Thou*; the latter reduces the *Other* to an Object-*It*.[99] For Ong the authentic literary work is essentially an evocative presence: "Literature exists in the context of one presence calling to another."[100] The evocative quality of literature establishes it in a relation of interiority with the interpreter, for literature is a quality of voice, and commerce between interiors is most readily attained through voice. Voice is the most interior sensible phenomenon not only because it emanates from bodily sources that are visceral as well as laryngeal but also because in order to be received it must penetrate another physical and psychological interior and literally enter the body and imagination of another through the ear in order to be re-created in the imagination so that it can live. The speaking voice lives solely from interior to interior as it passes between one bodily and imaginative center and another. The power of the speaking voice to bring interiors into communion is the essence of the true literary work. The one who *hears* the poem receives its interior into her or his own. On the basis of this awakened receptivity an audience attains belief *in* the poem, and actors or interpreters, belief *in* the truth of what is going on.[101]

The possibility for true communion between interiors depends first of all on the individual's ability to perceive the *Other* as a *Thou* living within her or his own being. Ong describes a kind of inner dialogue, in which the speaking voice is also heard by the one who utters it forth. This dialogue is not so much the ability to objectify oneself—to be seen or heard by oneself as a body-subject, as in Merleau-Ponty's phenomenology of perception—but an inner openness to a quality of otherness that is within each person. By hearing the *Thou* within, a person becomes self-comprehending and thus ready to hear other voices of being also calling to her or his interior as a *Thou*. James Hillman notes that only when a person has attained genuine love of self (not as ego, but as *being*) and is filled with faith in her or his personal being is it possible to enter an authentic encounter with an *Other* as a *Thou*. Only then is it possible to recognize truly another being's presence and to meet that other being without jabbing and probing it or trying to discover it on a level of mere curiosity.

Curiosity is capable of undermining all true spirituality and all true relationships, because it tries to tear apart areas of the *Other* that can only be known through mutual yielding and mutual listening in an interior dialogue.[102] The phrase "interior dialogue" best describes the relationship between poem and interpreter, for the interpreter speaks and listens to the poem from within her or his own body and, at the same time, tries to enter into the interior of the poem's world in order to participate in the perspective of that truly *Other* world.

The interior quality of sound places human beings in the midst of things, at the active center of reality, unlike vision, which situates us in front of things that are separate from us and on the outside. The effects of the simultaneity of sound are in contrast to those of the sequentiality of sight. Aural perception takes in what is happening and so enters into it as it happens, situations seeming to form an all-at-onceness and an immediacy that cannot be closed off. We cannot close our ears the way we can our eyes. The poem as word belongs in the world of resonance and acts there as an intensification of being. The sounding of voice into the world becomes an amplification of life and being in general. Voice is a quality of the interior, but of the interior manifesting itself, *outering* itself, for voice is primary expression. The interior resonance of voice *is* the *I-Thou* world, where beings can enter relationship with one another at the deepest level, in ways never possible with objects: functional things denied interiority, observed as all surface, and speechless.

For Maritain poetic experience takes place at the center of the soul, where world and subjectivity are known together in a nonconceptual manner.[103] The *Other* as subject can only be known in nonlogical mode, the "mode of affective connaturality," by which Maritain means a mode of intuitive feeling in which the universe and the subject are revealed together to the subject in an experience of mutual awakening. The poetic act is a manifestation of real, resonating creative intersubjectivity that includes both poet and interpreter moving together as one. Thus, when the artist's deeper self is disclosed with the deeper nature of the poem, there is an authentic intersubjectivity in interpretation. This intersubjectivity is revealed in performance as a new being, created from the union of poet and performer, moving and acting together as one. Thus, interpretation as incarnation arises from the joining of two natures in a kind of hypostatic relationship. The poem as subject proceeds, not from itself alone (not having the power to realize itself in isolation), but from itself through its interpreter or actor.

In theological terms incarnation is an action or operation concerning the subject from which it proceeds, but one doubled because of the interaction of two natures (which remain separate and distinct) in a single act. Dionysius the Areopagite may have been the first to describe the union of divine and human operations in the Incarnate Word as a *theandric* action—one in which the divine operation joins with and makes use of the availability of the human operation.[104] The one operation by itself is incapable of bringing about the effects proper to it in its situation: in the theological sense, the Incarnation of the Word and, in the interpretational sense, the incarnation of the word.

In the interpretation situation the two operations are not divine and human, but poetic and human, the poem needing a human voice in the human situation of an art event as the divinity needed a human voice in the human situation of redemptive incarnation. Through the intersubjectivity of two modes of being in Christ an incarnation took place and the Divine Being was revealed as a hypostatic (personal) being, capable of entering intersubjective, bodily voiced relationships with humanity in the human situation. Through the intersubjectivity of two modes of being in the interpreter (her or his deepest self and the poem's deepest nature) an incarnation takes place and the poem is revealed as a hypostatic (personal) being, capable of entering an intersubjective, bodily voiced relationship with an audience in the interpretation situation.

The poem shows itself as a personal existence—though not as the interpreter's personality or even as the person of the interpreter. By *personal existence* is meant an existence that has "a dynamism, a complexity, a diversity-in-unity, that can never be expressed in terms of inert thinghood," and by *person* is meant "an embodied self in the world."[105] The interpreter acts as a creative self in relation to the subject-poem and responds to it in an act of spiritual dialogue: "The creative Self is both revealing itself and sacrificing itself, because it is *given;* it is drawn out of itself in that sort of ecstasy [*out-standingness*] which is creation, it dies to itself in order to live in the work."[106]

The interpreter loses herself or himself in the work and, paradoxically, becomes a renewed and more genuine self. George Herbert Mead, the social philosopher and psychologist, asserts that for a self to be a self it must exist in two or more perspectives at once.[107] A person comes to understand her or his own attitudes and behavior by participating in the attitudes and behavior of others. In taking the role of the other, or entering the situation of the other, one does not literally take on the identity of the other. The self is still a self, only in relation to others and through perspectives that are not her or his own:

> In order to be a self, then, one must also enter into the perspectives of others, but entering into their perspectives does not obliterate one's own. The seller must take the attitude of the buyer without being the buyer. The I component of the self, in contrast to the Me, is the actor, the innovator, the creator, and the problem at hand is to show how this is possible.[108]

For the interpreter the creative self is realized through a complex process of dialogue and transformation leading to the creation of the interpretation event.

The Russian philosopher Berdiaev views creativity as "the self-revelation of the powers of being."[109] For him as for Maritain the creative act is an ontological act, centered on something outside the creator. For Berdiaev it even becomes a religious experience overcoming dualistic divisions between subject and object. Creativity is "an original act of personalities in the world."[110] Berdiaev contrasts the mimetic tendency that he believes is prevalent in Western art and religion with the Russian Orthodox attitude toward Christ. Christian piety in the West strives to imitate Christ, whereas the Russian does not strive to imitate Christ, who is known to be within the human soul, to live in the core of the believer's being. In the West Christ is the object of love; in Russia Christ is the loving subject within. The way to God is not through imitation, but through the reality of the Incarnation and the divine presence within. Thus, what Buber and Marcel describe as a dialogue in relationship is for Berdiaev a participation in presence. What is of significance here in the description of the Russian attitude toward Christ is its implication for creativity. In the creative encounter with Christ the Russian Christian meets Christ as the subject and lovingly receives God into her or his own self, "into the depths of the heart." This union happens without any passionate hunger or uneasy striving, but as a growing spiritual abundance, an overflow of energy and life.[111] Creativity as participation is also a hypostatic relation achieving a perfect unity of movement, as if a single movement contained two lives, two realities brought together in one act and allowing only a general light to pass between them. This progressive participation is a movement of life into life and lives into lives.[112]

The Christian application of hypostasis to Christ is a paradoxical expression of an incomprehensible reality: How can two become one and yet be two—one in substance, two in nature? The union of the divine and human natures in Christ has challenged descriptive efforts throughout the history of dogmatic formulation. It is essentially something that defies conceptualization; it is a reality too large to be contained in any rational dictum. Yet, in an unyielding attempt to comprehend the incomprehensible, theologians have developed what has come to be the orthodox view of the Incarnation as a hypostatic union.

The Eastern theologian Vladimir Lossky describes hypostasis as a personal quality implying a unique being to be expressed only in terms of itself. In Christ "The hypostasis includes both natures: it remains one though it becomes the other; 'the Word became flesh;' but deity did not become humanity, nor was humanity transformed into deity."[113] Deity and humanity were consubstantial in Christ, since there was that in Christ which was consubstantial with God and that which was consubstantial with human beings. In interpretation, hypostasis involves *consubstantiality* (rather than *transubstantiation*) between the poem and interpreter. In the new being shown in performance there is that in the performance which is consubstantial with the poem and that which is consubstantial with the interpreter. Hypostases do not exist permanently within each other except in the Trinity. In art as in human life hypostases are formed, not by the melting of one being into the other, but by a coalescence between them.[114]

Transubstantiation would mean that the interpreter would cease to be a flesh-and-blood individual and would literally and physically "turn into" the poem. *Consubstantiation* means that the two beings of poem and interpreter move together in a coalescence of being and so create, for the time of their joining, a new presence. The Council of Chalcedon in 451 presented an orthodox definition of the hypostatic union in declaring that in one person two distinct natures are present without confusion. "The differences in the natures are not suppressed for a moment by reason of the union; rather, the properties of each are guarded intact. Yet they are joined together in one Person."[115] Humanity is not literally changed into divinity or divinity into humanity in the Person of Christ, but both natures exist together.

In interpretation the transformation spoken of is not the transformation of the interpreter as being into the poem as being, nor is it proper to say that the poem is "clothed" by the interpreter, as Tertullian said that the Word was "clothed" in flesh in Christ. In interpretation, transformation involves both poem and performer, as both are transformed into a realization of *presence* in the final interpretation event. They are not transformed into each other, but each is transformed into a greater fullness of being, and each comes together with the other to create the living body potential within the word of the poem. The end of interpretation is neither "clothing" the poem, nor *essentially* transforming either poem or interpreter, but *realizing the poem fulfilled in flesh,* the bringing of two subjects into communion, the transforming of each, not into each other, but into larger aspects of themselves in order to meet each other in an ambience large enough to contain an audience. The *word* of the poem is transformed into a more truly present word, authenticated by a living voice. The being of the interpreter is opened and enlarged by coming into intimate contact with, and being made available to, the world of the poem. The two subjects exist together for a time, not in confusion, but in true communion.[116] As the formula of Leo the Great states regarding the two natures manifested in Christ, "They were joined together in one Person, while the property of each nature was left intact."[117]

Certainly there is no exact point of comparison between the hypostatic union of the divine and human natures in Christ and the process of interpretation, but, as was pointed out in the beginning, it is not the purpose of this study to make such a comparison. The language used to describe aspects of the numinous in theological speculation, since it is metaphorical to begin with, may also apply to aspects of the process of interpretation and illuminate a way of access to certain dynamics of interpretation that have as yet remained undisclosed. The notion of intersubjectivity expressed in various ways by philosophers whose common focus is, from whatever viewpoint, dialogic and incarnational, and the doctrine of hypostasis in the sense described above, may be of significant value in understanding the interpretation process itself, and the application of these terms cannot extend beyond this purpose. In being too explicit these terms not only can tend to become less adequate as descriptions of the incarnating process of interpretation; they also can become less adequate in describing the philosophical or theological situations from which they originated. Philosophy, theology, and art need to recall that they are dealing with aspects of ontological disclosure and that all *being,* insofar as it expresses the ultimate mystery which is its unique self, steadily eludes being grasped by determinating concepts and fixed in descriptive molds whose boundaries *being* always tends to overflow, as it is not something to be grasped—it is not a fixed and static thing.

Theopoiēsis/Synergia

In *The Art of Interpretation* Bacon speaks of literature as a *presence* to be actualized and asserts that it is not a thing, or a sign standing for a thing, but truly and wholly itself. The interpreter's task is to actualize the presence of literature, "and the task can be achieved only through understanding (intuitive or not)."[118]

Understanding is the beginning of interpretation as an actualizing moment. In Christian theology understanding of God is achieved only through communion with God, or participation in the divine life, sometimes called "deification" or—by the older, more explicit term—*theopoiēsis (God-making)*. The true theologian, says Lossky, is only God, for only God can truly understand the divine nature. If one wishes to become a theologian, to *understand* God, one must enter into the life of God. For Lossky there is no theology apart from experience, and experience is the only means to knowledge of God, which involves the whole person. To know the divine nature, it is necessary to draw near to God, to open one's being to the divine being, to change, to become a new person: "The way of the knowledge of God is necessarily the way of deification."[119] "Deification" is a highly metaphorical term. It stresses the fact of total involvement and change of the human person who seeks to know God. To know God is to *become* God, that is, not to take God's place, but to enter, almost to disappear, into the life of God, to become thoroughly assimilated to it, truly to live its glory. As said earlier, the interpreter comes to live the life of the poem. For the interpreter *theopoiēsis* becomes *being-making*. The interpreter must enter the life of the poem in order to know it, in order to understand it, in order to actualize it.

Lossky describes *theopoiēsis* as an attitude of the whole person, a willingness to conform to the life of the *Other* (God), beginning with a general openness to the *Other* as presence. When the soul opens itself to God, divinity can enter it, and this leads to a union between the soul and God, which St. Maximus calls interpenetrative: "the Divinity, having once penetrated the flesh, gives to it an ineffable faculty of penetrating the Divinity."[120] Such was the nature of the hypostatic union in the Incarnation, which made possible the participation of all believers in this process on a spiritual level. St. Gregory Nazianzen wrote of *theopoiēsis:* "I must be buried with Christ, arise with Christ, be joint heir with Christ, become the son of God, yea, God Himself. . . . This is the purpose of the great mystery for us."[121]

Not only is mystery a quality of being in which one is involved, but Nazianzen sees the divine mystery as a determinating power capable of transforming human life. For him participation in the divine mystery is participation in being for the sake of restoring the status of true image of God to the human soul. For St. Maximus *theopoiēsis* is implied in the Incarnation as a mutual movement toward each other between the divine and human natures.[122] St. Basil also defines the "supreme goal of human appetition" as the yearning "to become God," a bold-sounding phrase reminiscent of Aristotle's famous statement of the ultimate human goal: "to live the eternal life so far as is possible for a human being."[123]

Theopoiēsis in a broad sense means *to live the life of another*. But it does not mean that one ceases to live one's own life. Life becomes changed through contact and interpenetration with other lives. Intense concentration on participation in a specific life of a specific *Other* is entailed in the interpretation process. The interpreter concentrates her or his energies on entering the life of the poem. All energies are brought into play with the energies within the literary work. *Living the life of another* thus means bringing into interplay all of the energies available within oneself and the poem. In the performance situation this fullness of life includes the energies available within the audience as well. The interplay of energies in order to create something larger than the sum of the energies is called *synergy*. In theology *synergia* has a specific meaning directly connected with *theopoiēsis*.

Throughout the writings of the Cappadocians (Gregory of Nyssa, Gregory Nazianzen, and Basil the Great) the themes of *theopoiēsis* and *synergia* recur. In Gregory of Nyssa the concept of synergy is the idea of cooperation between grace and human will, the latter seeming to have a priority, being itself a gift of the Spirit.[124] Grace is the gift of eternal life through the Spirit, but the tireless human *eros* to actualize faith in actions enables human beings to receive and enjoy the gifts of the Spirit. For Nyssa *eros* is the striving outward, the yearning to show, to deliver, to relate, in order to attain a wholeness of being through act. The same use was made of *eros* in terms of developing an erotics of interpretation in chapter two. *Eros* as relatedness and outgoingness is central to the theological notion of synergy. The Cappadocians speak of synergy in terms of the relationship between divine and human energies, both engaged in the human process of becoming whole. Synergy is of keen practical interest in their discussions. It recovers a sense of human nobility manifested in an *active* cooperation with grace.

Clement of Alexandria, in contrast, spoke of synergy as an almost passive human cooperation with a wholly active divine Spirit. For Clement the human soul is like a passive receptacle in which God plants the seeds of *gnosis* (passive illumination). The Cappadocians refuted this view entirely in asserting the importance of the human will in terms of the human process of becoming whole. It almost seems that the divine Spirit cooperates with the human spirit rather than the other way around. In thinking of this discussion on synergy in terms of its possible significance for the interpreter, what is chiefly of value is the emphasis on *both* beings joining their energies mutually (if in varying degrees) in order to realize the coming into being of one of them—in the theological discussion, the human participant; in the interpretation situation, the literary work, but also, if indirectly, the *true* being of the interpreter.

Gregory of Nyssa recognizes the place of the Word in *synergia*: "God, in creating all things, creates himself in all things."[125] Gregory Nazianzen holds that "Humanity must be sanctified by the Humanity of God."[126] Synergy involves the final good of all its parts, when all energies work together toward that end. For Nazianzen reason and faith work together toward ultimate union with God. Unlike Basil, who was a strict realist, and Nyssa, who was boldly speculative, Nazianzen believed that all methods of interpretation of Scripture were equally valid, as long as their goal was to bring the hearer of the Word into communion with the Word. He criticized Christians who rejected reason because of its associations with pagan learning. But, he insisted, reason derives its value from faith and is of value only when its limits are acknowledged: "Take for your guide faith rather than reason; from the realization of your weakness in regard to the things that are nearest to you judge the value of your reason and understand that there are things that are beyond it."[127] Faith, says Nazianzen, reveals the truth of the (scriptural) text; reason shows us how it is true.

The aim of *synergia* is the same as that of the Incarnation: to renew creation by reuniting, in human life, the creature with the Being in whom it participates and from whom it originated. The material elements of creation participate in this synergy as much as the spiritual, or interior. Nyssa says that none of the *qualities* of the body—size, shape, color, and such—*are* the body in themselves, but their concourse, nevertheless, does make the body. From this dynamic theory of matter it is possible to conceive of interplay between bodies on varying levels of energy and to consider all bodies together in their interplay as constituting the *body,* which is the sum of creation. "All things exist in each other—says St. Gregory of Nyssa—and all things mutually support each other, for there is a kind of transmuting power which, by a movement or rotation, causes the terrestrial elements to pass from one to the other and gathers them in again to the point from which they started."[128]

Artists apply these same principles to the work of creation according to Raïssa Maritain. She speaks of the sources of poetry and creativity as vivifying forces that either overflow in immanent acts or work together to form a new creature.[129] She quotes Heidegger writing of the poet Hölderlin that in poetry the human being is concentrated on the depth of her or his own reality. In this concentration the poet "accedes to quietude; not at all, it is true, to the illusory quietude of inactivity and emptiness of thought, but to that infinite quietness in which all the energies are mutually in action."[130]

In the creative work of *poïēsis* the energies are concentrated and directed. In interpretation energies are directed to participating in the poem and working the poem phsyically and spiritually into the interpreter. The vitality of energies at work in performance is communicated to an audience: "The energy flows from you into the body of the audience; the feeling should be that the story is propelled outward."[131]

Both the poem and the performer are constituted by elements of consciousness, activity, and vitality. All of these elements come into play in performance in a certain arrangement. "The perceptive reader, reading the poem," says Bacon, "activates it."[132] The interpreter, in a full sensory response to the poem, matches her or his own form with the form of the poem, all the while looking into the text, hearing into the speaking poem;

and through bodily utterance the interpreter manifests its full and felt meaning by exploring it with all available resources. When the reader comes into relationship with the literary work, she or he becomes "an environment in which the poem is placed, and from which it must draw the energies that give it life."[133] The interpreter's past experiences, conscious and unconscious, participate in the relationship. But the poem has its own energies, its own constituents, and as the interpreter takes these in, both beings are enriched, and finally a new being emerges from the process.

Stanislavski describes this process through a metaphor of chemical change: A chemist tries to find the real essence of two chemicals and then to bring them into some kind of retort. Then the chemist waits, perhaps for a long time, until some sort of synthesis occurs. This process between actor and text Stanislavski calls *creative acting*.[134] Interpreters are not just intermediaries between the writer and the public, not just convenient mouthpieces, but creators in their own right. For the interpreter creation is a process of concentrating the inner faculties on an external image— that of performance—and adjusting one's whole being to it. What is most important is that while the interpreter focuses her or his inner energies on the poem in order to become one with it, she or he is not absorbed, or faded, into the poem, but remains an active participant in it. The interpreter must lose *self*-consciousness, but not consciousness. Stanislavski writes that an actor develops a character from her or his own nature. There is a relatedness between poem and interpreter, or they could not find a way into each other. The interpreter finds a way of becoming the manifestation of the poem, of growing into it, not through means outside herself or himself, but through her or his own nature at its deepest level. This manifestation involves two aspects. Stanislavski says that it is like dividing oneself into two personalities—one of whom works as the actor (or interpreter), the other working as an observer, a detached witness—and these two personalities exert energies together that combine to manifest the work.[135] This comparison calls attention to the double aspect of the interpreter's relationship to word: the interpreter incarnating the word and, at the same time, speaking as a witness for it, proclaiming it—being and showing at the same time.

When the interpreter works to combine energies with the poem, the process of embodiment begins. The interpreter begins with her or his own bodily, factual existence and then moves to accept the poem as an embodied and factual existence, to release it from print and free it by allowing it to enter her or his own bodily being. The work is successfully embodied when all of its parts are manifested through an "irreducible significant gesture" proper to each one. Roloff speaks of the "irreducible significant gesture" in the Burkean sense when he describes the complex act of embodying multiple *personae* in a single work. Don Geiger also describes the joining and manifesting of energies in the creation of performance as finding "behavioral synecdoches," or the creative projection of a certain illuminating aspect of a character's expressive pattern.[136]

Synergy in performance not only is a matter of associations, however, but also involves the final effectiveness of these associations. If energies are united in an effective pattern, the resulting performance must reflect their interplay through a certain *charged* quality of vocal and bodily power. This means, not a "loudness" or "heaviness," but a potency or vitality exactly suited to the work in all its aspects. This power is the manifestation of spirit working between poem and performer in order to bring all present into its own unity, sometimes by similarity and sometimes by contrast.[137] It may manifest itself in performance as a steadily directed concentration. Roloff illustrates this power by the use that can be made of stage fright, a negative and troublesome force that can be converted into a positive energy of concentration by a shift of attention from the performing self to the speaking poem. When this positive conversion takes place, stage fright becomes what Roloff calls "presentational energy."[138]

It holds true for synergy that what makes it possible is again a certain outgoingness or other-directedness. A moment's relaxation in which focus returns to the performing self can destroy the effect of synergy. It depends entirely on the preposition "with"—moving, acting, becoming *with* an *Other* who is also doing these things. Attention is on the other and on the action. Bacon writes: "The sense of the other person's or thing's existence in and of itself is what we mean, an existence to which we pay homage by giving in to it. This sense of the otherness of persons is a kind of miraculism, drawing us out of ourselves into a communion with the rest of the world; it is a responsiveness." The interpreter responds holistically as body, voice, mind, heart, spirit—all the parts that constitute her or his being—and "must in the process learn to make each of these parts so flexible and sensitive that they can together encompass the experience of literature."[139] Experiencing the world of the poem is a matter, not of gaining or relaying information, but of paying homage to a mystery by concentrating all available energies on it and uniting them with it.

Synergy means always becoming more than what one is and always becoming more oneself. It is true for both poem and performer that each alone is more than the sum of its individual functions and that together they constitute a new being that is really a new dimension of being expressing itself through the combined energies of both, yet also beyond them, larger than even the sum of their energies. In some cases of performance the interpretation act seems larger than the poem deserves. In these cases synergy has not taken place, for the performer has joined energies with something other than the poem and created, not an authentic new being, but a distortion of being. Synergy depends on exactly matching energies between poem and interpreter. This matching results in a moment of performance that is authentic and powerful. A synergy with the audience is also experienced in this moment.

Synergy as communion between the acting interpreter and the acting poem results in the creation of a new being shown in performance. Stanislavski wrote of a demonstration of this new being to his students, one of whom was baffled. Tortsov (Stanislavski) gave an enactment of the character Famusov from the play *Woe from Too Much Wit,* and when he had finished, he asked, "With what was Tortsov in contact?" A puzzled student tried to remember the change his own feelings underwent as the center of his attention was transformed from Tortsov to Famusov. He concluded that he himself must have been in contact with Tortsov's inner spirit, but he could not be clear about it. Tortsov responded:

> "You were in contact with a new being," he explained, "which you may call Famusov-Tortsov—or Tortsov-Famusov. In time you will understand these miraculous metamorphoses of a creative artist. Let it suffice now that you understand that *people always try to reach the living spirit of their object* and that they do not deal with noses, or eyes, or buttons the way some actors do on the stage."[140]

Stanislavski illustrated that the actor's soul does not leave her or his body. The actor or interpreter is still an integral self, even while being someone else at the same time. The interpreter as the embodiment of the literary work is bigger than either of the two alone, and this is what is meant by the synergy of performance.

Apophatic/Cataphatic

Experiential knowledge of the literary work can be received in one or both of two ways. In theological language these ways may be either negative (apophatic) or positive (cataphatic), and they may be in opposition or complement to one another. Apophatic theology is believed to originate with Dionysius the Areopagite (or "pseudo-Dionysius"), who said that the soul attains union with God through a process of elimination. Apophatic theology is "an attitude of mind which refuses to form concepts about God."[141] Such an attitude excludes all abstract and purely intellectual tendencies to adapt the mystery of divine wisdom to the methods of human analytical thought. The negative way stresses conforming to the other by, in vertical terminology, rising to God, whereas cataphatic theology stresses that God comes down to us on the ladder of theophanies or divine manifestations in creation. Lossky explains the apophatic and cataphatic ways simply as two directions in the process of union. Apophatic theology describes God by saying what God is not, whereas cataphatic theology tries to describe God positively through the divine theophanies. God's self-revelation in the cataphatic way is not through rational means, but through images that enter the soul directly as energies dispensed by the *Logos* into the world of creation. These energies constitute revelation.[142]

In art the negative way is equivalent to the illumination of being by nonbeing, or the framing of incarnate being by discarnate space. The ontological vastness within a painting may be revealed only by means of seemingly empty space, which is not empty at all but is charged with positive possibility. In some instances inner depth can only be revealed through potentialities suggested by space. Rudolf Otto writes of the differences in the negative expression of reality in Western and Eastern art. What can only be expressed in Western art through silence and darkness is revealed in Eastern art by potent emptiness and empty distances or remote vacancies. These spaces, distances, or vacancies frequently have the power of the numinous and express what can be expressed in no other way, "the sublime in the horizontal." In his study of the relation between the sublime in art and the numinous in religious experience Otto believes these vacant spaces to have a real sublimity and the power to "send out vibrating chords of the numinous."[143] In a silk painting the trailing-off of a branch into nothingness implies, not dead space, but the fact that the branch does indeed trail off and reach into a realm of reality inexpressible through any positive means. Such suggestiveness has the power of reaching the *is-ness* of a being when no positive statement of it could. It is almost electrically charged. For those who have the patience to see into the world of the painting, what is found there is invaluable and inexpressible, yet truly expressed in the juxtaposition of being with nonbeing and perceived by the insightful beholder. The play between half-light and shadows in Gothic churches has a similar effect in the West. In the aural arts, music and utterance acknowledge the numinous moment by sinking into stillness and creating a silence that is positively charged with the presence of the *Other*.[144]

The viewpoint of the Chinese artist is apophatic—the way of affirmation of being through nonbeing. A spokesman for oriental art is recorded in saying to a Western critic: "You are always trying to express yourselves. We never do—neither in art nor in life. You aim at expression and fail. We aim at repression and succeed—and incidentally achieve expression as well."[145] What is achieved is achieved by means of its opposite: the way up is the way down.

Insofar as the mystery of a being reveals itself, the process is cataphatic; insofar as the one to whom it is revealed is emptied or freed of presuppositions and is receptive, the process is apophatic. The only appropriate response to the self-revelation of an *Other* in a truly numinous experience is speechless humility, a silence that pays homage to the being showing itself. The mystery of a being is something beyond conception. "Mystery" is applied to something that can be expressed in no more positive terms.

What seems to be enunciated in the word is negative, but what is meant is something absolutely and intensely positive. This positive "something" can be experienced through feelings, which can help to clarify the percipient's recognition of it.[146]

Robert Ornstein describes a particular instance of the positive (cataphatic) approach by citing this story of an encounter between a Westerner and a dervish, who asked him:

> "Are you prepared to leave the world as you know it and live in a mountain retreat on a very basic diet?"
> I signified that I was.
> "You see," he nodded his head regretfully, "you still feel that to find knowledge you must seek a solitary life away from impure things. This is a primitive attitude. . . . Can you comprehend the uselessness of abandoning the world for your selfish development?"
> "You may need a course," he went on, "at a Sarmoun Center, but that will not mean total abandonment of . . . worldly activity provided you do not allow it, nay invite it, to corrupt you. If you have enough skill you can actually harness the negative forces to serve you, but you must have enough skill."[147]

Whether the way to a particular source is by positive or negative means depends on the nature of the source as well as that of the seeker and the situation in which the two meet. Another dervish saying emphasizes this point: "When it is time for stillness, stillness; in the time of companionship, companionship; at the place of effort, effort. In the time and place of anything, anything."[148]

Another way of looking at this particular dynamic is through the Dionysian and Apollonian motifs. Sam Keen views these motifs as two modes of being in the world, and he further states that authentic selfhood, wholeness, and creativity depend on the integration of the dominant emphases of these motifs.[149] Keen perceives the wisdom of the Greeks in requiring the temple at Delphi to be the place of honor of both Apollo and Dionysus, for either god worshipped alone would lead to madness. The way of Apollo and the way of Dionysus are two ways of viewing the world. Keen notes that psychological studies reveal the interplay between primary and secondary process-thinking (id and ego) in the creative process. Creativity is an oscillation between work and play, realism and fantasy, conceptualization and imagination. Creative perception and creative action coincide. Both of these complementaries are necessary for the fulfillment of the creative process. The human intensity of the creative urge is an oscillation between these poles.[150] Out of the Dionysian condition the artist sometimes attains, for lingering moments, the Apollonian vision. But if the vision is to be more than an escapist side trip, the artist will bear the tensions and problematic character of the experience from which it was born and be faithful to the authentic expression of speech characterized by a degree of tensiveness.

Victor White discusses creative revelation in terms of two comparable contrasting dynamics by placing the theory of Thomas Aquinas in the light of analytical psychology's view of the soul.[151] Aquinas applies the term *cognitio* in his treatment of revelation. *Cognitio,* explains White, is subject to rational investigation but is itself a form, not of grasping, but of experiencing, and is in sharp opposition to the processes of direct thinking. The apprehension of revelation is "a kind of clouded awareness mixed up with darkness" (*De veritate* xxi. 12). The normal vehicle of revelation is not the rational concept but the concrete image. It affects the recipient by "an agitation of bodily spirits and humors," which produces shapes and forms directly in the imagination (*Summa theologiae* I. 111. 4). Whether these images are produced in perception of the external world or remain purely psychic phenomena makes no difference because the means of revelation must in any case act through the human body. Like prophecy, revelation is essentially physical in character. Unless an image is related to something else, it has no meaning for the recipient. Revelation provides judgment and relationship as well as an image and so increases the intellect's ability to connect or disconnect the ideas it already possesses with the images presented to it. Revelation is essentially revelation of meaning added to or concomitant with a direct perception. Its twofold action may allow the recipient either to recognize an interior image or to understand an exterior idea.[152] Thus, reason and imagination—the grasping, positively forming and the experiencing, receiving areas of the mind—are brought into relationship through a seemingly contradictory operation.

In the case of artistic creation there is probably a balance between apophatic openness and cataphatic perception. There is a time when the artist waits for the art work to show itself, and this time must be marked by freedom from imposing opinions and grasping. There is a time when, the work having shown itself, the artist enters into an active, positive relationship with it and contributes her or his own personality to the work. This process is true for the interpreter as it is true for the poet. There is a time when the interpreter must wait on the poem, but this is also a time for preserving a vigorous imagination in order to insure that the poem will be able to present itself at all. What is needed is a balance between concentration and free-playing receptivity.

The interpreter is poised between a growing need for utterance and the patient waiting for the self-revelation of what is to be uttered. When the poem comes forth into light for the interpreter, dynamics of more overt cooperation enter in. But these two attitudes mingle all along the way, for, just as the poet discovers the poem while making it, the interpreter discovers the poem while hearing and speaking to it. What is true for the poet is here true for the interpreter: the interpreter does not force the poem to show itself, but she or he allows this to happen by encouraging the poem to come forth into light. Without the poet's and interpreter's collusion the poem can neither make nor show itself. Both creative artists must wait, however, for conscious and unconscious processes to reassemble and make themselves known in a new and unique light cast by the poem. The interpreter waits for the various energies within to come together in preparation for joining with the poem. The first part of this process is *apophatic* in nature. The interpreter frees herself or himself from distractions and presuppositions as much as possible and refrains from molding the poem to personal intentions. Finally, the poem shows itself in *cataphatic* illumination, and a creative synthesis emerges between poem and performer.

The interpreter waits on the poem as the poet must wait on it. It is difficult to imagine a more explicit description of how this waiting, receiving, and cooperating works than in the following passage from *The House at Pooh Corner*. The ever-wise and ever-simple Pooh Bear has promised his friend Piglet that he would make up a song about a heroic thing that Piglet did in saving Pooh and Owl from the flood:

> "But it isn't Easy," said Pooh to himself, as he looked at what had once been Owl's house. "Because Poetry and Hums aren't things which you get, they're things which get *you*. And all you can do is to go where they find you."
> He waited hopefully. . . .
> "Well," said Pooh after a long wait, "I shall begin *Here lies a tree* because it does, and then I'll see what happens."
> [A wonderful hum is what happens.]
> "So there it is," said Pooh, when he had sung this to himself three times. "It's come different from what I thought it would, but it's come. Now I must go and sing it to Piglet."[153]

Matching in interpretation comes differently from what one thinks, but it comes. The interpreter has only to sing its outcome to others.

Kenosis/Plerosis

A parable from Zen archery says that the more one aims, the farther from the target one strikes. There is wisdom for the interpreter in this lore. What is first necessary in an encounter is to abandon self-interest and all claims upon the other subject. This implies a certain intentionality of consciousness, yet eradicates its aggressive thrust. James Hillman attributes these qualities to the *art of listening*. Listening, he says, is akin to prayer: "Prayer has been described as an active silence in which one listens acutely for the still small voice, as if prayer were not asking and getting through to God, but becoming so composed that [God] might come through to me."[154]

In order to converse with an *Other,* one must actively engage in listening. Hillman illustrates this activity as a kind of "negative capability": in
order to make room for the *Other* to become present, I must withdraw at a
certain point. Through an intense act of concentration I can make a space
for the *Other.* In the Jewish mystical doctrine of Tsimtsum, withdrawal is
of the essence of creativity. God the Creator, asserts Tsimtsum, is omnipo-
tent and omnipresent, filling all space. In order for creation to occur, God
must withdraw, not through literal absence, but by means of creative
concentration. In order to create a not-God, God must undergo intense
self-contraction and self-concentration. From this doctrine much speculation arose concerning the hidden glory of God contained in active, creative concentration. For the love of creation God withdraws. For the love
of the poem the interpreter withdraws to make a space, to listen. Withdrawal of the self aids the *Other* to come into being. Yet, withdrawal is not
an end, only an acted attitude in a complex process of dialogue. The *Other*
needs space in which to expand but also needs the encouragement or
invitation of a compassionate call. The space made by the interpreter—
like the creative space of the theological paradigm—is not a negative
emptiness but is positively charged with receptive love.

The chief obstacle to genuine creativity is the self-interested ego. The
self-aware ego places us in a subject-object relationship not only to others
but to ourselves. The ego is identified with the Me, which demands
attention. The true self is identified with the I, which is the genuinely
creative self, authentic being. The way out of the ego is through attention
toward others, especially through intense concentration on an *Other.* In
Zen Flesh, Zen Bones there is advice for the person who seeks to enter
authentic relationship and be liberated from the bondage of the ego:
Wherever your attention is fixed, there *experience,* feel, the consciousness
of the subject of attention as your own consciousness; leaving aside concern for yourself, become the being you contemplate.[155] A Zen story
speaks of this process as a self-emptying receptivity:

> Nan-In, a Japanese master during the Meidji era (1868–1912), received a
> university professor who came to inquire about Zen.
> Nan-In served tea. He poured his visitor's cup full, and then kept on
> pouring.
> The professor watched the overflow until he could no longer restrain
> himself. "It is over-full. No more will go in!"
> "Like this cup," Nan-In said, "you are full of your own opinions and
> speculations. How can I show you Zen unless you first empty your cup?"[156]

What is essential was indicated in the Zen archery parable: Do not seek
graspingly after the truth, "only cease to cherish opinions."[157]

William Johnston compares the effects of Zen with Christian *agape,* for
in both states "psychic life is penetrated with the silent supraconceptual-

ity" of integration.[158] Unity of body and spirit brought about through disciplined meditation involves the banishment of all superfluous thoughts, images, feelings, plans, ambitions, and such. The mind is emptied—freed—from all extraneous distractions that could weigh it down or hinder it from *seeing* clearly. The various techniques used in Zen practice aim at the total abolition of dualism on all levels: the ego must be forgotten in order for the individual to become one with the universe. Identification is stressed, so that the subject-object barrier is completely broken down. In the intense moment of enlightenment, of pure perceiving, the seer and the seen are undifferentiated. It is like "music heard so deeply / That it is not heard at all, but you are the music / While the music lasts." (T. S. Eliot, "Dry Salvages," V, 27–29). This pure perception and identification demands a continual surrender of self to something more valuable.

Eliot wrote of the necessity of the writer's subordination of personality to the subject—the art process itself—in connection with finding the objective correlative. He wrote that the poet can reach the impersonal emotion of art only by complete self-surrender to the work to be done.[159] In studying the relationship of Christianity to Zen, and of Eliot's writings in particular in that connection, William Johnston concluded that Eliot's emphasis on depersonalization was none other than the crucifixion of the ego in the process of attaining a higher, "resurrected" or renewed, personalism. Eliot attempts to eliminate the "empirical ego" in order to find the true poetic self. For Eliot participation in creation contains "high moments" in which the artist feels conscious of the whole universe existing within herself or himself.[160]

The chief difference in the approaches of Zen and Christianity to this state of oneness is that Zen is ultimately monistic (the self is literally lost, absorbed into the universe) and Christianity preserves a duality in which relationship is always possible: there is always an "I," though a purified I, which knows that it is participating in another. In Zen enlightenment *union* is all. In Christian mysticism *union with another* is all, union with God and through God with the universe. The *I-Thou* relation is maintained, but the union (not fusion) between *I* and *Thou* becomes a new subject in its own right, constituted by the two subjects participating in it. In Zen the individual becomes transparent through fusion with the All. In Christianity the individual becomes illuminated from within by union with God and filled with a knowledge of "connaturality," in Thomist language. The emptiness of the Zen practitioner is bliss, final and complete. The emptiness of the Christian mystic is charged with love and filled with wisdom imparted through union with God. The void is only apparent and never an end in itself.

Maritain speaks out for the distinction between ego and true self and the importance of the latter in the creative process. He criticizes Eliot for not making this distinction clear. The ego-self is the "small self" that is lost or forgotten in creativity, but the poet-self, or "true self," as integral personality is preserved and even enlarged.[161] Creativity for Maritain is a kind of "selfless self-revelation."

The humanistic psychologist Rollo May warns against the illusions that the aggressive ego presents to a person. Personal convictions, he says, will always have some element of self-distortion and blindness, and the most deadly illusion of all is the belief that one is free from illusion. He notes that some scholars believe the Greek phrase "know thyself" to mean "know that you are only a human being with limitations." This interpretation implies that something must be "worked through" or surrendered, and that "something," says May, is "the tendency arising in human infancy to play god and the omnipresent demand to be treated as though we were god."[162] Thomas Merton connects this infantile tendency with the over-emphasis on the rational, controlling faculties whose purpose is to gain dominance through analytically gained knowledge. "Differentiation—the splitting-up process that leads to mindlessness, instead of the mindfulness of seeing all-in-emptiness and not having to break it up against itself."[163]

To be emptied of ego demands . . . to see all in emptiness: What does this mean? What is the place and significance of "emptiness" for the interpreter? The Zen viewpoint can throw light on an important aspect of interpretation, and the Christian viewpoint, which preserves the notion of relationship that has been emphasized in this study, may more deeply illuminate the issue at hand. "Emptiness" has a special place in Christian theology and is expressed in what has been called the "kenotic motif."[164]

Kenosis is a word derived from the Greek verb "to make empty." In Christian doctrine it refers to the passage in Philippians 2:5–11, in which it is said that Christ "emptied himself, taking the form of a servant" (v. 7, RSV) through becoming human and, further, through undergoing the humiliations of death in order to redeem creation. The Incarnation involved a *self-emptying* on the part of God, for in entering the space-time dimension the divine nature had to *withdraw* the fullness of its power in order to create an Incarnation of itself. The language of *kenosis* is paradoxical and richly metaphorical. It speaks of an *emptying*, but this emptying is not a cessation of being. It has to do, not with a change in the nature of God at all, but with an act of love in the Incarnation: "What is meant is that the heavenly Christ did not selfishly exploit His divine form and mode of being. . . . The essence remains, the mode of being changes—a genuine sacrifice. . . . 'he became a beggar even though (of himself, and up to this point) he was rich.' "[165]

In *kenosis,* according to the absolute semimetamorphic theory, Christ did not undergo a loss of the divine nature but willingly allowed it to be disguised for the purposes of the Incarnation. The divine attributes were retained in Christ but were used "only in the time-form appropriate to a human mode of existence." These attributes were retained in such a way that they could be expressed only as appropriate to the human situations and needs that presented themselves to Christ.[166] God yielded to the limitations of human existence without ceasing to be God. Only through setting aside aspects of the divine nature could Christ become human flesh, but only through incorporating them at some deep level of reality could Christ continue to be God. A change in the being of God is not possible, but a self-giving attitude expressed in an act of God as the divine humility was in fact necessary for the creative redemption of Incarnation. The Russian philosopher Bulgakov sees *kenosis* as "a quality of self-giving, the deepest attribute of divine nature through which all creation comes into being, an out-pouring of divinity."[167] The self-emptying of Christ is a self-outpouring into the world; accepting the limitations of human life is his greatest, most total gift to human life. The various kenotic controversies in the Western church center around the question of the place of Christ's divinity: Was Christ no longer divine in the Incarnation, was the divine nature lost, or just how was it present if it was? These questions arise from a tendency to make the general metaphor of *kenosis* too explicit and to dogmatize it almost into meaninglessness. The Eastern church simply sees *kenosis* as an act of love, essential to the doctrine of creation. It cannot threaten the Godly nature of Christ.

In the paradoxical terms ever-present in Christian spirituality Christ's glory could only come about through a self-emptying humility; perfection consists in self-abandonment. When a person ceases to exist for herself or himself, that person becomes a true self. Self-expression occurs most truly through the indirectness of self-renunciation. The self-emptying of Christ in the act of redemption (in becoming as a servant to that work) made it possible for the *kenosis* of the Holy Spirit to take place, in the sense of the Spirit's self-emptying into the human world.[168] *Kenosis* is also seen as the renunciation of one's own will in order to accomplish the will of another. In accepting his death Christ's *kenosis* was in being emptied of the fear of dying in order to accomplish God's will. Through conversion of a human abhorrence of death into a complete willingness of self-giving, Christ was literally poured out in order to give fullness to others, by emptying divine fullness into creation without changing the Christ-nature in any way.[169] The self-emptying of Christ has been taken as an example to be followed by Christians. It is seen as an enrichment of life: "I came that they may have life, and that they may have it abundantly." The newness of creation is in this abundance of life.[170]

The implications of *kenosis* for interpretation are twofold. There is a self-emptying undergone by the interpreter in the willing subordination of her or his will to the will of the poem in order for a new creation to be accomplished; and there is a *kenosis* of the text as well, in that the poem pours itself into the life of the interpreter. Emptying, or *kenosis*, and filling, or *plerosis*, are two aspects of a single process. The interpreter is self-emptied of self-centered tendencies that may be irrelevant or harmful to the poem in order to be filled with the true nature of the poem. But the interpreter never ceases to remain a person. There is no loss of consciousness or self in interpretation, but only of self-consciousness and ego-centric self, in order to reveal the true self so that it can become engaged with the poem. *Kenosis* for the interpreter is a loving attitude of humility and nonresistance toward the text.

In Russian spirituality *kenosis* is a spontaneous way of life centered in participation with the Incarnate Christ. *Kenosis* is simply self-forgetfulness expressed in acts of love toward others. Ippolit in Dostoevsky's *The Idiot* expresses an insight into *kenosis*: "You are giving away, in one form or another, part of your personality and taking into yourself part of another; you are in mutual communion with one another; a little more effort and you will be rewarded with the knowledge of the most unexpected discoveries."[171] *Kenosis* is thought of, not as suffering, but primarily as loving obedience, the appeal to an active fidelity. The Russian word for obedience (*poslushanije*) suggests hearing and following, as hearing a call and responding to it, or hearing a person or being and responding. The interpreter can hear the call of the poem and obey it in terms of enacting or completing its own creation.

Kenosis involves an asceticism which, for the artist, means that she or he must be emptied of anything that distracts attention from the end of the art. From the viewpoint of the good of the work the artist needs to maintain the virtues of humility and generosity, the chief virtues of the creative personality. Generosity takes the form of self-giving. Keats wrote of the limits to which the self-giving of the poet can go and said that the poetic character is not itself, is everything and nothing, forms itself according to the work: "A Poet is the most unpoetical of any thing in existence; because [the poet] has no identity [but] is continually . . . filling some other Body."[172] The interpreter even more than the poet is called always to be "filling some other body." But the interpreter is also aware that these bodies are *other*, that the nature of the filling is of the nature of encounter and exchange, that there is an *I* and a *Not-I*, and that these two are in intense dialogue.

Kenosis in the dialogue between beings in interpretation means that the interpreter does not try to force responses by direct contact with her or his own responses but is emptied of these and is attentive to the responses acting within the work itself. This attentiveness requires that the artist approach the poem in simplicity and reject her or his own everyday masks, to consent to the experience of the poem and value the communion hoped for. Such an attitude makes possible an integration between the interpreter's self and not-self.

Kenosis as the essence of creativity implies that creativity is self-transcendence. A. H. Maslow views creativity as an elimination of blocks against the matter-in-hand, so that "we let it flow in upon us."[173] Maslow observes that a person is most integrated, unified, directed, and all of a piece when totally organized in the service of the creative matter-in-hand. He views creativity as systemic—as a Gestalt involving the whole person. In genuine, concentrated creativity there is less dissociation and splitting of facets and more here-now-allness. Maslow attributes part of the integration process in creativity to the recovery of unconscious and preconscious aspects, including the primary process, which he sees as poetic, archaic, and metaphoric. The primary process is marked by a kind of childlike or innocent quality—the Taoistic quality—of receptivity. In the artist this innocence is an achieved innocence, comparable to Blake's "innocence of experience," rather than the truly naïve innocence of the child. It is characterized by aesthetic perceiving rather than abstracting. For Maslow abstracting amounts to active interfering, whereas perceiving is more Taoistic and caring. Perceiving concentrates on one thing—the matter-in-hand—and this narrow fascination Maslow compares with the Japanese concept of *muga. Muga* is a state of total wholeheartedness, in which one acts without distraction or hesitation: "This is possible only when the self is transcended or forgotten."[174] It is possible when the mature, experienced human being enters the *second innocence,* or the *innocence of wisdom.* Perceiving in this way, the creative person comes to recognize the characteristics of being. Maslow calls this perception, or total concentration, *Being-cognition,* or *B-cognition.* B-cognition often happens when the senses and spirit are educated through silence and wonder. The doors of perception open when words and silence, feelings and ideas, concepts and sensations, act in a vital relationship.[175]

Being-cognition may have been a characteristic experience of the Desert Fathers of the early centuries of Christendom. They literally followed Christ into the desert (where the mission of the Word was inaugurated), a place where the spirit could drive inward, where silence and word compenetrate and complement each other. The Christian ascetics who emptied themselves of the world and sought the vast horizons of the desert were attempting to respond to the total gift of God (in creation and Incarnation) by making a total gift of themselves.[176] The *ascesis* of the desert required nothing less than total self-giving; through it the Desert Fathers attained a new innocence and purity of heart from living lives concentrated on Christ as their center. They no longer acted on objects from without but acted toward all things from within, with limitless cosmic charity. The intensely contemplative life of the desert was not life-denying: "The hesychastic tradition stresses the body's participation in the exercise of the spirit. Its ascesis does not seek suffering and affliction but endurance through abstention, resistance to distractions, and attention of the heart to essentials. The great truth of the Gospel is clearly affirmed; the spiritual [person] is such entirely, soul and body."[177] Contemplative receptivity is structured by the unconditional offering of oneself. It is humility that has become a state of being—humility become act.

The receptivity of the Tao, the contemplative activity of the Desert Fathers, the creativity of the artist—all have the intrinsic requirement of liberation from the greed of the ego, the natural enemy of creative life. Maritain equates the essential disinterestedness of poetic activity with the elimination of the controlling ego. Disinterest—the ascesis of the artist— amounts to unself-conscious commitment, a concentration on the work, and a profound engagement with it. Meister Eckhart's "On Disinterest" describes it as a state of humility leading to maximum capacity. To be filled with things, he writes, is to be emptied of God. One must become empty in order to be filled with new being, in order to admit the life of another into one's own. Disinterest is thus a state of preparation and sensitivity: "[I]f a heart is to be ready it must be emptied out to nothingness, the condition of its maximum capacity. So, too, a disinterested heart, reduced to nothingness, is the optimum, the condition of maximum sensitivity."[178] One who bows down in deep humility will rise up in the glory of a new life in God.

Leslie Gillian Abel and Robert M. Post have proposed an application to interpretation of the ascetic (essentially kenotic) theatre art of the Polish director Jerzy Growtowski.[179] Growtowski believes that the actor's training should be a "via negativa—not a collection of skills but an eradication of blocks."[180] He calls the actor thus trained the "holy actor," whose technique is that of elimination, in contrast with the "courtesan actor" who accumulates and applies skills. The latter works on the text from without; the former works with the text from within. The courtesan actor sells her or his body publicly; the holy actor sacrifices her or his whole bodily being to the work through making a gift or total offering of self. The function of the holy actor in performance is to make an act of transgression—by setting a challenge for herself or himself to challenge others—and to reveal her or his true self by casting off all false masks, and so make it possible for the audience to experience a similar process. Such a task demands the total presence of the actor or interpreter in performance, a keen concentration of energies into the work itself.

Growtowski teaches his actors not to "pretend" to be a dog when they are playing a dog, because they are not dogs. Instead they should try to discover and amplify their own doglike qualities. Thus, in playing a dog the actor (or interpreter) would seek to eradicate her or his undoglike qualities in order to be reborn, to reemerge as a dog. Growtowski instructs actors to match the essences of their subjects through intense concentration. Whereas Growtowski would tell the actor to concentrate within herself or himself, Bacon advises the interpreter to concentrate on the subject of the text at all times. It is not what the interpreter does, but what she or he watches, that is important:

> Keep your attention off yourself as much as possible and on the objects of the poem. You are trying not to dramatize yourself but to be an accurate observer. Watch and listen! Your own feelings are important only insofar as they help you to respond fully to the poem. . . .
> In creativity and in the process of perceiving a poem, absolute concentration is a prerequisite. *There is no substitute for concentration.*[181]

This is one application of the motif of *kenosis,* focusing on the creation of a "holy interpreter" who is self-emptied of all ego-inclinations that might threaten the text.[182]

Growtowski views the holy actor as a model of the healthy human being, integrated through opening the self to another mode of existence manifested in performance and through finding the self in this act of outgoingness. The goal of the holy actor or holy interpreter is realized in performance, when actor or interpreter and audience are led together to new levels of human reality and understanding through confrontation with the living text. Interpreter and audience participate in different ways in the life of the text during performance. The audience participates receptively, while the interpreter functions in an active gift of self to the work and through it to the audience, in order to lead the audience into new insights through the literature. Roloff describes the artistry of the interpreter as lying in the capacity to make her or his "imagination freely available to the stimuli of the literature—to allow them to flow within the flexible confines of the literary experience" creating "a sense of inevitability" in the performance.[183]

The discussion of emptiness as disinterest, *ascesis,* or receptivity, is relevant to the interpreter in terms of the literary text. The interpreter's creative intention is the realization of the literary work, or the phenomenon of reverberation of the work within her or his own body. Reverberation has the significance of being resounding within being, not within a lifeless emptiness, and it is possible through the permeability of one being to the other and through sensing, perceiving, and experiencing in a common situation. Reverberation occurs in a self-transcendence that is intentionally toward an *Other,* and it is the fullest experience of the *Other* on a level of being. *Kenosis* as a prerequisite of reverberation means that the interpreter does nothing to interfere with the experience of the poem.[184]

Kenosis is not an end in itself and cannot even be discussed in isolation from its purpose, which is the good of an *Other* through an act of self-giving love. It finally involves the action and interaction of two powers and two dynamics: emptying and filling in a context of relationship. Self-emptying implies a filling of those who are to profit by it. *Kenosis* as an act

of Christ in the world can be translated to interpretation as an act of the
interpreter in the becoming world of the poem. The process is an inner
movement, making a space for the *Other* and finally acting with the *Other*
in mutual filling and outpouring. The kenotic theologian P. T. Forsyth
sees *kenosis* as incomplete and meaningless in isolation from *plerosis*. Everything depends on an outgoingness in the act of creation. Self-emptying is a
means to self-communication on the deepest level, that of self-giving.
Forsyth's application of *kenosis/plerosis* to Christ might well apply to the
interpretation process as well:

> Alongside the Kenosis and its negations there went a corresponding
> Plerosis, without which the Kenosis is a one-sided idea. More and more, as
> he laid by what he eternally was, he came to be what he began by being. . . .
> His obedience was his divinest achievement. And out of that obedience grew
> his vast creative, commanding, and even coercive, effect upon the whole
> world.[185]

Unconscious/Conscious

The self-emptying motif points to the broader area of the relation
between conscious and unconscious elements at work in the interpreter's
psyche. It was suggested that self-emptying applies to the shallow, superficial self, to the purification of the ego and the elimination of the *personae*
that tend to diminish, falsify, or disengage the true qualities of existence
on a deep human level. The present age is one in which rationalism and
ego-consciousness are nearly worshiped as instruments of conquest over
all of nature, within and without.[186] The symbol of the crucifixion por-
trays the spiritual dilemma present in modern psychology, for the only
remedy to the disproportionate emphasis on ego-dominance, allowing a
return to the deeper powers (which are the life-giving forces) of the
psyche, is a literal crucifixion of the ego, through which the true self may
reemerge in a genuine rebirth.

The disease of our times may be described as "the hubris of consciousness," a refusal to recognize that human beings are not, after all, entitled
to control and destroy nature. June K. Singer writes of the hubris of
consciousness as destructive conscious arrogance, the absence of humility.
She quotes the insight into this hubris of one of her analysands:

> The striving after awareness—as though awareness were something you
> could "get" or "have" and then "use" is pointless. You don't seek awareness,
> you simply *are* aware, you allow yourself to be—by not cluttering up your
> mind. To be arrogant about consciousness, to feel you are better than
> someone else because you are more conscious, means that in a similar
> degree you are unconscious about your unconsciousness.[187]

Psychologists who are concerned with this particular pathology of the soul are beginning to explore more fully the possibility of developing a receptive, holistic mode of consciousness as a cure and replacement for the hubris of consciousness. Psychologists such as Robert Ornstein are looking to Zen, others to Taoism, and still others to Christian mysticism, as sources that can throw light on the mode of consciousness being sought. Ornstein writes that Zen and psychologies concerned with the *soul* both seek a balanced development and integration of intuition and intellectuality.[188] Since our scientifically oriented culture has provided educational development of intellectuality, what seems to be needed, for Western persons at least, is a means for developing the receptive, intuitive mode of experience. This development would seem especially important for artists of all sorts, because the art process itself is highly dependent on the successful operation of this latter mode of perception and response.

Jung writes of the balance described above as a creative balance or dialogue between the conscious and unconscious portions of the psyche. Jung believes that artistic creativity originates in unconscious depths, that the creative process has (in his terminology) a feminine quality that arises from the unconscious matrix of human life—"the realm of the mothers."[189] When the creative process is at work, human life is molded by the unconscious in contrast to the predominant, active will. In genuine creativity the conscious ego is, for the most part, carried along by creative forces independent of it. For creativity to occur it is necessary that the conscious ego assents to taking a passive position at some point in the process. The artist lets the work of art act upon her or him, and it is perceived, not as something being formed, manipulated, and controlled, but as a being that forms and shapes the artist. In order for the work of art to be perceived accurately, its percipients or audience must yield to being shaped by it, just as the original artist had to yield. This necessity is particularly true in interpretation, for the interpreter, as an original artist in her or his own right, yields to forces that are, to an extent, beyond conscious control, in order to come into a truly creative and original dialogue or relationship with the art work as being. During performance the audience is presented with the work of art and is subject to undergoing a similar process of yielding to it, to allow the work of art to enter and do its own creative work from within.

According to Jung the art experience draws from the redeeming, healing powers of the personal and collective psyche underlying consciousness. These powers must somehow be allowed to penetrate consciousness and to shape the person receiving them. This effect generally means that conscious barriers need to be broken. In Zen there is a specific technique that has just this effect of breaking through the apparent wall between the conscious and unconscious. The *kōan,* or illogical problem, has the power to work on the mind of the recipient in such a way that she or he has finally to "give up," to give in to the inner realities beyond all discursive reasoning, even beyond the shell of paradox. The stubbornness of the ego is manifested by its unwillingness to yield to mystery. Frustration seems to mark the way as long as consciousness clings to its dominant role. Finally, in relinquishing the frustration itself, along with the complexities of applied logic, there is a breakthrough, emptying the mind of extraneous ideas and images, opening it to mysterious subliminal elements that are now free to rise from the depths of the psyche.

Just as Christian spirituality differs from Zen on the question of emptiness and union, analytical psychology differs at this point on the question of conscious abandonment. In Zen a real loss of ego seems to occur; the novice undergoes an "imitation psychosis" that constitutes a spiritual death. When she or he emerges from this state, integration will have taken place, and enlightenment, or *satori,* is achieved. For Western persons, however, there can be no question of total extinction of the ego, for this would result in total loss of consciousness and the complete dominance of the unconscious and would amount, not to enlightenment, but to insanity. What is needed, says Jung, is a creative balance, a way of access between conscious and unconscious, not the annihilation of either. Nothing the unconscious produces ought to be taken for granted, writes Jung, but should be subjected to a just criticism.[190] The chief work of the unconscious is the formation of symbols, and these have a necessary and illuminating effect on conscious life. The conscious faculties are given symbolic meaning and can only come to accept this meaning through a certain critical observation. Symbol, here, simply means the best possible expression of something that has no other—and no better—means of being understood.

Jung's interest in the creative process led him to the theory of the *transcendent function* of the psyche in artistic creation.[191] This is a term he borrows from mathematics, in which it refers to the combining of real numbers with imaginary integers. In analytical psychology it has to do with the permeability between the conscious and unconscious. Jung sees these as distinct autonomous entities between which there is a kind of wall. This wall, however, is penetrable. For the artist there is usually a high degree of permeability between the two sides, and this permeability is the artist's greatest asset. (This same permeability, in larger degree, is dangerous and troublesome for the neurotic and totally victimizes the psychotic, for whom there is no longer any wall at all.)

The artist, having been granted a way of access to her or his own deeper psychic structures, is given a rich source of vitality in the form of symbols, images, and gestures, which may be incorporated into the incarnating work of creation. At this level the creative psychic elements are in a state of *deformation* and *discarnation,* but, through passing into consciousness and coming in touch with the discerning and discriminating faculties there, they may pass over into the *transformation* and clarification of reality which we call art and so shape themselves into an authentic and viable *incarnation*. For the interpreter this transformation involves a doubling, for the term *art work* or *art working* is always in two senses in interpretation. First, the art work is something already given and present in the form of the literary work that comes to meet the interpreter. Second, the art work is a process in which the interpreter finds herself or himself in a unique relationship with the poem, and the result of this process of *art working* is a unique, authentic creation called performance. By entering a subliminal dialogue with unconscious life through the *transcendent function,* the poem undergoes a real deformation and disincarnation, because its own symbols and images mix with those in the interpreter's psyche, and for a certain disruptive time this mixing seems nothing more than chaotic. But this mixing is only an aspect in the total, complex process of interpretation.

Bacon refers to this element in the process in citing Harold Rugg's theory of imagination and the creative psyche:

> Harold Rugg speaks of the "off-conscious" functioning of the mind-body relationship in creative work as a process, a technique, for "inducing trans-liminal states." He sees creativity as involving a conscious preparatory period of struggle [i.e., meeting the text on a conscious analytical level], an interlude of "giving up" [i.e., the *kenosis* of the ego and the *transcendent function*], a subsequent flash of insight and statement [i.e., *plerosis,* or emergence and organization into consciousness], and a period of verification or reconstruction. In essence, this is what occurs too in the matching process of the interpreter: there is a period of coping with the outer form (reaching toward inner form) of the text, a plateau in which the reading seems not to be going anywhere, a fresh gathering of forces involved in the act, and a final "putting it together." Unless the interpreter takes the time in . . . preparation to allow for the plateau period, he does not usually get all the way.[192]

The "plateau period" is the period of unconscious activity, the *transcendent function* in action on a subliminal (and seemingly chaotic) level. Bacon very wisely points out that it is really necessary to give all the time to it which this particular part of the process seems to require; otherwise the interpreter may never get beyond the apparent disorganization characteristic of this stage.

Through the *transcendent function* the interpreter can experience the revelation of what was present but heretofore unknown, an active mystery now ready to be incarnated in an art form: performance. Jung says that the new creation finding its elements here has the possibility, as a work of art, to be of general value to society. Not all of the elements presented to the interpreter will be of value, however. At this stage of the creative process "consciousness puts its media of expression at the disposal of the unconscious content."[193] The *transcendent function* becomes a dialogic process of the psyche in which the unconscious is striving for light and expression, and the conscious is striving for substance and form. The creative process for the interpreter seems to fall into specific phases that may be viewed as outlined above, or as a movement from *preparation* and *frustration* (conscious phases) through a period of *incubation* (the unconscious phase) to a final *illumination* of breakthrough between conscious and unconscious, which is followed by an artistic *elaboration* unfolding in the incarnational act of performance.

Another aspect of the plateau period, or incubation, is the particular way in which the artist responds to it. The interpreter may not recognize the source of new insights that emerge into consciousness and may try to grasp them and immediately place them under the rule and service of the ego. Or, on the other hand, the interpreter may humbly receive these insights and allow herself or himself to be guided and moved by them. The imposition of the former response is what Jung calls, in the context of the *transcendent function,* an introverted response, conscious energy pushed from the outside in. The latter he calls an extraverted response, unconscious energy moving from the inside out. In the former, the artist/ interpreter imposes the ego inward onto the process. In the latter, she or he allows the process to emerge in its own way. In terms of the present approach the introverted response would be the opposite of a kenotic response: it would be "taking over" on the part of the ego; whereas the extraverted attitude would constitute a true *kenosis,* or emptying, of the ego and its *personae.*

The matter of critical judgment in the interpretation process enters in at the point of what Bacon calls the "fresh gathering of forces," the reconstruction, or *elaboration,* period. Maslow describes the creative and critical phases of the artistic process as primary and secondary creativity. Primary creativity has its source in the unconscious and is characterized by discovery and imaginative play; it is the genuinely poetic quality of creation. Secondary creativity is conscious, precise, critical, and discursive.[194] As Jung calls for a balance between conscious and unconscious, which diminishes but does not altogether deny the participation of the ego, Maslow asserts that for genuine creativity to take place, and for the individual to become a whole person, primary and secondary creativity are both necessary. An imbalance or one-sidedness between them results in spiritual disintegration. A person who completely suppresses the unconscious and remains walled off from the primary processes becomes the obsessive-compulsive psychological type. One who experiences many insights, yet cannot make practical use of them because she or he is too much totally experiencing and not enough self-observing or critical—this person becomes schizophrenic.[195]

What is necessary is a synthesis of both primary and secondary processes, an openness between conscious and unconscious, deeper self and observing self. When the processes participate in each other, they change in character. The unconscious ceases to be frightening, and the controlling, reasoning faculties of consciousness are incorporated into the service of the work at hand.[196] When the whole person is thus functioning at maximum creativity, a change in perception occurs. When the person's resources become available to her or him on all levels, it is possible for the individual to experience B-cognition. In this state the person is able to perceive the *suchness* of things. For Maslow perception of *suchness* can be both concrete and abstract. When the characteristics of being are perceived in the total concentration of B-cognition, they are perceived as values of being. When one has B-cognition, one can return to the level of D-cognition (deficiency, or ordinary, cognition) with new insights. The perception of being can then incorporate the perception of what is lacking in order to make an adjustment or integration.[197] B-cognition simply sees things in their *is-ness* (or *suchness*), whereas D-cognition sees with the idea of making, shaping, and actively organizing in terms of time and space. The combination of the two modes of perception operates in the creative process to bring about a new being as the shaped incarnation of a vision.

James Hillman views the experience of the unconscious as the gaining of soul. When the inner dimension of being shows itself, it takes on substantial reality and gains influence over conscious decisions. Hillman speaks of a "third realm, a sort of conscious unconscious." Rather than any part of the person, it is something happening to the person, not directly connected with either inner or outer world, but a place where the two can meet. This reality is a psychic world of experiences, fantasies, emotions, visions, physical sensations, and dialogues. It is a free, open space of meaning, and it is possible because of the "rediscovery of soul through the unconscious."[198] Here is reached the "Within which is beyond," the "psychic reality beyond the ego level." This realm points beyond the self, calls for a process of transcendence, and therefore imposes a kind of morality that demands always going farther and deeper. Hillman calls this "the moral impulse of the individuation process."[199] Values are presented as limitations upon the ego, so that the ego is drawn into the service of transcendental values of transformation. The wholeness of the self that is coming to be places imperatives on all the powers available to it. Everything tends toward enlightenment through relatedness. William Johnston sees "There are ... enlightenments which are ... quietly spiritual, prompted by an aesthetic experience and penetrating deeply into the personality."[200] The interpretation experience can contain such enlightenment and has a morality of its own tending toward the individuation of the poem in performance.

The art of interpretation depends on the ability of the imaginative process to bring psychic realities and energies into consciousness. The interpreter has to create and incarnate an inner life and present that life before an audience. This presentation is accomplished by means of a breaking-through to unconscious sources of creativity and artistic truth. One of the main objectives of the art taught by Stanislavski was this method of stimulating the creative nature of the unconscious in order to enhance and enliven the conscious art of acting: "Our conscious technique was directed on the one side towards putting our subconscious to work and on the other to learning how not to interfere with it once it was in action."[201] Stanislavski considered acting to be the organic blending of physiological and psychological processes in a creative act: "Real art is a union of the deep substance of inner experience and the vivid outer expression of it."[202]

What is involved here is the overcoming of the limitations and boundaries of the empirical ego, literally a breaking-through into a larger reality. Certainly there are many kinds of experience of this breakthrough, but they all have in common the fact that the division between subject and object is eliminated. The notion of *becoming an object* prevalent in Japanese culture is central here and is expressed in the concept of *muga* already mentioned. *Muga* is participation in the nonself, in which the "small ego" *(shōga)* is lost and the "big ego" *(taiga),* as true self, partakes.[203] Bacon explores the relevance to interpretation of another Japanese concept—that of indirection. The poet is submerged in the subject—the experience or image—and speaks by indirection:

> The effect is gained, indeed, because the poet does *not* specifically say how he feels. Japanese poets often submerge themselves in the object in this way and hence symbolize the emotion by the presentation of the object, drawing forth a sense of the oneness of things. . . . One of the primary requisites of great poetry in traditional Japanese literature is the quality called *yūgen* ("mystery," "suggestiveness"). It is this sense of hovering between possibilities that gives such literature much of its life.[204]

The reintegration of the conscious and unconscious parts of the psyche appears as an illumination. It is the state of discovering one's true self through apparent loss of self, described by the Christian mystics in their loss of self in God and their joy in the discovery of subsequent new life. It is a sense of unification in which there is no awareness of mind apart from body or of being apart from acting. Johnston describes persons who come into this state as "vertical thinkers," able to move openly and expansively between levels of reality.[205] The world of reason and the world beyond reason need not be, indeed cannot be, in conflict at the deepest level. Vertical thinking holds for the reality of both worlds and affirms the consonance between rational and pararational knowledge. To transcend reason is not at all the same thing as to contradict reason. There can be no ultimate contradiction between horizontal (rational) thinking and vertical thinking, for at the deepest level they naturally penetrate one another.

The Christian mystics insisted that there is a point at which one must abandon discursive meditation for a superior, supraconceptual moment of contemplation. The inner realities cannot be finally contained by discursive knowledge but can be known only through *unknowing*—the *nada, nada, nada* of St. John of the Cross. This is the apophatic way of ascent in which the unconscious is allowed to ascend to conscious regions. The cataphatic, positively and richly imaginative way experienced by St. Teresa of Avila in her corporeal visions, attained this same end by another means. What is necessary is a dialogue, an openness between these two directions. Both ways require concentration of purpose and purity of vision and being, a deep psychic detachment for the sake of an even deeper engagement with reality.

This detachment is seen by the contemporary psychologist Erich Fromm as the natural and fundamental prerequisite for all human growth. One cannot freely move onward if one is symbiotically attached or fixated at immature levels of existence.[206] This detachment is progress into a deeper intuitive love for being. In prayer it is manifested as participation in Christ through an extension of being. One does not think about Christ; one is abandoned to Christ in an openness and availability that transforms the individual into the eternal reality of Christ, the living subject of the prayer. The Incarnation of Christ is prolonged in the being of the one who participates in it through prayer: I live, yet not I, but Christ lives in me. The Incarnation is prolonged in history through those who participate in it in belief, and this life quality begins in an internal detachment: "We must be still and still moving / Into another intensity / For a further union, a deeper communion." (T. S. Eliot, "East Coker," V, 33–35).

In communion perception is altered, "as though the spatial act of seeing were changed by a new dimension."[207] What happens is a whole new way of seeing, which calls upon the resources of both conscious and unconscious, a way of seeing potent with possibilities, bordering, it would seem, on a total vision. The Christian mystic and scientist Teilhard de Chardin describes his own experience of this transformation in perception as a spiritual renewal welling up from the center of his life, allowing him to make the claim, for the first time, of his existence *as a life*: "I had in fact acquired a new sense, *the sense of a new quality* or *of a new dimension*. Deeper still: a transformation had taken place for me in the very perception of being."[208]

Word/Icon

In *The Perception and Evocation of Literature* Roloff speaks of *the performer as icon*: the interpreter's "total behavior is iconic of the literature." Symbol and metaphor in performance are embodied in "sound, sight, and time."[209] The interpreter is transformed into a sounding and visible icon, a being filled with sensuous form assimilated from the structures of literature. The performer as icon *shows* and is *seen*.

The lore of Russian spirituality is almost entirely iconic, a quality summed up by the dying Abbot Vessarion when he said the Christian "must become *all eye*."[210] For the Russian Christian all of life is an icon of the divine, and all iconography is centered in the mystery of creation consummated in the Incarnation. In the icon the creature is not copied but is truly evoked through spiritual transfiguration in form.[211]

The interpreter becomes *icon* through a growing process of self-transformation (including *kenosis* and the *transcendent function* of the conscious and unconscious) and through growing with the word within the literary text: listening to it, learning it, becoming it. The interpreter *comes to see* the vision of the world within the literature, and as this vision is increasingly clarified, she or he is increasingly able to manifest it in her or his own body, *to be seen*, in performance, as the showing-forth (or bodying-forth) of that world. As the interpreter comes to recognize being within the poem, she or he is enabled to act that being, to present it through her or his own being to others. The literary work is iconic for the interpreter as it shows itself more and more, and through assimilation with it the interpreter becomes iconic of the literary work for an audience.

Being and image come together for the percipient through a certain inner light, and, as Gabriel Marcel writes, the process by which being is shown is

> a combination of spiritual forces through which this being is maintained in existence on the one hand, and on the other, the act, equally spiritual, by which it is given to a subject to apprehend this being from the outside as a distinct and visible individuality. We must bring ourselves to see . . . that in considering this individuality through some medium or go-between, of whatever sort, we make our own in some degree the powers that are immanent in it. The truth is that what presents itself from a certain perspective as something apprehended or grasped can from a complementary perspective be regarded as an appearance and as giving of itself.[212]

In this way a model gives herself or himself in presenting a visible manifestation of self to the painter. The painter tries to commune with and to express this being in still another form, which ought to convey a profoundly significant image of the unique inner being shown forth as gift.

The interpreter is first of all a bodily presence, and the audience *sees* this presence as a totality prior to utterance. The expressive self within the poem needs to be shown in the iconic presence of the interpreter, so that it can effectively fill the presential space and prepare the atmosphere, so to speak, for penetration by utterance. Roloff's presentational aesthetic of interpretation views the iconic aspect of performance as part of an actualizing process whereby the interpreter creates a sense of the coming-into-being of the artistic vision within the poem.[213] The interpreter's presence—as the embodiment of the poem—constitutes a kind of image-meaning, or a *sacramental meaningfulness.*

Merleau-Ponty views the body as a creative interaction of vision and movement, through which the artist, as a body, can transform the world into a work of art.[214] A certain ambiguity or tensiveness is intrinsic to this interaction, for the body-subject is both *seeing* and *seen.* It discovers, or is discovering, the vision of the visible world—approaching it, opening itself to it—and it is also being seen.[215] The interpreter sees the poem, and the audience sees the interpreter *as* the poem. The opposition of energies at work here makes for a certain unifying tension: everything is held together by it. Bacon describes the interpretation process in Wheelwright-ean language that expresses an aspect of this interaction and its effect. Both literature and performance are filled with *tensiveness,* the rhythmic movement between contrary pulls. "These oppositions create awareness in us if we attend to them without distraction."[216] There is also a *coalescence,* originally meaning "growing up together," "growing together as the halves of a broken bone grow together." Finally, there is "*perspective,* which is the attitude, the angle of vision of the work." The creation of the embodiment of literature depends upon the relationship between these factors: the qualities of *tensiveness* are held in their place so that they *coalesce* into a structured form, guided by a sustaining *perspective,* or angle of vision.[217]

These factors apply to the total work, the speaking as well as the visual dimensions of performance. For Merleau-Ponty speech reveals to the speaker as well as to the listener. The speaker *speaks* and *hears.* In interpretation the speaking-subject of the poem coalesces with the body-subject of the interpreter through a process of "coherent deformation" (Malraux) of significations that causes the available properties of poem and performer to arrange themselves in a unique way and take "not only the hearers *but the speaking subject[s] as well through a decisive step.*"[218] The body is a kind of incarnate cognition in this activity, as it teaches and mediates life to others and itself, because it is the subject which utters a speech that can transform and relate self and others. A being's corporeal or vital situation is constituted in speech and moves outward into world and between beings.

The body perceives and is perceived in performance from multiple points of view—especially in interpretation. Because the interpreter is working with a variety of perspectives in performance, she or he must find the right gesture or posture of presence to fit each perspective in the most economical way possible. Presence, perspective, and economy are essential characteristics of iconography. *An icon is not a mimetic representation of a being, but an embodiment of certain essential aspects of it, capable of evoking the whole presence of its prototype through a moment's perception.* The true nature of an icon may be explained by contrasting it with a figure.

A figure is a likeness or representation of something. It is designed to be an explicit imitation, like a photograph, and, like a photograph, it could be confused psychologically with its subject. An icon, on the other hand, is not a likeness but a true image: it does not represent; it evokes presence. A figure is a likeness attempting identification with its subject. An icon is an unlikeness embodying the real presence of its subject. An icon is sacramental in this sense: Like the bread and wine of the Eucharist, the material form of the icon is different from the presence it reveals. The bread and wine are not confused with body and blood and do not represent body and blood; they constitute the real presence of body and blood by making their material nature available to that presence.

The undiscriminating eye of the camera captures its subject and literally represents it. A portrait, on the other hand, makes a judicious selection of certain meaningful details that it amplifies in order to reveal more of the true inner quality of its subject than the camera could. An icon is a portrait of the inner being of its subject expressed in appropriate sensuous form. The sacramental power of an icon is its symbolic capacity for *anamnesis;* it is the best available (i.e., symbolic) means for *recalling* or invoking *the true presence* of its subject or prototype.[219] On a symbolic level the icon is a material body that moves on to a spiritual form, to unite the percipient with its prototype through the invocation of being and the evocation of presence. It is a meeting place, filled with the indwelling energy of its archetypal reality. Its energy is not that of *mimesis,* but of *logos.* It is a cataphatic presentation of being and an apophatic means of movement toward that being. The *logoi,* or intelligibles, pour themselves into the form of the icon; spirit resonates from within them as incarnation and revelation. "Honour rendered to the image passes to the prototype," writes St. Basil in *De spiritu sancto.*[220] The presence of *logos* in the image constitutes the seat of its energy. "For this reason Philo calls the Logos, which is the pleroma of the Forms, the Image of God."[221] The image becomes a repository of power transmitted to it by the primary repository, the subject of the image. For the Christian the power of the image is the divine *energeia,* which works in the world through human cooperation.[222]

The reality of the prototype is manifested fully and instantly in an icon by means that are indirect and nonliteral. The subject of the icon is expressed in a dimension liberated from historical necessity, as a poem might be embodied in a way suggesting its metahistorical significance:

An icon of a saint tells us nothing of his physical appearance and gives no biographical, historical, or sociological detail. It shows the radiating influence of the [person] beyond history. A saint bears history within . . . but . . . shows it in a different manner; he reveals a new dimension of it, in which its meaning is made clear by its last end. [The saint] constitutes a metahistorical synthesis. We must read the lives of the desert Fathers *iconographically,* just as we contemplate an icon.[223]

In traditional Russian iconography the straightforward position of the subject and the conventional wide-staring eyes were the vehicles through which the percipient could enter into communion with the prototype, and the "doors" through which the percipient could enter the suprasensible world through the sensible one.[224] A contemporary American iconographer, John Walstead, O.H.C., calls an icon the meeting place between heaven and earth. He explores the perceptual aspect of seeing and being seen: "Icons are a kind of window through which the inhabitants of the celestial world look down into ours. To look through the window of an icon would be to look straight into the celestial world."[225]

The interpreter as a living icon is like a window opening onto the world of the poem because she or he also contains it in the sensuous form of bodily presentation, just as the painted icon opens onto the eternal truth of its subject by containing an aspect of it in its sensuous painted form. The painted icon is different from its subject in being (*ousia*), says St. John of Damascus, yet there is a connection between them, precisely through the material, incarnate form of the image. The interpreter is also different from the poem and yet, in performance, becomes the same, also by means of an incarnate form that takes on certain evocative aspects of the poem: in the words of Cassirer, by a "degree of intensification and illumination which is the measure of the excellence of art."[226]

The effect of art on human feeling is made possible through the manifestation of dynamic, sensuous forms. The formative power of the structural unity of a work of art is an intensification of energies reflected in the percipient. As a bodily location where energies intensely interact, an icon is the visual contact point between beings, between "the immense life of Christ and our own lives in the world."[227] The interpreter as icon is the contact point between the immense world of the poem and the world in which the audience lives. The life of the poem pours into the lives of those who see and hear. Likewise, in theological terms "We often say that at Communion we are receiving our Lord into ourselves. If we reverse the process, we see that Christ receives us into His immense life."[228] The poem receives those who see and hear it, who receive it by participation into its own life. Communion amounts to a mutual interpenetration. Word and icon are connected in Christian spirituality through the powers of communion proper to both.

The word of the Holy Scriptures is called an image, and Eusebius referred to it as the true image of Christ.[229] So the image is also a word, for, according to St. Basil the Great, "What the word transmits through the ear, the painting silently shows through the image, by these two means mutually accompanying each other!"[230] The icon is placed on a level with the word conveyed in Holy Scriptures and is considered an authentic form of revelation and self-communication of the holy, a form in which two wills (divine and human) and two actions have been blended and made to fit one another. Word and image both reflect something within and beyond them; each is symbolic of the spirit contained within them: "The Image and the Word are significantly the same. Each transmits teaching and expresses . . . life."[231] Oral speaking connects word and image in that it lets something be seen, shows something, in an active sense.[232] Vladimir Lossky writes that the principle of the Incarnation of the Word is at the root of the cult of holy images that express the inexpressible and make visible the invisible. An icon does not exist simply to direct the imagination during meditation; it makes the subject of meditation present in an active way, as it is a material center for this real presence, which is manifested as an energy uniting itself to human art.[233] The hypostatic union of *Logos* and flesh in the Incarnation is in a sense prolonged in the artistic icon; the *word* is somehow present and life-giving within the image, just as the image is intrinsic to the word.

The contemporary Russian poet Andrei Voznesensky, in trying to discover new modes of poetic expression, has come on this iconic notion of the word: "before the word there is an idea or an image. There is *something* before sound. My new work . . . is an attempt to go right to the image."[234] Whether image precedes word or word precedes image is not as important as the actual interpenetration of these two in artistic expression. The creative imagination strives to engender a work through word and image, as it attempts to give form to the inner word through a work that is both material and spiritual. This work is the work of incarnation: "The Incarnation of the Word makes God personally and visibly present, . . . it is no longer a presence unseen."[235]

Roloff illustrates the transformation of an image in performance by the power of verbal energy. Hyperverbal meaning can transform language into the experience it strives to become in performance. The image within the word needs to be taken into the body and transformed into a sensual form appropriate to it through sounding and showing: "The language of literature is image-bearing; when the imagination receives the same images through sound and behavior, the result is image-amplifying."[236] The interpreter first sees and hears from within the experience of the poem in her or his own body what is happening in the poem, and the behavior that goes into informing the poem in performance gives shape to the experience and reveals the inner life of the text to an audience. Images have the power to affect the senses in the holistic perception of literature. The primary communication between images creates tensiveness as they flow into and move against each other, to progress from visual to auditory to kinesthetic levels. Word and image blend in the process and act of interpretation-incarnation: "In the effective performance of literature, there is a sense of something being revealed; through the unique impact of sound and physical presence emanating from a performer, the perceiver senses an art form working upon and within him. What [the perceiver] sees and hears happening ... is both *the literature and the performer attaining a state of being.*"[237]

The body can be transformed in creating verbal images by giving aspects to and taking them from the surrounding space, to shrink or expand itself. An action can move the body-image from one place to another and can intend and effect a change in the shape of the body-image.[238] Perception has a direct effect on muscular action and can cause a change in the body-image, or the way in which the body is perceived. Not only can the psychic attitude connect with muscular states but so close is their interrelation that every shift or sequence of tension and relaxation causes a specific attitude. A specific motor sequence changes attitudes and alters the inner situation and can even provoke a fantasy to fit the muscular activity. The body-image can spread itself out into a space and can incorporate realities into itself. We perceive the body-images of others as expressions of emotion, and emotions emanate from personalities. They are primary data in perceiving and relating to others.[239] In interpretation the performer expresses her or his inner experience of the literature by presenting, or *outering*, its qualities through a visible and audible body-image.[240]

Stanislavski believed that inner states could be produced by enacting the outer muscular movements characteristic of them. An actor was taught to perfect the outer physical aspects of her or his roles in order to stimulate and create the inner psychological states that they reflected and to evoke the actual feelings belonging to them.[241] Thus, the images that the actor or interpreter gathers within are not merely means of reproducing prior experiences; they actually constitute experience.[242] Images constellate in the interpretation process as the poem's aesthetic drive for self-actualization joins with the interpreter's intentionality. This drive does not aim at the reduction of tensiveness between word and image, poem and interpreter, but creates and organizes tensive qualities in the service of realizing possibilities for carrying the work through to its end in the particular experience or situation of performance.[243]

Word and image coalesce in the incarnating process of interpretation. They function together to bring about the showing of an inner state—the *epiphany*, in iconic language—of an internal world. The Christian view of spirit and matter shows the nature of the dialogue between inner and outer in terms of a wholeness. Spirit and matter are not two separate dimensions of reality that exist side by side but signify two constitutive elements of the one reality of being, a reality in which inner and outer are always directed toward each other. Spirit and matter move together as aspects of lived experience,[244] and they can, in fact, only be known in combination. It follows that neither aspect can be completely known, so there is always a certain mystery in the result of their interweaving in actual experience. Matter, says the theologian J. R. Illingworth, is the language of spirit and its realization: "In every case contact with matter strengthens the spiritual fibre, forcing vagueness into outline, confusion into clearness, doubt into decision, hesitation into act. It is the necessary means by which our spiritual life becomes actual, concrete, real."[245]

Reality turns upon the interpenetration between aspects of existence that we call inner and outer. An icon is the outer manifestation of an inner state; it is the material center for a presence, the embodiment of an inner reality. The interpreter as icon undergoes a process of matching that Bacon illustrates by the following diagram:[246]

The poem presents itself to the interpreter through the outer form of its physical text: printed words on a piece of paper. This form is lifeless, but the interpreter can bring it to life by discovering its inner form: the spoken poem, the *word* speaking itself through the interpreter's own body and heard as a kind of inner voice. Everything depends on the interpreter's ability to create a coalescence between her or his own inner form and the inner form of the poem. When this happens, the inner reality of the poem is projected outward again, but in a different way—an alive way, through the living, sounding, visible body of the interpreter. An iconic presence is created. The interpreter has discovered the inner reality of the poem by *hearing its vision, hearing and feeling what it looks like inside.* Hearing, seeing, and feeling function together on the inner level of the performer's matching process with the poem, and they act together in the outering event of performance.

Illingworth suggests that images and thoughts tend to become more real for us as they are presented in external space.[247] As image becomes word and word becomes act and act becomes image again, but fully realized, there is an increasing sense of fullness, simply because more and more of our whole personality becomes involved at each stage. In uttering and enacting what is within we give it the power of our intention in putting our will into it in a way that shows we *mean* it. Image and word in performance are realized in the gesture of utterance and take on sacramental power. In his definition of gesture in language R. P. Blackmur echoes the catechetical formula for a sacrament ("an outward and visible sign of an inward and spiritual grace"):[248] "Gesture, in language, is the outward and dramatic play of inward and imaged meaning. It is that play of meaningfulness among words which cannot be defined in the formulas in the dictionary, but which is defined in their use together; gesture is that meaningfulness which is moving, in every sense of that word: what moves the words and what moves us."[249]

George Herbert Mead speaks of gesture as a meaning-act. It is the part of a social act that stimulates another form (or person) "to make an adjustment, and this adjustment is both a later phase in the act and the meaning of the gesture."[250] Gesture acts on those who perceive it, and their act of perceiving completes it by giving it meaning. The art work of performance is an iconic gesture that is not only an incarnation but an extension of meaning in physical terms, to make its subject accessible to others and invite them to engage in its experience. As an outer form through which inner form is perceived as real, interpretational performance is a sacramental way of access to reality. But the perceiver must be prepared to allow the vision to be perceived as a sacrament, to complete itself from within. In other words, as *sacramental meaningfulness,* the art of interpretation calls for response from those who experience it. It calls for engagement: "Sacramental truth is not an unlocated, eternal truth we try to assimilate in our lives or try to bring to ourselves. It calls us to be our body-selves. It is something into which we step, and it keeps us stepping. The sacraments are the same mode of meaning our bodies are; they are meaning we must live, not just think about."[251]

It is the responsibility of the interpreter to create and maintain the sacramental icon throughout the performance. This is done, as has been said, by profound concentration and attention on the subject at hand. The controversial phrase "aesthetic distance," so much discussed in interpretation studies today, may be clarified in the context of the interpreter as icon. It is possible to speak of aesthetic distance from two opposing viewpoints: one that sees the interpreter as *only* herself or himself and one that sees the interpreter as *not* herself or himself. The former view sees interpretation as a kind of stylized art, in which the interpreter's close or direct relationship with the audience would make too intense a presentation of the poem a source of embarrassment to both interpreter and audience. This view holds that it is impossible for the interpreter to fool an audience into believing that she or he actually *is* the character or subject being performed, so she or he ought not to attempt this illusion at all. Here aesthetic distance would mean the interpreter's frank admission, throughout performance, that she or he is *not* the embodied poem, but a sensitive interpreter, and sometimes critic, responding to it with the audience. This position is clearly incongruous with the point of view of this study.[252] It sees the interpreter as a would-be *figure*, in contrast to *icon*, and, acknowledging the inadequacy of this role, says that it would be foolhardy for the interpreter even to attempt a sustained illusion of convincing likeness. Of course, what is presented here is an extreme view of the position, but it shows the limits to which such an aesthetic can go.

The other position sees the interpreter, *not* as herself or himself during performance, but as the embodiment of the inner form of the literature being presented. In this viewpoint the interpreter is an icon of the poem. From this position the interpreter does not need to be warned against feeling too much or being too expressive, for it is not the interpreter feeling and expressing, but *the poem expressing itself through the performer.* The interpreter is also present, but in a state of heightened consciousness and intense concentration. Unless for some reason this concentration is broken and the interpreter falls back into her or his own *persona,* the *personae* speaking will be those of the poem, with which the interpreter is in a state of coalescence, or consubstantiation.

The sacramental quality of performance changes beings from their ordinary context. They are perceived differently and become charged with an *otherness* and an *innerness.* The consecrated bread and wine of the Eucharist are no longer perceived as mere bread and wine. They are present in a different context from their ordinary one, and their reality is intensified through the sacramental meaning which they form. As physical entities, the bread and wine are *distanced* from their ordinary context and gathered into the larger, heightened life of sacrament and mystery. The interpreter is also distanced from her or his ordinary context and gathered into the larger life of the poem in performance: a sacramental act. Distance in this special, sacramental sense is not maintained through "empathy," for even though empathy is "feeling into" another, it is still not feeling *from within* the other. Empathy still involves a self-conscious ego aware of its own feeling, even though it tries to identify with another.[253] What is needed is a sustained *participation in the life of the other.*

Stanislavski observed the effects of concentration during performance and connected its power with true creative inspiration, manifested as a kind of distance. It is at the very time when the actor's total attention is on the work itself, "when the actor's attention is not turned toward the public, that he acquires a special hold on them, forcing them to participate actively."[254] In this situation the actor's energies are concentrated in a "circle of attention" that excludes her or his own *persona* and manifests the *persona* or *personae* of the literary work. The actor—or interpreter—is not an impersonation of the drama or its characters, but the icon of its inner essence. Distinguishing between these two types of interpretation, Stanislavski describes two contrasting types of theatre: the theatre that is a spectacle, designed only to entertain by seducing the eye and ear, and the theatre whose "effect on your eyes and ears is only a means to penetrate the soul of the audience."[255]

In interpretation the performer creates presence through tensive distance and compels an audience to participate in the world of the poem by offering a way of access to it through the sacramental act of iconic incarnation.

Substitution/Participation

An audience is allowed (or even compelled) to participate in the life of the poem in performance only if the interpreter's participation in the poem is total and authentic, free from ego-centric designs. Such participation requires a sustained, active intentionality on the part of the performer: "The oral process involves active participation in the perceptions of the poem. Passivity is a completely impossible state for the oral reader."[256] Participation means more than perceiving the poem; it means to perceive what the poem perceives.

A person who participates is different from one who is merely a passive spectator—who watches something as if it was a spectacle that cannot touch or involve the person and has no claims on her or his commitment or attention.[257] Participation involves the whole person in an active relationship with another. It acknowledges and acts in the mystery of interpenetration between self and world or, in this case, poem and interpreter, performance and audience. Illumination is interior to participation. Meaning becomes clarified when beings share existence. Participation begins in a perception or recognition at a preconceptual level and emerges into consciousness as an intentionality toward another—in the case of performance, toward the poem being enacted. Participation requires an affirmation of the poem in place of affirmation of the personal ego. Human beings rob their own existence of its meaning whenever they affirm themselves in isolation from all else; human individuality is reduced to an empty form. Egoism is in reality the self-negation and destruction of true individuality. Through love we come to know another, not in abstraction, but in the truth of concrete reality, and we actually transfer the center of our lives from our own separate and isolated ego to the other. The Russian philosopher Vladimir Solovyov writes of love as a power of realization. By going out of ourselves to another or others in love "we manifest and realize our own truth, our own absolute significance, which consists precisely in the power of transcending our actual phenomenal existence and of living not in ourselves only but also in another."[258]

The *Other* in whose existence we can participate must be a real and objective reality as we are but must also be different from us, so as to be truly *Other* and not merely a projection of ourselves. The *Other* has an essence like our own, but it shows itself in a completely different form. Because of this element of polarity all of our vital energies can meet in the *Other* in a creative exchange based on tensiveness and intentionality. The coming together of two beings that are different in form but one in intentionality has the power of creating a new being and is at the same time the source of an individuation process for both beings engaged in this interaction. Solovyov describes the meaning of love in these terms. Love is important, he says, not as a type of human feeling, but because it constitutes "the transference of our whole vital interest from ourselves to another, as the transposition of the very center of our personal life."[259] There is love between poem and performer that has these effects during the act of performance and that is indeed powerful enough to contain and move an audience. This love relationship is a tensive, intentional outgoing toward the other and a dynamic and ongoing exchange with the other.

The way of exchange, or substitution, is at the center of the Christian doctrines of the Incarnation and Atonement. The doctrine of substituted love, or the doctrine of coinherence, lies at the center of these mysteries.[260] The Christian writer Charles Williams describes the doctrine of substitution as a reality in which human beings can participate on many levels. First and foremost, the Divine Word coinheres in God the Creator and the Holy Spirit, as they do in the Word; but also the Word substitutes for humanity in the mysteries of the Incarnation and Redemption, or At-onement. Christ's life was given for others, that is, instead of and on behalf of others, an offering for the ultimate good of others. Substitution is first of all an intentionality toward another for the good of that other. Its actualization in power has two results. The first is a state of mind that may be called humility, not as an acquired virtue, but simply a recognition of fact: seeing things as they are and seeing oneself in right relation to others. In the second place there arises within one a "faint sense of what might be called 'loving from within.' One no longer merely loves an object; one has a sense of loving precisely from the great web in which the object and we are both combined."[261]

The way of exchange, or substitution, is at the heart of the interpretation process. When the interpreter meets another speaking-subject in literature, whether as a dramatic character or simply the speaking poem itself, she or he must adopt an attitude of intentionality toward that being which amounts to a willingness to *perform* or *realize* that other being, to allow her or his own personal being "to be the sounding voice and behavioral body of another."[262] Williams says that in substitution one has a flicker of a sense of living within the other. In interpretation this sense becomes a pervasive and steady light, as the interpreter comes to realize the "sounding-body-voice" of the literary work.[263] This knowledge can never be complete because each true being remains a mystery never entirely accessible to any other. But the interpreter knows the *Other* in the literary work as much as possible through learning how that *Other* feels. Such knowledge is true participation.

Everyone who *lives meaning creatively* participates in meaning by affirming her or his own personal being in receiving and transforming reality through the creative realization of it.[264] For Paul Tillich "participation" can be used in three ways, each one of which is applicable to the interpretation process. Participation can mean "taking part": (1) in the sense of sharing a space, (2) in the sense of having in common or having-with another (the participation of the individual in the universal), and, finally, (3) in the sense of being a part of something larger than one's self. In each of these cases "participation is a partial identity and a partial non-identity. A part of the whole is not identical with the whole to which it belongs. But the whole is what it is only with the part."[265] In interpretation what the interpreter strives for is not identification, but participation in this sense: being an indispensable part of the whole process of actualizing the poem. The "identity" in this participation is not the same thing as "identification": "Literature does not ask for identification, . . . but it does ask for participation in the ongoing feelings of the poem."[266] The identity in participation is a corealization of the powers of being that exist in the self and the world or in the poem and the interpreter. The interpreter is existentially involved as a whole existence in the existence or situation of the poem. In performing an existential breakthrough the interpreter comes to know the poem in the situation of the breakthrough: "You must participate in a self in order to know what it is. But by participating you change it. In all existential knowledge both subject and object are transformed by the very act of knowing. Existential knowledge is based on an encounter in which a new meaning is created and recognized."[267]

Another way of considering participation is from the standpoint of the *interface*. This term is borrowed from neurology, where it was first used to refer to junctions at which energy is transferred or transmuted. George Whalley means by interface the place where beings meet and embrace, "the interface being a pliable and permeable membrane extending infinitely both upwards and on either hand. This membrane is to be regarded as a medium joining, not separating, subject and object; as I conceive it, the interface has depth, some spatial characteristics—one can 'move about in' the interface."[268] Everything within the interface is in a state of constant flux of dynamic movement in the complicated process of mutual adjustment. The interface is the location where values cluster that cannot merge outside of the relatedness that takes place there. Although the situation at the interface is highly complex, the experience of it is simple and direct. It is a matter of engagement in a reality that presents itself only through engagement and shows itself to be of value. The mystic and the poet both work at the interface, but the mystic tends to see through it, while the poet *looks at and along* it in order to discover what it is like at the interface and to manifest what she or he sees in an incarnate art form.

Incarnation in an art form—the word becoming flesh—is the substance of performance. It comes to be through a process of unself-conscious participation and exchange between poem and performer, and is finally shown to a perceiving audience that, if the work is true, cannot help but be drawn into it and through it to another mode of reality where beings discover their true selves. This kind of interpretation is not an interpretation of spectacle without substance. It is not all surfaces. It has a dimension of depth to it and a transforming power over the lives of those engaged in it. Its end is to be a presence for an audience, an actual, incarnate *presence*. Stanislavski's vivid illustration of this kind of performance and its effect on an audience can illuminate the particular kind of performance that is interpretation:

> But there is also another kind of theatre. You have come in and taken your seat as an onlooker, but the director of the play changes you into a participant in the life that is unfolding on the stage. Something has happened to you. You are carried away from your position as a mere onlooker. As soon as the curtain is drawn you say to yourself:
>
> "I know this room, and there's Ivan Ivanovich, and there's my friend, Maria Petrovna. . . . Yes, I recognize all this. Now what happens next?" You look at the stage and you say:
>
> "I believe it all, every bit of it. . . . That is my mother there. . . . I can tell. . . ."
>
> When the performance ends you are stirred, but in a different way now. You have no desire to applaud.
>
> "How can I applaud my own mother? It feels rather strange."
>
> The components of your excitement are such that they force you to concentrate, to turn your eyes inward.[269]

A coalescence or at-onement is created between poem, performer, and audience. It is created because the interpreter has assented to becoming one with the poem, to growing into it, and, finally, to stand *for* it, in the sense of the doctrine of substituted love. The interpreter offers herself or himself as the bodily means whereby the poem becomes an audible and visible presence. Through the process of incarnation the interpreter becomes the living icon of the poem. Through the sacramental power of this icon a circle of energy is created in which poem, performer, and audience are transformed in the experience of communion.

four

AND DWELLS AMONG US

The last two chapters have explored the nature of the poem and the process of the interpreter's meeting with it and becoming one with it. This process begins in a dialogue with the poem. First there is a meeting between the outer form of the poem and the interpreter. Then a dialogue begins to take place between the inner forms of both poem and interpreter. This dialogue presupposes that the interpreter has learned as much as possible about the poem in terms of structure, pattern, and style and is prepared to become engaged with it at a deeper level of intensity. At some point in this engagement a *kenosis* takes place, in which the interpreter empties herself or himself of the demands of the ego, irrelevant and idiosyncratic *personae,* and as much as possible of all other elements that might interfere with the authentic realization of the poem. The poem also undergoes a *kenosis* in the sense of outpouring; for, given the right situation of receptivity, it pours itself into the interpreter's body so that both poem and interpreter experience a mutual *plerosis,* or fullness, in mutual self-giving. This exchange of participation takes place through dynamics of tensiveness, coalescence, and perspective, as the interpreter's vision of the poem is assumed by her or his total bodily being, so that the interpreter finally *is* an iconic presence revealing that same vision to others. When this revelation happens, the poem is realized in communion with the bodily being of the interpreter as an *incarnation.*

Just as both poem and interpreter have experienced a transformation (in the form of growth or amplification of being), the energy field created by their incarnate presence has a transforming effect on an audience. All of these dynamics interplay in the whole process of performance. Though it is necessary to study them separately and, to an extent, sequentially, they are in reality neither separate nor sequential. The complex dynamics of the interpretation process overlap and are intricately interwoven: their synergy is the very power that creates a meaningful performance. They are all present at once in the manifestation that is performance: First, there is the word; the word becomes flesh and so dwells in our midst, to reveal itself to us, make us one in its light. We see and hear it in its own reality. The word becomes act and is alive, and so has power over us.

Having explored various aspects of the interpretation process leading up to and involved in performance, this study will now look to performance itself as a transforming act, a kairotic event, and a moving communion. *Transformation* effects a change in poem, performer, and audience. *Kairos* is the decisive moment of transformation. *Communion* is the enspirited situation in which transformation takes place.

Transformation

Stanislavski writes that artistic performance is the transformation of everyday human realities into *"crystals of artistic truth."*[1] In the perception of performance a transformation takes place in feeling, as the *felt sensing*[2] of the poem takes hold of interpreter and audience and brings about a metamorphosis in awareness. Lev Semenovich Vygotsky's psychological theory of art asserts that the significance of the metamorphosis of feeling in art is its transcendent quality: the movement of feeling from the individual to the social plane, where it achieves true personalism.[3] The function of a poem is not to convey the poet's emotion to the reader (that would be unfortunate for art, remarks Vygotsky), but to change that emotion in such a way that something new and truly unique is formed.[4] Likewise, the function of interpretation is not to convey the interpreter's sensitivity or emotional reactions to an audience, but to transform those qualities into a presentational form that allows the essence of the work itself to shine through, to reveal something new and pertinent to humanity on a higher level of truth. Only the high quality of an artist's work can bring about this transformation, says Vygotsky, and the process itself is hidden. Yet process is everything. The viewer of the art work does not see the process but sees only a finished product. In interpretation, however, the process is not obscured, for performance is not an art work frozen in clay or paint. It is active, alive, vibrant; in performance, form as process and form as being are perceived as one, for being emerges through motion.

Vygotsky has a dynamic, dialectical theory of emotion in art, which he calls the "opposition of feelings." This term suggests that the affective qualities of a work move in two opposing directions which, however, come together in a single crowning point. This intersection constitutes a joining or closure, in which feeling is transformed and clarified. The resolution of an individual conflict is transformed into the revelation of universal human truth. Emotion is outflow, movement outward. Vygotsky's "single pole energy outflow law" states that emotion moves out from one of two sources: periphery or center. Increased activity at one pole immediately causes a decrease at the other. Ordinary emotion originates at the periphery and moves outward in some form of external action or expression. In the experience of art this single-direction flow of feeling is not true. The emotion of aesthetic perception flows from the center, where powerful feelings converge at high levels of intensity but do not tend toward outward action. The activity at the center is greatly increased.

According to this theory aesthetic feeling differs from ordinary feeling by its intense concentration at the inner source of energy, which leads to an activation of an extremely intensified imagination. In the experience of art the emotions aroused are intelligent emotions, not inciting the individual to overt acts of violence or passion, but acting inwardly, released through images of fantasy. Vygotsky goes on to say that the stimulus of art sends opposing messages to opposing muscles in different parts of the body, so that one is inclined to move in opposite directions at once. Vygotsky explains by this "opposition factor" the delay in the manifestation of feeling that usually distinguishes aesthetic responsiveness from ordinary feeling. Catharsis takes place as painful and unpleasant effects are transformed into their healing opposites: passions are converted into virtues by a complex transformation of feeling.[5]

Not only are feelings but also the whole person is affected in the art experience. The experience of literature in interpretation is an open, dynamic process of the self-revelation of the art through performance. Understanding comes about through the experience of literature as a relationship: an encounter between an *I* and a *Thou*. Understanding takes place as this encounter unfolds and changes. The audience experiences a changing relationship with the poem just as the interpreter does. As the audience comes to terms with this relationship, it comes to terms with itself and, in a way, with the human situation. Insofar as the experience of the poem is an experience of a world, changes in that world bring about changes in its participants. Active perception in the audience constitutes active receptivity, which is a true form of participation. The audience undergoes a transforming process of understanding as a new reality emerges in the performance and unfolds as the self-creation or self-revelation of a whole event having a whole meaning. But the audience can perceive this meaning and event only as it unfolds. The understanding exists in the anticipation of the whole in the unfolding. This is an existential view of performance, assuming that "reality as a whole is not yet complete, and is still in the process of becoming."[6] Meaning can only be experienced moment by moment, as the wholeness of meaning in the reality of a given situation diffuses itself into significant particulars.

In interpretation, meaning unfolds through the process of speech and gesture. Günther Müller points out that metamorphosis is intrinsic to language:

> The sentences themselves, by the sequence of their words, constantly introduce something new that enters into manifold connections with what has already been said. . . . The form-giving pattern of meanings which emerges

from [words] presents an abundance, growing with each sentence, at every point of the sequence of sentences, and is manifest as a growing form.

Now, the "growth" does not just add something "more" or "longer," but it changes what has already been said by further fashioning of the whole.[7]

Performance coheres for the percipient because of the interpenetration of all its parts, which come together in a power that draws and sustains total attention. The impact of performance can be such that the percipient believes it to be permanent and far-reaching. What is perceived is a kind of truth and reality that both challenges and moves the audience. According to Iredell Jenkins this kind of art in performance "has changed us as persons because it has radically altered the ways in which we view things."[8] Performance as icon, as suggested in chapter three, alters the very perception of being. One cannot look deeply into the eyes of an icon and ever see the world in exactly the same way again. The icon changes one by bestowing the vision of another world. This is the effect described in performance as well. To enter the world of the icon is to take on that world by spontaneous and largely unconscious response to it. The gesture of the icon is repeated in the one who perceives it. This gesture is the performance itself. In *The Perception and Evocation of Literature* Roloff expresses this aspect of performance: "The performer of literature translates language into a behavioral act, into a moment that is pure transformation."[9]

In the aesthetic experience of performance what is necessary is to let all that is present in the literary work reveal itself in the fullest and most vivid manner possible. The poem in performance becomes the guide, and the audience submits to its direction as the interpreter did. Performance constitutes a transformation, not of the poem, but of the performer and audience by the poem. Transformation by the poem implies cooperation on the part of the percipient, and this implies pliability and the availability of the body. According to Merleau-Ponty responsiveness as a psychic state implies the body in the forming of new structures.[10] For him bodily involvement is true of any change. The will is involved in this process only initially, in giving consent to it. The will is what allows one to enter a situation. Then it is the participation of the body that is of vital importance. Merleau-Ponty illustrates this point in describing the process of falling asleep. The person lies on the bed, closes the eyes, excludes all projects from the mind. And here the power of the will or of consciousness stops. This initial act is an invocation of sleep. By acting as if one were asleep one invokes sleep: "There is a moment when sleep comes. . . . I succeed in becoming that which I make believe I am."[11]

We do not will a situation, but being in a situation, we assent to it and find that the existential circumstances we are in make us be one kind of person instead of another and cause us to will one way rather than another. Our existential circumstances arise, finally, from the body. The body assures metamorphoses and is the means whereby ideas and images are transformed into realities and acts. The body converts elements of a situation through its total gesture in response to it. Movement toward another is movement of and in the body, changing the situation by a true inclination. When the body opens itself to others, it finds its own voice in an active coexistence beyond itself. Intention toward another transforms one's bodily existence, which is itself a perpetual incarnation. Even though we do not know how this transformation happens, it does happen.[12]

What is involved in the creative act of performance is the whole human person—performer or percipient—and the fact of the transformation of human nature and character, for creativity as transformation (change, growth, renewal of being) concerns the full development of the whole person.[13] Rollo May writes that it is in the context of dialogue that we experience the structures of creativity.[14] Meaning emerges through the ability of two beings to question and answer each other in the right way. May points to the ability to hear questions and to put them together meaningfully, which typified the dialogues of Socrates. Socrates tuned his mind to discovering the question that would cause his dialogic partner to understand, to break open the shell of meaning that lay in the midst of the spoken relationship with another human being. Understanding is possible, says May, by the structure of language, and more so by the structure of relationships. This analysis holds true for interpretation, for performance is the final moment of actualization in a process of a spoken relationship between poem and interpreter, now experienced in the context of an audience. What is essential is the *becoming* of each of the members of this triadic relationship: "In the process of becoming, the whole reader becomes, just as the whole poem becomes. It is full communion between reader, poem, and audience toward which interpretation as an art and as an act moves."[15]

The structures of communion allow for communication, and communication is dialogic encounter through which beings develop and transform, always to change more and more into their true selves. May illustrates the importance of participation in the meaning structures of dialogue by contrasting communion with daimonic possession through the example of the importance of dance among the Yoruba. The dance draws the individual into deeper participation and relatedness in the community, while daimon possession has the opposite effect of isolating a person from the community. The daimonic is present in both manifestations, but in the dance the daimonic is creative, whereas possession destroys human liberty and is the opposite:

The former makes the daimonic personal and conscious, whereas the latter not only leaves the daimonic unconscious but sets in motion a whole train of new repression. The integrated daimonic pushes the person toward some universal structure of meaning, as shown in dialogue. But daimon possession, in contrast, requires that the daimonic remain impersonal. The former is transrational, the latter—daimon possession—is irrational, and succeeds by virtue of blocking off rational processes. The former makes the vitality of the daimonic available for the use of the self; the latter projects the daimonic outside oneself on someone or something else.[16]

Both instances constitute a transformation, but only the former—the transformation into communion—is creative.

Another psychologist, Sidney M. Jourard, connects transformation with revelation through dialogue. The person who reads or listens to authentic human experience outside her or his own is enriched by it: "In ways that we do not yet fully understand, at least in a scientific sense, the disclosed experience of the other . . . enables us to see things, feel things, imagine things, hope for things that we could never even have imagined before we were exposed to the revelation of the discloser."[17] The experience constituted by listening can shape our essence and change our lives just as firsthand experience can.

Art is the coming together of forms, and though it does not incite the perceiving person to direct, overt actions, it does change lives because it suggests a change of purpose.[18] Hence, the transforming power of literature is great, and the more alive the form in which it is presented, the more likely it is to be known and felt as authentic, creative experience.

The art of interpretation takes the form of performance, which is the transformation of the form of literature.[19] The literature is not transformed from printed word to living form, for the printed word is not the literature at all, but only its vehicle. Literature in all cases can come to life only within the human body, whether it is read silently, seen and heard strictly from within, or read or performed aloud. Performance is, rather, the transformation of literature into its true, vital nature, from a potential state to *act*ualization through the entelechy of incarnation. Thus, works that exist only in potential in print yield to the body of the person who physically takes in their form, so that they can come to life within the imagination of that person. Most works of literature will also yield to the "transformation of space-time-sound"[20] and in the context of presentation in performance will reveal their values, which may have remained hidden and unrecognized on the printed page—perhaps even in silent reading if the reader is so conditioned to print that she or he does not know how to see and hear a literary world from within.

In the inner dialogue created by the presence of literature, spirit manifests itself as a vital energy that moves lives. Tillich's description of the revelation of spirit speaks to the moment of interpretation as transformation: "The Spirit can awaken you to sudden insight into the way you must take your world, and it can open your eyes to a view of it that makes everything new. . . . Spiritual Presence may break again into our consciousness, awakening us to recognize what we are, shaking and transforming us."[21]

Kairos

The moment of interpretation as transformation suggests an attitude toward *time as moment,* descriptive not of measurement or duration, but of content, quality, and affectivity on those participating in it. The Hebrew notion of time expressed in the Old Testament is understood from the point of view of *time content.* Time is not a measured dimension, but a mode of being that is filled with all kinds of energies and content: "the times . . . that went over him" (I Chr. 29:30, KJV) serves as a graphic example of this attitude. What is suggested is not duration, but "the circumstances that came upon him."[22] In the New Testament the Greek word *kairos* was adopted and used in a more specific sense as the *appointed time* or the *decisive moment.* An examination of *kairos* in its biblical context, and of the Hebrew concept of time leading up to the notion of *kairos,* may illuminate the nature of interpretation as a transforming event, effecting a change in the perceived quality of time and relating event to creative incarnation as act.

There is no abstract word for time in the Old Testament. Expressions relating to time are concrete and in terms of content. The most frequently used word that can be translated as "time" is *'ēth,* meaning the moment or point of time at which something happens. Whether the event that characterizes this point of time is of long or short duration is irrelevant. Time is identified with neither space nor duration, but time and content interpenetrate without logical distinction. The Old Testament word for the appointed time (comparable to the New Testament *kairos*) is *mô'ēd,* meaning "place of meeting."[23]

In the New Testament *kairos* is generally used to mean "the essential point."[24] The Greek word *chronos* designates the "space of time" and is clearly used to express time as measured quantity. *Kairos,* on the other hand, expresses a quality rather than a quantity of time. It suggests the opportune moment, filled with possibility. *Kairos* has a double emphasis depending on its context: in one sense, it indicates the present moment that is God-given and ripe with possibility and that demands a decision in favor of obedience; in another sense, it points to a unified alignment toward a goal *(telos)* set by God.[25] Oscar Cullman's articulation of the Christian view of time describes time as a system based not in an initial point, but in a center: the Christ-process of creative redemption extending throughout all time from the Incarnation.[26] He points to the antithesis between the Christian, linear concept of time and the Hellenistic determinism of a notion of circular time. For the Greeks time was a prison out of which one could escape into the other, eternal realm only through death. Eternity was seen as existing spatially outside of the circle of time and as totally inaccessible to those within that circle.

The Christian understanding of time is that it is a small part of the unending dimension of eternity that contains it.[27] Time and eternity are not in opposition but coexist and mutually interpenetrate. The revelation of the Eternal Word in time made clear the fact that eternal life is not a "place" or a state outside of time but it is a quality of life that begins in time because that is where human life begins as an incarnation of being. *Kairos* as a felt quality of time is a concept expressing moments of clarity, events in time that have the sensed quality of eternal life in the present situation. These are moments of changed perception, a transformation in the way of seeing the world, the gaining of true insight.

Paul Minear's understanding of the biblical point of view on time calls for an attitude of openness to states of being other than those determined by *chronos*. The personal experience of time is nonmetrical. It requires that we adopt an attitude of humility toward one's own unique, internal time mode and an imaginative openness to qualitative changes in the perception of time. Minear points out that a person's sense of time can be revolutionized by a particular crucial or transforming event in her or his life:

> Recall that moment when time has stopped, or has raced by at whirlwind rate, when time has been forgotten, when every second seemed a year or the whole year seemed a second? Any profound conversion involves a transformation of calendar as much as of character; it may be described as the receiving of a new, inner chronometer. . . . And with a shift in the sense of time, our whole universe shifts into new focus.[28]

The experience of *kairos* illustrates a contrast between two different rhythms—those of the solar and lunar bodies and those of the human body—and the impact that events in personal history (which are fluctuating and occasional) have on the bodily spiritual being of the individual. In those moments or events time loses its ordinary disposition of metric thrust: as a state of measure it seems to disappear. The only time that exists is the time within us, along with the time our present situation fills, and this may not correspond at all to the information ticked out by the clock.

Minear also observes that *kairos* is related to the destiny of a particular being, for it describes the moments that transform a being into its own authentic form. In this sense *kairos* is a creative function, as it marks events, acts, and relationships that are part of the creator's design for the fulfillment and actualization of the creature. *Kairos* is creative time and purpose-charged time, through which something comes to pass or comes into being. In biblical terms it is the synchronization of God's creative will with human responsive will, enacted as call and response in the purpose of life-formation.[29] *Kairos* is a gift of God manifested as an event in the history of a being, an event both revelatory and redemptive. The gift exists in a relation between God and humanity and exposes the dramatic conflicts present in the creative process. God's purpose for creation is manifested as a sequence punctuated by calls and judgments, through which creative intentionality increases its work. Insofar as this work is opposed or interfered with and the creative purpose of in-forming is hampered, conflicts are revealed that can threaten or, through transformation into creative energy, engender true creation.[30]

Kairos as qualitative time preserves the synthesis of the fundamental self, whereas restriction and replacement of the qualitative aspect by the quantitative dimension break up the creative process. *Kairos* emerging from a purposive and creative center does not have to do with the duration of clock-time so much as with events as meanings and with the creative "momentum of our dominant desires."[31] *Kairos* is the moment of fulfillment, the actualization of possibility for being. It sometimes appears in the form of a conversion from an ordinary state to an extraordinary one. When one tries to escape time, it seems endless; but when one is unconscious of it, time (as measure) loses its tyranny over us.[32] Minear refers to the biblical notion of divine purpose as changing the sequential character of time to simultaneity; for those who cooperate with the creative purpose through faith and obedience the time process ceases to affect their lives as succession and takes on the quality of all-at-onceness, or the eternal present.

Time is ingathered as part of the process of creation and becomes subordinated to the purpose of the created will. *Kairos* includes revelation of purpose in the sudden breakthrough of its realization. *Kairos* and *logos* come together in creation: "God creates time with [a] word and ends time with [a] word, the work being simply God's revealed purpose in action."[33] *Kairos* is the revelation and communication of a will toward being. It cannot be measured by objective calculation but can only be inwardly and obediently received. The true *time of one's life* is manifested at a spiritual center where one is deeply engaged with the reality and will of another being that comes to meet the self in creative encounter. Time for Minear is the manifestation of will; *kairos* penetrates duration as significant and creative intentionality coming to dynamic fulfillment ("when the glory of God comes"). *Kairos* is the moment when a being's *time has come;* it is the *time of* that *being* which is revealed through a coalescence of will toward that end in a given situation.[34] *Kairos* is the expression of spirit; its power is the movement of spirit toward its goal.[35]

Sam Keen describes *homo tempestivus* as a person whose wisdom consists in knowing what time *(kairos)* it is.[36] Keen opposes this person to the opportunist, whom he places in Kierkegaard's "aesthetic" mode of existence: the pejorative connotations of this mode suggest a moral deficiency in which purpose and decision are lacking in the individual. The timely (kairotic) person, on the other hand, has a strong sense of ethical commitment to a situation and an equally strong sense of the ambiguities within which that commitment must be lived out. Wondering sensitivity and responsibility are combined in this person, whose chief intention is to discover the appropriate response to a situation and to act appropriately. Keen defines the wise person as one whose ethical ideal is to act appropriately. In the experience of *kairos* human action breaks forth as a spontaneous response to the time of ripeness or fulfillment. *Kairos* as the prepared moment, rather than *chronos* as the correct moment, reveals values and gives quality to life events.[37] Keen writes that creativity as the union of action and incarnation depends upon the continual dialogue between conscious and unconscious and between the quantitative and qualitative aspects of time as *chronos* and *kairos*.[38]

Incarnation is related to *kairos* as the Word is to time. In becoming flesh the Word became the ultimate symbol of unity between sense and spirit, time and eternity—the ultimate symbol of wholeness in which the totality of time-experience is relative. In attaining incarnation the Word also attains intemporalization and so reenters the mystery of its own nature through an added complexity of dimension.[39] According to St. Augustine time is in God and in humanity as well. Time is the unfolding of creation: The Word speaks forth creation, and humanity perceives it in time.[40] The Word, in reality, is eternal speech and has no extension, duration, change, or progression, but simply IS. Eternity is manifested in time under the conditions of progress and limitation proper to temporal, creaturely existence. The *kenosis* of the Word consists in assuming these conditions. Incarnation in terms of the dimension of time is intemporalization. But the presence of the Word in time gives to time an irreversible quality. For Augustine the Christian (incarnational) understanding of time perceives it not just as simple past, present, and future, but as *redeemed* time in which all events are eternally and simultaneously present in the Word: the present of the past is perceived as memory, the present of the present as immediate vision, and the present of the future as expectation.

Merleau-Ponty's view of time, though it is not Christian, illuminates the relationship between time, incarnation, and ontology. For Merleau-Ponty we are fundamentally conscious of time only because we are *embodied:* "Time and being become present only from a certain point of view through the intentionality of consciousness. Since the world and things are thus the linking of perspectives, they exist only as lived and constituted by some subject. . . . There is time and meaning for me only because I am incarnate."[41] *Kairos* as the manifestation of spirit absolutely depends on incarnation: spirit only exists effectively *as* spirit on condition of becoming flesh.[42] Marcel speaks of the "supratemporal level," or "the level of time's other dimension of depth or inwardness."[43] In the notion of time as depth the future and past are somehow interwoven, clasped together in a mystery perceived from the point of view of interpersonal heres-and-nows converging as an absolute Here-and-Now. *Kairos* becomes a meeting that takes place at a level of creative development, or inwardness.[44]

The kairotic perception of time is related to contemplative activity in which the time of human experience is concrete and present time.[45] Thomas Merton speaks of a new and qualitative time that can be perceived through the exercise of the spirit:

> The contemplative life must provide an area, a space of liberty, of silence, in which possibilities are allowed to surface and new choices—beyond routine choice—become manifest. It should create a new experience of time, not as stopgap, stillness, but as *temps vierge*—not a blank to be filled or an untouched space to be conquered and violated, but a space that can enjoy its own potentialities and hopes—and its own presence to itself. One's own time. But not dominated by one's own ego and its demands. Hence open to others—compassionate time, rooted in the sense of common illusion and in criticism of it.[46]

From this contemplative activity there can rise up sudden spurts of clarity, which can throw light on a being or situation and pierce through obscurity as a flash of lightning would. The most important aspect of this sudden clarity is its power to penetrate the solitude in which we grope. These are moments in which communion with other beings is included in the forms that emerge into light.[47]

Cassirer focuses on the "highest moments of phenomena," to describe them as neither a mere overflow of strong feeling nor imitation of physical things, but "an interpretation of reality—not by concepts but by intuitions; not through the medium of thought but through that of sensuous form."[48] The artist does not arbitrarily invent these forms, says Cassirer, but discovers them and then presents them to us in their true shape. By choosing a certain aspect of the reality of a being, the artist creates a phenomenon in which we both see and recognize that being through the perception of form. Once we have yielded to the artist's perspective, or the perspective presented in the art work, our perception itself has changed, undergone a permanent transformation. One might say that it has grown: "It would seem as if we had never before seen the world in this particular light. Yet we are convinced that this light is not merely a momentary flash. By virtue of the work of art it has become durable and permanent. Once reality has been disclosed to us in this particular way, we continue to see it in this shape."[49] The particular shape of performance is a dynamic form and does not contain a perspective in the same way that the plastic arts do.

Yet the form of performance in its own high moments penetrates the imagination of the perceiving audience, and its perspective, or unique angle of vision, will remain there, consciously or unconsciously, to work its permanent effect from within. Performance is a happening, an event in time, and its material is the unique time within the world of the poem it brings to life.

The Perception and Evocation of Literature explores the time aspect of literature and performance extensively:

> What is crucial for life and literature is *how time is* felt, its psychological effect. . . .
> The performance of literature exists in a present tense moment—it happens. The performer transforms the present tense moments of performance into the time of the literature. We feel that the literature becomes what it is at the same time it is being performed, that it springs into being, that it seizes and focuses all our sense of time upon the time contained in the literature. . . . The highest achievement in the performance of time is a congruence between the performer and the experience contained in the literature.[50]

The sustained vision that unfolds in performance enters the imagination of the perceiving audience as a shared reality. This moment of focus is the content of *kairos* in performance. The apprehension of such moments as qualitative and affective is possible through the engagement of feelings at a level of inwardness, perceived as an inner quality composed of many elements that overlap and permeate one another imprecisely. Perception of form is the perception of images that seem to exist in each other rather than one after another or side by side.[51] The perception of forming images is the perception not of an object, but of an act, of experience as quality, emerging in a moment in time and changing time.

The interpretation event, like all of human life, is "time-filled, time-bound, time-centered." Roloff examines performing time as containing essentially three kinds of time: "event time," "set time," and "symbolic time."[52] Event time in performance has to do with carrying through the situation to completion. Event time can exist in performance only when it has been presented in its entirety. Set time, in performance, is the time prescribed by the literary form itself, and the accurate enactment of its mode in terms that are appropriate and necessary to it. Symbolic time has no set time. It is experienced as the seeming dissolution of time. The values established by clock-time disappear as the values within the experience of the poem take hold of performer and audience and transform them into a dimension that seems to move outside of ordinary perceptions of time. It is like receiving a different inner chronometer (cf. Minear) for the special *time of the performance*. Roloff asserts that performance, while it constitutes an event, is usually concerned with the enactment of symbolic time above all else.[53] Symbolic time in performance is the unfolding of *kairos*.

Related to symbolic time are psychological and mythic time. Psychological time is manifested in sparsity or density—sparsity being characterized by the presence of silences, density by the profusion of language in a literary work.[54] Roloff expresses what may be called the *kenosis* of *kairos* in performance: "The performer's artistic responsibility is to evoke the psychological time of the material, not to project his own psychological time onto or into a piece of literature."[55] Mythic time is also outside of clock-time. It is felt as the eternal present, a haunted time evoking holiness and mystery, like the recurring *circumstance of time* as human ritual described in the Old Testament (*'ēth*). Psychological and mythic time may be simultaneous but may also function separately. Both time forms can function in great literature as a movement "from internal states of being into associational patterns of thinking that have universal meaning."[56]

Dorothy Sayers relates the perception of time quality as the self-revelation of the word in time through the event of performance. While the performance is going on, she says, we wonder "how it will turn out"; we anticipate the completion of an event in time. When the set form of the drama is over (assuming the given structure of a literary form) and the event time has taken place, we can perceive it imaginatively as a whole and see how all the moments of the event came together and related to each other in such a way that they produced a vision or reality inside our minds that is greater than the sum total of the emotions we experienced as members of an audience. In speaking of the drama, and in the context of her own theological analogy, she writes of the play: "It is in this timeless and complete form that it remains in our recollection: the Energy is now related to the Idea more or less as it was in the mind of the playwright: the Word has returned to the [Creator]."[57]

When we see a play with which we are familiar, we can carry out this associational thinking or relating part to whole from the beginning. As the performance proceeds, we perceive the activity of the Word relating the time sequence to eternity at every point. The complete event is already present as a whole in the unconscious imagination and reveals itself as a wholeness through the unfolding of performance. Sayers writes that it is as if the work had moved from eternity into time (from potential into actuality) and then back into eternity again (penetrating the unconscious of the perceiver and remaining there as acquired potential). In this process the literary work has remained the same, but as it moves back and forth (and it does this many times as it is performed again and again), it becomes charged with a different emphasis of power or spirit, which comes to it as creative response from audience and performer.[58]

Kairos as the decisive moment in performance that demands appropriate response places a responsibility on the performer to be prepared for the contingencies surrounding performance. While *kairos* is purpose-charged time, it requires the cooperation—or humble obedience—of human will. The meaningful moments that are always potential in performance cannot arise if the interpreter rebels by refusing to cooperate. An uncaring (careless) interpreter can destroy the possibility for *kairos* by ignoring circumstances that may alter the nature of a performance and distort the artistic experience of the poem. Alethea Mattingly warns, "The interpreter cannot follow his own taste entirely but must examine selections for their appropriateness to a given audience and creation." It would be *untimely* indeed to perform the murder scene from *Othello* on Valentine's Day to a group of men and women![59]

Kairos requires a basic decision or affirmation on the part of the interpreter, as well as active receptivity from the audience. The interconnections that constitute *kairos* can come about only as a result of the interpreter's organic growth or coalescence with the poem. *Kairos* in performance occurs as it does in daily experience, as a combination of the unexpected and a certain readiness in the one who experiences it. A moment can only be significant if one is prepared to perceive significance and to create it by appropriate response or action. *Kairos* is a quality emerging from an act and dependent on the coalescence of all available energies. Energies and perception converge in a single high point: one sees and hears, and at the same time in the very seeing and hearing one's being is changed. But this change can happen only if one is prepared. The interpretive artist has control and can take responsibility for preparation of her or his consciousness by fidelity and obedience to the laws of dialogue and relationship with the poem. Through conscious fidelity to the poem unconscious preparation for *kairos* also takes place: "Acts are not engendered fortuitously by the pressure of various external conditions but emerge as the results of an inner preparation. Reactions to life do not occur by accident or by compulsion but grow out of a specific background, the basic decision which a [person] has made."[60] Only habituation and practice—in interpretation, the discipline of rehearsal—can prepare the artist for the revelation of meaning in power in a performance. *Kairos* as the creative transformation of time can occur only if enough *time* has been given to its content in preparation.[61]

Kairos breaks through time experience as a creative or renewing moment of incarnate meaning. It occurs in the context of an act or event in process. *Kairos* must be fleshed out in order to create a truly new and unique experience of the present moment. Time as *kairos* is in reality a continual newness, a process of unfolding genesis. In interpretation "The interaction of creative disposition and creative act assures that every literary act is fresh and novel."[62] Stanislavski taught his students the uniqueness of the incarnation, which is the moment or event of a performance: "When actors try to repeat what they did the night before, the

theatre stops being art because it stops being living theatre. Every performance in a living theatre is as different as all days are different."[63]

Just as in the coming together of poem and interpreter a new being is
created, in the communion between poem, interpreter, and audience a
new time is created. This new time provides the coalescence of all parts in
an appropriate expression of the true time of the literature, so that the
three members involved in the triadic relation of performance are prepared for and receptive to the moment of transformation. Failure in the
breakthrough of *kairos* as the felt quality of transformation is failure in the
entelechy of the poem (assuming that it is worthy literature and has the
capacity for such transformation within it): its *moment* never comes; its
time of coming into being is lost: "During the performance an emotional
time is created that makes the nature of personal/psychological time more
real, more felt. Indeed, unless a performance of literature achieves this
shared and common time, all that may be felt is the passing of clock
time."[64]

The new time created in a true performance (performance that is an
appropriate and authentic incarnation of the literary work, that is both
revelatory and transforming: *kairotic*) presents the inner being of its
subject and the nature of its existence in a totally new and unique way,
because it arises from a unique meeting of beings.[65] The poet (the maker
of imaginative literature) expresses the quality of a unique moment in
poetic experience by discovering the right language and the appropriate
style to embody it. The performer realizes this quality by discovering the
appropriate bodily gesture to incarnate and intemporalize it in a unique,
creative, and transforming moment. All of the elements involved in a
performance have an immediate effect on this process of discovery and
enactment. Since the performance of a poem is always new if it is to be
authentic, "It should be re-embodied for each occasion. Strangely
enough, you may even find that the context (the other poems surrounding it in your performance) will alter your perspective and hence, subtly,
your reading. In order that you may not be misled by the context, you
must practice the reading in context—always, always."[66]

Kairos may be viewed as the prepared moment of a revelatory experience in the present. George Herbert Mead's philosophy of time asserts
that reality exists as an emergent event in the present.[67] The locus of
reality is an act in time: "An emergent event is an event containing novel
features not wholly derived from antecedent presents"; the present overflows into the past and future rather than being solely determined by
either.[68] The power of the truly new present moment can overflow into
the past as well as contain selected conditions of the past within it. The
emergent event can create the future and change the effects of the past; it
transforms in both directions of time. It is an appearance that is more than
a deduction from the past. It is a completely new moment through an act

that both creates newness and establishes a relation to this newness by a process of adjustment. Performance as an emergent event communicates qualitatively through " 'timeless' *time,* acoustic *space,* and oral *sound*"[69] in the live context of an interactive situation in which poem and performer reveal values through the emergent dimension of interaction with an audience. In the evocation and perception of *kairos* in communion, performance is liberated from the tyranny of clock-time and opens out onto a larger dimension of movement and transformation. Everything depends on the dynamic quality of the act of interpretation and the active receptivity and interaction from an audience: Event and participation are inextricably bound together.

A. H. Maslow speaks of the necessity for absorption in the creative moment. The artist must be immersed in the present and focus all energies on the here-now matter-in-hand. The artist's self-expression in the creative act should be "I am utterly lost in the present."[70] The concentration of activity in performance must be centered on the now-quality of the experience. Loss of attention or transfer of attention from the act to the audience or self can be a loss of *kairos.* When the performing self loses the tensiveness of the present-tense moment of the poem, she or he turns away from the act, to vitiate its energy and move away from "the space available, the space in which both the text-as-presence and the audience for the moment must exist."[71] Sustained tensiveness and attention, on the other hand, generate a feeling of the inevitability of experience unfolding from the incarnate poem. When the performer creates this sense of inevitability, she or he is creating "an excitement in the present moment" which "has the power to change the quality of an auditor's life, to create within that auditor a never-ending memory of what a piece of literature is."[72]

Bacon speaks of "certain large moments where things seem to end, or to come sharply into focus."[73] "Large moments" may be a better description of *kairos* than "high moments," for what is sensed is not so much a heightening as a fullness of being, processes perceived as the revelation of beings in their *is-ness,* and the feeling that these beings have somehow entered and changed our lives through the encounter of a single moment—no matter how long or short that moment may have been. This is the final effect of reverberation: "to fall into the vertical dimensions of time."[74] Beings act themselves toward us and into us in time through incarnate relationships. In the experience of their presence we seem *to know* them and ourselves in a totally new and often dramatic light. Interpretation is the containing experience or framework of this process. The powerful and transforming experience of performed literature extends meaning into us, as participants, and part of the effect of *kairos*—as the moment of communion, or corealization—is the recognition that these meanings link us with the experiences of all human beings in all times.

The goal of interpretation as an art form is to body forth reality. The meaning of reality shows itself as the intersection of time and the timeless, and is expressed in a moment of time as an act or gesture of being uniting values and persons. Interpretation's art form exists as an act in time, which places time against time—*kairos* against *chronos*—and so creates a new time, translucent time in which beings show themselves and reveal their *time of being*. The experience of *kairos* in performance constitutes an illumination and recognition and is an *epiphany* in its own right. Bacon describes epiphany as the dramatic coalescence, through tensiveness and perspective, of all the parts of a literary work in a vivid point, toward which the whole has been moving. The *kairos* of revelation in performance also seems to be a point standing "before us like a living presence, in a kind of utter nakedness of perspective. We are not *told,* we are *given.*"[75]

In the poem "Choruses from 'The Rock' " T. S. Eliot relates the whole of the action of *kairos* to the Incarnation as the one redemptive act in time and through time. Part VII begins, "In the beginning GOD created the world."

> Then came, at a predetermined moment, a moment in time and of time,
> A moment not out of time, but in time, in what we call history: transecting,
> bisecting the world of time, a moment in time but not like a moment of time,
> A moment in time but time was made through that moment: for without
> the meaning there is no time, and that moment of time gave the meaning.

Then, after the Incarnation, it seemed that all beings "must proceed from light to light, in the/light of the Word."[76] Through this unfolding beings discover themselves in communion. This discovery is the goal of interpretation as incarnation, in the moment of union between spirit and word, performance and audience.

Communion

In *The Art of Interpretation* Bacon writes: "When the reader performs for an audience, the audience in turn participates and shares, even while it remains part of the external environment affecting the poem. Between poem, reader, and audience there is communion. This communion is in effect the pleasure of literature."[77] Communion and communication are not interchangeable terms. Communication is a projected exchange between beings in which a specific content or message is conveyed and understood. Communion is an ambience that draws beings together in a circle of energy through a common act or shared experience at a level of inwardness. Words are projected as messages in communication. In communion, words and silence are experienced together and accepted as energy and power, or felt as meaning, before they are understood as content. Communication is possible in the experience of communion as a certain aspect of communion, at the level of comprehended meaning. Communion, however, exists prior to communication and can only contain it rather than be contained by it.[78] The experience of communion depends absolutely on the degree of preparedness of its participants. As Maud Bodkin notes in her psychological study of imagination, no effort or attempt will succeed in conveying an idea or image (especially if it has a *felt* quality) to a person who has no means of grasping it inwardly; it is not assimilated by mere contact: "Some inner factor must cooperate. When it is lacking, the experienced futility of attempted communication is the most convincing proof that it is."[79]

In the situation of performance, communion depends on the sacramental power of the incarnate word *and* the degree of readiness in those who come to partake in it. An audience comes together to share a common act: to perceive the forms presented to it in performance. The perceptual quality of the audience creates an energy field that enters into relationship with the dynamics of performance, for good or ill.[80] But if this energy field does indeed serve the art working in performance, interpretation is experienced as a shared reality of communion, in which the audience comes to participate in the communion manifested between poem and performer. This communion is characterized by the presence of a new energy emerging from an intense experience that has the power to transcend human solitude and create inner relationships. Coparticipants brought together into a single reality are not conscious of themselves as isolated personalities. All are intent upon the common task. Thus poetry and the dance, through the integrative rhythms of gesture on the one hand and speech on the other, encourage the participation of the body from those whose inner receptivity becomes congruent with these rhythms.[81]

In performance the rhythms of gesture and speech function as one. The integrative form of performance effects communion through concentration of energy on the matter at hand. The interpreter achieves fullest communion with an audience when she or he is not directed toward the audience but is intent on creating an ambience or circle of energy large enough to contain the audience. Thus Stanislavski taught that an actor can achieve closest contact with an audience through the concentrated development of relationships within the literary work. The same law holds for interpretation. If the interpreter tries to commune directly with an audience, the energy between poem and performer may be lost, and neither the poem nor communion will be realized: as Bacon says, "the audience is likely to come away with spirits unfed."[82]

Attention on the poem creates a focus of act in performance, and through this focus, interpretation gains the power of drawing different persons from their separate spaces into one time and from different times into the one space of the locus of performance. This concentration can only be experienced through the body, as bodily participation in revelation. The self becomes a place in which the universe within the acted poem can realize itself organically. Revelation, then, is always "our sudden awakening to the upsurge of the body" focused on a single, compelling perspective.[83]

Merleau-Ponty uses the word "intersubjectivity" in a way uniquely different from Marcel, and his application of the concept is relevant to the communion achieved through shared focus in the acted event of interpretation.[84] For Merleau-Ponty intersubjectivity is not direct involvement between subjects, but an objective act simultaneously shared by subjects. Perceiving body-subjects are not described as intersubjective, but the event or act which they commonly perceive becomes intersubjective as a stabilizing focus for mutual perceiving and knowing. An event or act is intersubjective when it is known by me as others know it, and when it is available to a number of perceiving subjects, not as an idea, but as a concrete reality that is accessible through the senses. As the poem and performer experience an intersubjective relationship in Marcel's sense through the interpretation process, the performer and audience share a common focus of perception in the intersubjective concrete act, in Merleau-Ponty's sense, of the performed, self-revealing poem in the interpretation event.

Performer and audience meet, not directly in performance, but only through the work being performed, through the common act of attention on the literary work as a presence that involves all participants. There is an inner connection in communion. It does not rise from the same source as the direct projection of meanings in communication. It is a contact between beings from within, as they share the same time, and experience the same time-content. As James Hillman writes, "for if I am connected to this moment just now as it is I am also open and connected to you. The ground of being in the depths is not just my own personal ground; it is the universal support of each, to which each finds access through an inner connection."[85] Communion in this sense depends, not on the effect that beings have directly on one another, but on the effect of "critical moments, archetypal events, welling up from within and reflected in our meeting."[86] This description is of the nature of the communion experienced by an audience in a performance situation if that situation is characterized by the circle of transforming energy of *kairos*. In such situations persons in the audience express themselves afterward with words such as "I was deeply moved" or "it was a profoundly moving experience." These words are in fact literal, for those participating in the moment of the experience did undergo a movement, a deep inward motion, a transformation in perception and being. They will never again be just as they were before.

In such instances of communion in the art experience of performance, interpretation creates an ambience in which persons—audience and performers—"may be in the same psychological place, constellated by the same state of soul, in communion without demonstratively sharing." Hillman continues:

> In each such moment some need of the common human soul is being expressed, and my needs and your needs are being reflected and met without a body interchange on the personal level. . . . Plunged suddenly to this level of the impersonal and ever-recurring one-time-only moment, the turning-point at the cross-road, two people stand together experiencing the event, together attempting its meaning.[87]

Performer and audience do not find themselves conscious of each other as such but are mutually absorbed in the incarnation taking place in their midst as the performance moves and expands its universe to contain all the bodily beings present.

The speaking-subject in communion has the effect of calling other beings into its ambience, by penetrating those beings from within, at a level of interiority and reverberation. Walter Ong writes that the speaking voice is an utterance—outering—of interiority through which the speaking-being invades the surroundings, to make "its terrible demands on those persons who hear it." The performing poem, the interpreter as speaking-subject in unison with the poem, can have an incredible power over an audience once this quality of interiority is unleashed: "For this invasion, under one aspect a raid or sally into others' interiors, is also a strangely magnetic action, which involves not so much one's going out to others as one's drawing other interiors into the ambit of one's being."[88] The welling up and outering of an interior state of being can have the power to captivate its auditors. Communion is formed from this state as sound manifests interiority and contains other beings within its space and time, to penetrate other interiors and fill them with the same energy.

The theological metaphor parallel to this experience is the sacrament of Holy Communion, in which the Incarnate Word is present as flesh and blood under the species of bread and wine. The power of the Incarnate presence of the Eternal Word as a bodily gift, offered to other bodily beings who will receive it into themselves, has the power of drawing these beings together unself-consciously through itself, and through the sacramental focus of prayer and praise centered on the gifts of the sacramental act. As it was pointed out in the discussion on icons, the total process of Communion is the communicants not only receiving Christ into themselves but being received into Christ's own immense life. This mutual reception happens through the word and act of liturgy (literally, a work done in common) and in the moment when those present do receive the Incarnate Word spiritually and bodily into themselves.

The moment of communion is the moment of a largeness or beyonding in the Burkean sense.[89] By perceiving an act or a being in terms of its inwardness and in terms of its spilling over into the beyond—the whole life suggested within it—members of an audience find themselves acting together, or consubstantially.[90] An experience is felt to be large when it seems to spill over into a region beyond itself. We feel a promise being made, while we experience its fulfillment.

The aesthetic position expressed in *The Art of Interpretation* describes the *right* performance (in the sense of a performance that is a true revelation of the literary work) as "a movement of all concerned into the act of the poem." The interpreter does not *tell* the audience what is going on, in order to have them respond, "Oh, yes, I see," or perhaps, "I don't see." Rather, it is up to the interpreter to evoke communion by bringing the audience bodily into the experience and reality that she or he is embodying: "This is the act and the art of interpretation; it is the *felt sensing* of a work of literature. . . . It is the poem being loved for itself. It is the poem made incarnate."[91]

five

CONCLUSION: AN INCARNATIONAL AESTHETIC OF INTERPRETATION

In the beginning is the word; the word becomes flesh and dwells among us, and we see its reality. Thus the process of interpretation unfolds as creation, incarnation, and revelatory transformation in communion. None of these aspects can be isolated from the others in the total artistic experience and performing event of interpretation. This process has been studied in the light of a metaphor: the original metaphor expressive of the Incarnation and revelation of the Divine Word in Christian theology placed side by side with the metaphor of the human word becoming flesh and showing itself in the incarnational act of interpretation through performance. The metaphoric expression of the biblical paradigm is taken from the Prologue to the Gospel according to St. John:

> In the beginning was the Word; . . .
> The Word was made flesh, and lived among us,
> and we saw Its glory . . .
>
> Indeed, from Its fullness we have, all of us, received.
> (John 1:1, 14, 16. Paraphrased from *The Jerusalem Bible*.)

In the biblical paradigm creation takes place through the Word. When the Word became incarnated in human form, its life was made visible and audible; the creative Word revealed itself as Christ and showed itself to all who would listen. The Spirit was with the Word and came to those who were faithful listeners, who participated in the Word's life and creative, renewing activity. The Word-made-flesh acted in the world as a living utterance, to renew and enliven others. When the Word returned to its Source in the Creator and was no longer seen in the flesh, the Spirit remained with those who had known the Word and had been drawn into its life, been made more alive themselves by this contact, through this communion. Their lives had been transformed by its power and presence, and the work that had begun in union with the Word was continued through the Spirit that remained.

The process of interpretation as incarnation does not constitute a thorough one-to-one model of the Holy Trinity of Christian theology. The poem is not exactly like the Creator in form and function, or the interpreter like the Christ, or the performance like the Sanctifier. But the relationship among the Creator, Savior, and Spirit may illuminate the relationship between poem and interpreter in performance, which shows the two as one and unites them with an audience in a common circle of energy. The Holy Spirit is sometimes called the love between the Creator and Savior, so great that it forms a whole new aspect of divine life! Imagine the *right* performance taking shape because of the love—or communion—between poem and performer!

The aesthetic position of this study is that interpretation is indeed a process of incarnation through which the word as poem becomes flesh, by means of interaction with a human interpreter, and that the communion between these two subjects reveals the truth of the poem to the audience in a transforming experience of power and energy that may be described as spirit-charged. This position is supported by two interpretation textbooks—*The Art of Interpretation* by Bacon and *The Perception and Evocation of Literature* by Roloff—which have served throughout the study as the spine along which the double helix of the sustained metaphor has ascended and descended and from which the various ganglia of complementary pairs have extended in a complex pattern of energy design. As a creative process, the art of interpretation can by no means be contained in a single approach or captured through one method of exploration. This study has as its intention the exploration of the creative process of interpretation from one viewpoint, expressed in the phrase "An Incarnational Aesthetic of Interpretation." This viewpoint alone cannot exhaust the many dimensions of interpretation. It has merely offered a certain perspective, an angle of vision from which a light—one among many others from many differing angles—may be thrown on the nature of interpretation as an artistic process, in the hope that through it this particular creative phenomenon might show itself more clearly and emerge in the strength of its own power as a creative art.

The juxtaposing of the theological dimension with the aesthetic dimension has had only one purpose in this study: to illuminate the nature of the process of interpretation. This is to say, not that theology has been "used" in the service of art, but that the two dimensions are in fact related at a deep level of human experience and that their common expression of truth through imaginative language and metaphor makes their yoking in the service of a human truth not only justifiable but also natural. Art and theology are not the same thing, but they touch human life at the same level of inwardness, and a profound experience of artistic truth has the power to change lives just as a deep experience of theological truth does.

The process of creation described in terms of Christian theology and the process of creation implied in the present aesthetic of interpretation may be recapitulated here in a final metaphoric illustration in terms of creation, incarnation, and transformation.

Creation

This study began with the facticity of the poem (the literary work) as a subject in its own right and defined interpretation as the realization of that subject through dialogic encounter and embodiment. The First Person of the Christian Trinity may be placed beside the creativity of the poem: The Creator creates the world from nothing through the Word. The poem creates a world from imagination through the word. In the Creator as in the poem the Word is alive and active but is not yet seen and heard as a discrete being that presents itself directly to the human senses. If the Incarnation of the Eternal Word was, from the beginning, part of the divine plan for creation, as the theologians Irenaeus and Duns Scotus in particular affirm, then it may be stated that the Word existed in the Creator from the beginning, to await its *kairos*. The creative Word of God required utterance, in order to complete the redemptive plan of creation, in a living form that could be seen and heard, a voice needing a body to fulfill, thoroughly to become, itself. In the sphere of the word-arts the poem, as word, exists in the text as potential, to await its *kairos:* the moment of realization when it will be seen and heard through a human form and will achieve its entelechy through human act.

Incarnation

Christ is the Incarnate Word showing, and bodily speaking, being into the world. The interpreter is the incarnate poem showing a world, bodily speaking its being into a presence. The interpreter is spiritually and bodily open to the voice of the poem as a speaking-subject, and through a process of self-giving, dialogue, and embodiment, utterance takes place in human form as the entelechy of the word-poem. A new being shows itself as the incarnate word. The Divine Word shows itself as Christ; the poem shows itself as the bodily presence given to it through the cooperation of the interpreter. A unique experience is created in the person of Christ through the totally unique coming-together of two natures in one being. A unique form or mode of existence is created in interpretation as two unique subjects come together to form a new creation shown to others in the moment of incarnation in performance.

The Word became flesh through a human act of receptivity, availability, and profound cooperation. When the human person Mary of Nazareth responded to the possibility of Incarnation, she said, in the old language, "Be it done unto me according to thy word." By her own affirmative words she allowed the Word to take upon itself the flesh of her flesh. The holy interpreter is like Mary in allowing the word to be born. I can say, as actor, that this moment is holy, that my flesh becomes flesh of the poem, my blood is the living word flowing toward realization with others. All of this through me! my spirit, my body! So much abundant life mediated through a process that in itself is Yes to the *word*.

The interpreter is the mediator who makes congruence possible between poem and performance. It is only through the interpreter that the poem can be seen and heard. The Creator is revealed in Christ through the flesh of Mary—ready, humble, and creative—and the poem shows itself through the interpreter. Unless the interpreter shows the poem, she or he is not creating an authentic performance or revelation of it, for the interpreter, as interpreter, exists only to do so. Only through the clarity or translucence of an interpreter's enactment of the poem in a revelatory performance can an audience come to know the poem and participate in it through belief. In a like sense, Jesus speaks of himself and his relationship with the Creator and the world:

> No one can come to God except through me. If you know me, you know God too. From this moment you know and have seen God. . . . To have seen me is to have seen God, so how can you say, "Let us see God"? Do you not believe that I am in the Creator and the Creator is in me? The words I say to you as from myself: it is the Creator, living in me, who is doing this work. You must believe me when I say that I am in the Creator and the Creator is in me; believe it on the evidence of this work, if for no other reason. . . . Those who do not love me do not keep my words. And my word is not my own: it is the word of the one who sent me. (John 14:6–7, 9–12, 24, paraphrased)

The act of performance is the visible moment of incarnation, when word is revealed in its full power, in its own reality, in its own time. The moment of performance is the moment when the word's body becomes coherent and shows itself in its own world and ours, in its own time and ours. This is the art of the poem, speaking itself into world, into flesh, uniting inner and outer, spirit and form. Interestingly, the word "art" comes from the Latin noun *artus*, meaning joint. Strictly speaking, art joins things together, unites different aspects of reality. We see how the different plastic and process arts do this joining in different ways. The process art of performed poetry is the word's joining together with its own body through an active relationship with a performer.

Some of the key words we use to describe this process have *form* as their root with a prefix indicating a particular motion of form. The word's body is the word's form, and it exists, not on the printed page, but in the spirit and body of one who *hears* it speaking from within. The word's body comes to be in several stages as it moves to find itself. First of all, *form* is the shape of something, its image, or its nature as it is sensed in some way. The dictionary tells us that the form of something is its *body* and also that it is something that gives shape to something else, as the performer's body gives shape to the word's body: form yielding to form making form. The dictionary goes on to say more precisely still that form is "the particular way of being that gives something its nature or character." Form is the unique body of something that allows itself to be seen, offers an image of itself in this particular, enfleshed way.

In the incarnational process of interpretation, form applies to the several dimensions at play and at work simultaneously in the whole development of a text from print to life. First of all, there is the form of the poem, the image showing itself through an internal dialogue with the person who comes to meet it. This person also has form, the whole physical and psychic makeup of humanity that she or he *is*. The goal of the meeting between these two forms in the process art of acting or interpreting is the performance itself, realized more nearly with each deepening of relationship along the way.

The *form* of *perform* derives from the word *fornir: to accomplish*. Combined with the prefix *per,* the word becomes literally *to accomplish through;* and since the preposition *through* must refer to another something, so in this case we can say that performance is the accomplishment of the poem through the actor by means of the uniting of these two forms in a lively embodiment. *In performance the word finds its body.* It is accomplished. It is brought to completion, but only in this moment, since incarnation is not a dead givenness, but an ongoing, renewing, prolongation of life in the body in time. This prolongation in time is why the uniting that takes place in interpretation is so dependent upon unique, continuing interaction with the human body. The same is true of the drama we experience in music and dance. The visual and tactile arts also depend on entering the human body so that they can come to life from within, but their forms in a sense constitute their own performance. They are realized through their own medium, whereas the word-arts require the mediating process of incarnation/revelation through the performing body of another. This requirement is true of sound and motion alike in the arts, for the visual or tactile art allows itself to be seen or touched and so experienced by another, then to have effect on that other from within; but the aural and motion arts of word, music, and dance must make themselves heard, seen, and felt in an assertive, iconic way, in order to move actively into and penetrate the bodies of others through joining with forms in the bodies of their performers. The eye can close out and invite in at will. The ear cannot. It is invaded by sounding motion; the body is filled with it by the active penetration of some other body from the outside. This body can also be internalized, as in the case of the solo performer who reads "silently" but hears actively once the word comes to life inside her or his own body. It may be said also that once a painting is seen or a sculpture seen or touched, it speaks from within to its percipient. In formal performance the word is heard *and* seen! *Logos* and image are one whether *logos* dominates as in the aural arts (literature, music), or image dominates as in the visual arts, or they are combined as in dance. Incarnation takes many forms and shows delightful variety of self-realization in all the arts, the same energy playing at different speeds.

Since we are considering how the word finds its body in the special way of interpretation/acting, we can take a final look at the process from the standpoint of interacting forms. First there is a mutual *in*forming: the form or image of the word flows into the form of the interpreter, and the interpreter, from the first tiny psychophysical response, begins to put bodily form into it. This first stage is the meeting. Then comes the *kenosis,* the block, the breakdown, which may be called the *de*formation stage. The actual form of the meeting breaks down; poem and interpreter/actor seem to move away from form, both in the sense of the image within the word and its accomplishment in the bodily form of the other. Finally the movement of forms flows together again. The interplay of unconscious/ conscious energies at the stage of seeming unproductivity and breakdown spills over, breaks through into the rewards of *trans*formation: the forms have come together at a deep level and have been changed. Bacon calls this coalescence. Forms become consubstantial; they exist with one another. The image form of the text is changed into bodily presence, and the physical form of the interpreter/actor is changed into the icon/servant of the word. All of this change comes about in *per*formance, as the word's form is brought to *fulfillment through* the interpreter/actor in the whole process that is finally seen and heard in the *kairos* of incarnation. The literal meaning of performance is manifest: "to act on so as to accomplish or bring to completion . . . to . . . fulfill, as a promise or command." The promise of the word is fulfilled because the interpreter heard that word speaking deeply, the speaking deeply being the command, the hearing deeply being the obedient response allowing them to act together to bring this moment to reality.

The gift of performance is the celebration of the word's body. It is a true birthing, a process enacted through love's genuine labor.

The interpreter can realize, or actualize, a poem by recognizing the poem's form within herself or himself. An interpreter has the possibility of access to all forms within. The doctrine of original sin claims that the *propensity* for good and evil exists equally in all human beings. Jung's belief in the underlying presence of a collective unconscious, binding all human beings to all human experience in all human times, also implies the presence within each of us of every possible form or condition of human experience. If one goes deeply enough into the self, one can find there the sources for all human behavior. The act of creative art is redemptive by nature, for art finds a way of access to these underlying propensities and then transforms them, to draw them out and convert them into artistic virtue through creative expression. The way of art is the way of purification, a view suggested by Aristotle so long ago. Through the sacramental act of coalescence between her or his own interior and the interior of the poem, the interpreter coincidentally achieves a kind of baptism in spirit, for the artistic enactment of good intentions and bad intentions in an art form comes to the same end: that of creating from all available and contributing human materials a new form that constitutes authentic being. The interpreter can unite with the form of an Iago or a Becket with equal results for good, since the good attained is the good of the art work itself. The virtue of art is autonomous from the virtue of morality, but as the realm of morality is larger than the realm of art, it includes it, so that the moral good of the work of art consists precisely in its sacramental powers of self-expression in the achievement of authentic being. The good in the making of an art form consists in finding the form proper to the work. The artist as prophet—one speaking on behalf of another being—is, *as artist,* required, not to practice goodness of morals, but only to demonstrate keen goodness of imagination.

The imaginative goodness of the interpreter is manifested in her or his ability to create revelation through becoming an incarnation of the work. Performance is a work of art that contains and fulfills the art work of the poem. The poem becomes a speaking vision, as the Word of God was revealed to the prophets sometimes as a speaking vision. The opening of the Books of Amos, Obadiah, and Micah have formulas that combine word and vision: "The words of Amos . . . which he saw"; "The vision of Obadiah. Thus says the Lord God"; "The word of the Lord that came to Micah . . . which he saw" (KJV). The major prophets Isaiah and Jeremiah also speak of the visible utterance of the Word of God: "The word which Isaiah the son of Amoz saw" (Isa. 2:1, KJV) and "This is the word that the Lord hath showed me" (Jer. 38:21, KJV). Revelation came to the prophets through their receptive imaginations, and the prophets passed on revelation through the participatory act of their own speaking and showing bodies. The process of revelation came to a climax and was consummated in the Incarnation of the Word in human flesh, and this revelation also constituted the redemption of all creation: "Behold, I make all things new" (Rev. 21:5, KJV). The Incarnate Word is the One in whose body are realized all of the meanings of the prophets. The symbols of the prophets are perceived in this person who does not merely convey meaning but *is* meaning, whose bodily presence in human existence touches and transforms the existences that perceive this particular self-revelation: "Now I am making the whole of creation new" (Rev. 21:5, JB).

Transformation

The presence of the poem as an incarnate being has power over those who perceive it, as the presence of the Incarnate Word was shown to have power over those who saw and heard Christ. The Spirit, according to biblical theology, is manifested as the power of love between the Creator and the Christ, overflows into creation, and touches human life directly, to transform it as if by breathing a new life into human beings. The Spirit and the Word move together to change the quality of—to redeem— human lives. There is a power manifested in the event of interpretation if all factors combine to reveal the communion that exists between the poem and the interpreter. This power forms what has been called in this study a circle of energy, and the audience, if the *kairos* of the performing poem has come, is taken up into this circle in the transforming experience of communion. The visible utterance of the incarnate word in the spirit-charged power of performance can have the effect of breathing new life into those who participate in its moment of revelation.

The incarnational aesthetic of interpretation presented in this study acknowledges the phenomenon of interpretation to be a creative metaphor, enacted through the at-onement between the poem as a speaking-subject and the performer as an embodying-subject. The environment created by their communion is the result of a complex process of dialogue, embodiment, and participation. The artistic event of interpretation as the revelation of *presence* in performance combines the dynamics of creation, incarnation, and transformation, as poem, performer, and audience are brought together in the moment of clarity and power that is communion. The interpreter prepares for the *time of the poem's life*—the *kairos* of performance—through an intricate process of encounter experienced in careful rehearsal. Fidelity to the poem as living word is expressed as time-giving and self-giving on the part of the interpreter, whose creativity leads to an authentic incarnation, described in this study in terms of the interwoven dynamics of complementary pairs: making/acting, *logos/eros*, intersubjectivity/hypostasis, *theopoiēsis/synergia*, apophatic/cataphatic, *kenosis/plerosis*, unconscious/conscious, word/icon, and substitution/participation.

The *becoming* process of encounter and coalescence between word and interpreter is consummated in the revelation of the poem's *being* through the interpreter as icon in the transforming moment of performance. Thus the word as speaking-subject is delivered from its potential state in the printed text and is realized through the entelechy of communion with the interpreter as an embodying-subject, giving sound and gesture to the poem and filling it out by becoming available to it, by being filled with it. The world of the poem is delivered from the silence and stillness of the word in potential and is revealed as it expresses itself through the interpreter as physical and spiritual icon. Through the loving cooperation of the interpreter the word is received into the lives of those who see and hear it in performance. Audience and interpreter participate in the world of the poem and act together in the ambience of its vitality and full self-giving.

Through its incarnate presence in performance the word interprets human life and speaks forth a new existence that includes those who see and hear it. *The poem makes us, and it makes us new.* In the ideal performance, the performance that the serious interpreter always strives for and frequently can attain, the experience of the poem is full and complete. From its fullness "we have, all of us, received."

notes

Chapter One

1. Martin Heidegger, *Being and Time,* 7th ed., trans. John Macquarrie and Edward Robinson (New York: Harper and Brothers, 1962), p. 51.

2. Richard E. Palmer, *Hermeneutics: Interpretation Theory in Schleiermacher, Dilthey, Heidegger, and Gadamer* (Evanston: Northwestern University Press, 1969), p. 128.

3. Jaroslav Pelikan, *Fools for Christ: Essays on the True, the Good, and the Beautiful* (Philadelphia: Muhlenberg, 1955), p. 119.

4. Ibid., pp. 120–31.

5. Rudolf Otto, *The Idea of the Holy,* 2nd ed., trans. John W. Harvey (1950; reprint ed., New York: Oxford University Press, 1968), p. 44.

6. Ibid., p. 46.

7. Ibid., pp. 58–65.

8. Wallace A. Bacon, *The Art of Interpretation,* 2nd ed. (New York: Holt, Rinehart and Winston, 1972).

9. Leland H. Roloff, *The Perception and Evocation of Literature* (Glenview, Ill.: Scott, Foresman and Co., 1973).

10. Bacon, *Interpretation,* p. xi.

11. Ibid., p. v.

12. Roloff, *Perception and Evocation,* p. i.

13. Walter J. Ong, *The Barbarian Within: And Other Fugitive Essays and Studies* (New York: Macmillan, 1962), p. 45.

14. Ibid., p. 45.

15. Ibid., p. 46.

16. Dorothy L. Sayers, *The Mind of the Maker* (New York: Harcourt, Brace and Co., 1941), pp. 22–23.

17. Quoted in Stanley Burnshaw, *The Seamless Web: Language-Thinking, Creature-Knowledge, Art-Experience* (New York: Braziller, 1970), p. 50.

18. Sayers, *Mind of the Maker,* p. 29.

19. Ibid., p. 30.

20. Ibid., pp. 40–41.

21. Another Christian aesthetician is more reluctant to imply direct relationships between the language of theology and the artistic process. Denis de Rougemont ("Religion and the Mission of the Artist," in *Spiritual Problems in Contemporary Literature,* ed. S. R. Hopper [1957; reprint ed., New York: Harper and Row, Torchbook Edition, 1965]), speaks from an almost Puritanical position, and one senses a genuine tension in the necessity with which he makes his statement and nearly retracts it in the same breath. Perhaps the artist's and the Christian's beliefs are not in harmony within his own mind, and this would explain the contrary forces in his theory of art; or perhaps for him *eros* and *logos* are incompatible, and one must choose between them in the creative process. He speaks of the art process and immediately uses the words of theology to describe what the artist does: artists *create* and *incarnate* certain realities in their work,

because they are *inspired;* but he instantly corrects himself: it is doubtless heretical and idolatrous to speak in these terms! These functions evoke the attributes of the Holy Trinity, and for this reason he rejects them. His theology of art, to my way of thinking, is anti-incarnational because it is not at ease with the juxtaposition of divine and human activity in one being or process, and this, of course, is the essence of the Incarnation.

This study *is* incarnational in its aesthetic position, and such language will not only be natural but necessary to it.

22. Sayers, *Mind of the Maker,* p. 45.

23. George Whalley, *Poetic Process* (Cleveland: World Publishing Co., Meridian Books, 1967), p. 5.

24. "Periphery: . . . in anatomy, the area surrounding a nerve ending." *Webster's New World Dictionary of the American Language* (Cleveland: World Publishing Co., College Edition, 1962).

25. Ong, *Barbarian Within,* p. 30.

26. See ibid., pp. 30–32.

27. Palmer, *Hermeneutics,* p. 197.

28. Ong, *Barbarian Within,* p. 35.

29. Ibid., p. 36.

30. Mary Rose Barral, *Merleau-Ponty: The Role of the Body-Subject in Interpersonal Relations* (Pittsburgh: Duquesne University Press, 1965), p. 175.

31. Abraham H. Maslow, *The Farther Reaches of Human Nature* (New York: Viking, 1971), p. 45.

32. Cary Nelson, *The Incarnate Word: Literature as Verbal Space* (Chicago: University of Illinois Press, 1973), p. 4.

33. Wallace A. Bacon and Robert S. Breen, *Literature as Experience* (New York: McGraw-Hill, 1959), p. 85.

34. Nelson, *Incarnate Word,* p. 4.

35. Ibid., p. 5.

36. Bacon, *Interpretation,* p. 451.

37. Jacques and Raïssa Maritain, *The Situation of Poetry: Four Essays on the Relations Between Poetry, Mysticism, Magic, and Knowledge,* trans. Marshall Suther (New York: Philosophical Library, 1955), p. 79.

Chapter Two

1. See Bacon, *Interpretation,* p. vii.

2. Ibid., pp. vi–vii.

3. Roloff, *Perception and Evocation,* p. 3.

4. See ibid., pp. 3–4, 17.

5. Ibid., p. 4.

6. Wallace A. Bacon, "The Dangerous Shores: From Elocution to Interpretation," *Quarterly Journal of Speech,* 46, no. 2 (April, 1960), pp. 148–52.

7. Ibid., p. 150.

8. Roloff, *Perception and Evocation,* p. 3.

9. See Bacon, *Interpretation,* p. xii.

10. See ibid., p. 165 and passim.

11. Ibid., p. vii.

12. Ibid., p. 7.

13. Bacon, "Dangerous Shores," *QJS,* p. 150.

14. Bacon, *Interpretation,* p. xiii.

15. See Roloff, *Perception and Evocation,* p. 4.

16. Bacon, "Dangerous Shores," *QJS,* p. 152.

17. See Bacon and Breen, *Literature as Experience,* p. 114, and Robert Beloof, *The Performing Voice in Literature* (Boston: Little, Brown and Co., 1966), p. 69.

18. Bacon, *Interpretation,* p. xii.

19. William F. Lynch, *Christ and Apollo: The Dimensions of the Literary Imagination* (1960; reprint ed., Notre Dame: University of Notre Dame Press, 1975), p. 23.

20. Ibid., p. 133.

21. Ibid., see p. 214.

22. Paul Campbell, *The Speaking and the Speakers of Literature* (Belmont, Cal.: Dickenson Publishing Co., 1967), p. 9.

23. See Bacon, *Interpretation,* p. 184.

24. See Bacon and Breen, *Literature as Experience,* p. 107.

25. Alethea Smith Mattingly and Wilma H. Grimes, *Interpretation: Writer, Reader, Audience,* 2nd ed. (Belmont, Cal.: Wadsworth Publishing Co., 1970), see preface.

26. Ibid., p. 5.

27. Ibid., p. 10.

28. Leland H. Roloff, "A Critical Study of Contemporary Aesthetic Theories and Precepts Contributing to an Aesthetic for Oral Interpretation" (Ph.D. diss., University of Southern California, Los Angeles, California, 1968), p. 144.

29. Ibid., p. 154.

30. Bacon, *Interpretation,* p. 34.

31. W. Keith Henning, "A Semantic for Oral Interpretation: A Wheelwright-ean Perspective" (Ph.D. diss., University of Southern California, Los Angeles, California, 1973), p. 6.

32. Ibid., p. 189.

33. Ibid., p. 200.

34. Ibid., pp. 156–57.

35. See Philip Wheelwright, *Metaphor and Reality* (1962; reprint ed., Bloomington: Indiana University Press, 1967), pp. 156–57, and Henning, "Semantic," p. 108.

36. Bacon, *Interpretation,* p. xi.

37. Roloff, *Perception and Evocation,* p. 4.

38. *"Longinus" On the Sublime,* trans. Benedict Einarson (Chicago: University of Chicago Press, 1945).

39. Henning, "Semantic," p. 6.

40. Philip Wheelwright, *The Burning Fountain: A Study in the Language of Symbolism* (1954; reprint ed., Bloomington: Indiana University Press, 1959), p. 15.

41. Thomas O. Sloan, "Oral Interpretation in the Ages Before Sheridan and Walker," *Western Speech,* 35 (summer, 1961), p. 157.

42. See T. S. Eliot, *From Poe to Valéry* (New York: Harcourt, Brace and Co., 1948), p. 26, and Lynch, *Christ and Apollo,* p. 163.

43. Bacon, *Interpretation,* p. xii.

44. For example, see Mattingly and Grimes, *Interpretation: Writer, Reader, Audience.*

45. James M. Robinson, "Hermeneutic Since Barth," in *The New Hermeneutic,* ed. James M. Robinson and John B. Cobb, Jr. (New York: Harper and Row, 1964), p. 7.

46. Ibid., p. 9.

47. Ibid., pp. 14–15.

48. Ibid., pp. 19–21.

49. Dilthey quoted in Robinson, "Hermeneutic Since Barth," p. 21.

50. Ibid., p. 25.

51. Barth quoted in Robinson, "Hermeneutic Since Barth," p. 25.

52. Ibid., p. 26.

53. Hans-Georg Gadamer, *Wahrheit und Methode: Grundzuge einer philosophischen Hermeneutik,* 2nd ed. (Tübingen: J. C. B. Mohr, 1965).

54. Gadamer quoted in Palmer, *Hermeneutics,* p. 42.

55. Palmer, *Hermeneutics,* p. 42.

56. Ibid., pp. 42–43.

57. Ibid., pp. 68–69.

58. Ibid., p. 76.

59. Ibid., pp. 80–81, 86.

60. Ibid., p. 92, citing Friedrich Schleiermacher, *Hermeneutik,* ed. Heinz Kimmerle (Heidelberg: Carl Winter, Universitatsverlag, 1959), p. 44.

61. Palmer, *Hermeneutics,* p. 93.

62. Ibid., p. 38.

63. Ibid., p. 13.

64. Robinson, "Hermeneutic Since Barth," pp. 27–28.

65. Ibid., p. 46.

66. See ibid.

67. E. D. Hirsch, Jr., *Validity in Interpretation* (New Haven: Yale University Press, 1967), p. xi.

68. Ibid., p. 4.

69. Ibid., p. x.

70. Ibid., p. 8.

71. Ibid., pp. 24–25. See also Emilio Betti, *Teoria generale della interpretazione,* 2 vols. (Milan: Guiffré, 1955), I, pp. 343–432.

72. Hirsch, *Validity in Interpretation,* p. 175.

73. Ibid., p. 177.

74. Bacon, *Interpretation,* p. 449.

75. Ibid., p. 365.

76. Ibid., see pp. 135–36.

77. Ibid., p. 137.

78. Robinson, "Hermeneutic Since Barth," p. 47.

79. Frank Ebersole, "Saying and Meaning," in *Ludwig Wittgenstein: Philosophy and Language,* ed. Alice Ambrose and Morris Lazerowitz (London: Allen and Unwin, 1972), p. 188.

80. Susan Sontag, "Against Interpretation," reprinted in *Literary Criticism: An Introductory Reader,* ed. Lionel Trilling (New York: Holt, Rinehart and Winston, 1970), pp. 610–19.

81. Sontag, "Against Interpretation," p. 612.

82. Ibid., p. 614.

83. See Bacon and Breen, *Literature as Experience*, pp. vii, 6–7.

84. Sontag, "Against Interpretation," p. 618.

85. Ibid., p. 619.

86. Wallace A. Bacon, "Reverberation: An Ontological View of Interpretation," an unpublished typescript circulated for teaching purposes in the Department of Interpretation, Northwestern University, p. 2.

87. See John Vernon, "Poetry and the Body," *American Review*, 16 (February, 1973), pp. 145–72.

88. Bacon, "Reverberation," pp. 2–3.

89. Ibid., p. 3.

90. Ibid., p. 4.

91. James Hillman, *The Myth of Analysis: Three Essays in Archetypal Psychology* (Evanston: Northwestern University Press, 1972), pp. 82–83.

92. C. G. Jung, *Mysterium Coniunctionis*, Collected Works 14, trans. R. F. C. Hull (London: Routledge and Kegan Paul, 1963), p. 179.

93. M. Esther Harding, *Woman's Mysteries: Ancient and Modern: A Psychological Interpretation of the Feminine Principles as Portrayed in Myth, Story, and Dreams* (London: Longmans, Green and Co., 1935), p. 143.

94. See Ann Belford Ulanov, *The Feminine: In Jungian Psychology and in Christian Theology* (Evanston: Northwestern University Press, 1971), especially appendix A, "A Note on Eros and Logos."

95. Harding, *Woman's Mysteries*, p. 223.

96. Hillman, *Myth of Analysis*, pp. 82–85.

97. Jung in Victor White, *God and the Unconscious* (1952; reprint ed., Cleveland: World Publishing Co., Meridian Books, 1965), p. 276.

98. Hillman, *Myth of Analysis*, p. 86.

99. Maslow, *Farther Reaches of Human Nature*, p. 61.

100. Bacon, *Interpretation*, p. xi.

101. Ibid., p. 34.

102. Roloff, *Perception and Evocation*, p. 314.

103. Ibid., p. 17.

104. Roloff, "Critical Study," pp. 423–24.

105. See Helmut G. Harder and W. Taylor Stevenson, "The Continuity of History and Faith in the Theology of Wolfhart Pannenberg: Toward an Erotics of History," reprinted for private circulation from *Journal of Religion*, 51, no. 1 (January, 1971), pp. 35–56.

106. See Roloff, *Perception and Evocation*, p. 23.

107. Jacques Maritain, *Situation of Poetry*, p. 60.

108. Harder and Stevenson, "The Continuity of History and Faith," p. 56.

109. Ibid., see p. 45.

110. Jacques Maritain, *Creative Intuition in Art and Poetry* (New York: Pantheon Books, 1953), p. 74.

111. Jacques Maritain, *Art and Scholasticism: With Other Essays*, trans. J. F. Scanlan (New York: Scribner's, 1947), pp. 12, 101–02.

112. Jacques Maritain, *Situation of Poetry*, p. 51.

113. Bacon, *Interpretation*, p. 250.

114. Roloff, *Perception and Evocation*, p. 303.

115. Don Geiger, *The Dramatic Impulse in Modern Poetics* (Baton Rouge: Louisiana State University Press, 1967), p. 36.

116. Don Geiger, "Poetic Realizing as Knowing," *Quarterly Journal of Speech*, 59, no. 3 (October, 1973), pp. 311–18.

117. Paul Campbell, *Speaking and the Speakers of Literature*, p. 20.

118. For both of these definitions see *Webster's New World Dictionary of the American Language* (Cleveland: World Publishing Co., College Edition, 1962).

119. Paul Tillich, *Dynamics of Faith* (New York: Harper and Brothers, 1956–1957), pp. 107–08.

120. Ibid., pp. 114–15.

121. Ibid., p. 116.

122. Heidegger, *Being and Time*, pp. 51–56.

123. John Macquarrie, *Principles of Christian Theology* (New York: Scribner's, 1966), pp. 65–66.

124. Ibid., pp. 67–68.

125. Ibid., p. 68.

126. Ibid., pp. 82–83.

127. Ibid., p. 85.

128. Ibid., p. 86.

129. Roloff, *Perception and Evocation*, p. 320.

130. Gadamer, *Wahrheit und Methode*, p. 350, and Palmer, *Hermeneutics*, p. 200.

131. Emil Brunner, *Truth as Encounter*, 2nd ed., trans. David Cairns (Philadelphia: Westminster, 1964), p. 10.

132. Palmer, *Hermeneutics*, p. 226.

133. See Bacon, "Reverberation," p. 4.

134. Fuchs quoted in Robinson, *New Hermeneutic*, p. 55.

135. Otto, *Idea of the Holy*, pp. 109, 135.

136. Ibid., p. 61.

137. Aarne Siirala, *Divine Humanness*, trans. T. A. Kantonen (Philadelphia: Fortress, 1970), pp. 54, 60.

138. Ibid., pp. 66–67.

139. Ibid., pp. 70–71 and 78.

140. Gerhard Kittel, ed., *Theological Dictionary of the New Testament*, vol. I, trans. and ed. Geoffrey W. Bromiley (Grand Rapids: Wm. B. Eerdmans, 1965), p. 239.

141. Brunner, *Truth as Encounter*, pp. 41, 102–03.

142. Roloff, *Perception and Evocation*, p. 12.

143. See "The Mustard Seed Garden Manual," in Mai-Mai Sze, *The Tao of Painting* (New York: Pantheon Books, 1956). See also Nathan A. Scott, Jr., *The Broken Center: Studies in the Theological Horizon of Modern Literature* (New Haven, Yale University Press, 1966).

144. Cited in Palmer, *Hermeneutics*, p. 199.

145. In Robinson, *New Hermeneutic*, p. 109.

146. See Amos N. Wilder, "The Word as Address and the Word as Meaning," in Robinson, *New Hermeneutic*, p. 207.

147. Bacon, *Interpretation*, pp. 184–85.

148. Roloff, *Perception and Evocation*, p. 62.

149. Robinson, *New Hermeneutic*, pp. 52–54.

150. Merrill R. Abbey, *The Word Interprets Us* (Nashville: Abingdon, 1967), pp. 20–26.

151. Brunner, *Truth as Encounter,* pp. 22–23.

152. Walter J. Ong, *The Presence of the Word: Some Prolegomena for Cultural and Religious History* (New Haven: Yale University Press, 1967), p. 22.

153. Ebeling, "Word of God and Hermeneutic," in Robinson, *New Hermeneutic,* p. 103.

154. Brunner, *Truth as Encounter,* p. 28.

155. Paul Tillich, *The Eternal Now* (New York: Scribner's, 1963), pp. 84–85.

156. Paul Tillich, *Dynamics of Faith,* pp. 106–07.

Chapter Three

1. Roloff, *Perception and Evocation,* p. 73.

2. Aristotle, *Nichomachean Ethics,* trans. W. D. Ross (New York: Random House, 1941), vi 3; 1140 a 11–20. See also Jacques Maritain, *Creative Intuition,* p. 67.

3. Jacques Maritain, *Situation of Poetry,* pp. 49–50.

4. Bacon, *Interpretation,* p. 373.

5. J. S. Johnston, *The Philosophy of the Fourth Gospel: A Study of the Logos Doctrine: Its Sources and Its Significance* (London: SPCK, 1910), pp. 21–23.

6. Ibid., pp. 39–79.

7. St. Augustine of Hippo, quoted in Johnston, *Philosophy of the Fourth Gospel,* p. 148.

8. Gustaf Wingren, *Man and the Incarnation: A Study in the Biblical Theology of Irenaeus,* trans. Ross MacKenzie (London: Oliver and Boyd, 1954), p. 88.

9. Albert Schlitzer, *Redemptive Incarnation: Sources and Their Theological Development in the Study of Christ,* 3rd ed. (Notre Dame: University of Notre Dame Press, 1962), pp. 2–3.

10. Ibid., pp. 57–58.

11. *The Interpreter's Dictionary of the Bible* [R-Z], ed. George Arthur Buttrick et al. (Nashville: Abingdon, 1962), p. 869.

12. Ibid., p. 869.

13. Ibid.

14. St. Athanasius, *The Incarnation of the Word of God (De Incarnatione Verbi Dei),* trans. by a Religious of C.S.M.V., S.Th. (New York: Macmillan, 1947), p. 26.

15. Ibid., pp. 29–30.

16. Ibid., pp. 44–47.

17. Roloff, *Perception and Evocation,* p. 73.

18. Ibid., see p. 158.

19. See Bacon, *Interpretation,* p. 63.

20. See Dallas M. High, *Language, Persons, and Belief: Studies in Wittgenstein's Philosophical Investigations and Religious Uses of Language* (New York: Oxford University Press, 1967).

21. Ibid., p. 114.

22. Ibid., pp. 124–25.

23. John Hospers, *Meaning and Truth in the Arts* (Chapel Hill: University of North Carolina Press, 1946), pp. 3–7.

24. Ibid., pp. 76, 123.

25. Arthur A. Vogel, *Body Theology: God's Presence in Man's World* (New York: Harper and Row, 1973), p. 12.

26. Ibid., pp. 23–24.

27. Ibid., p. 92.

28. Georges Gusdorf, *Speaking (La Parole)*, trans. Paul T. Brockelman (Evanston: Northwestern University Press, 1965), p. xxix.

29. Ibid., pp. 45–47.

30. Ibid., p. 76.

31. Noah Jonathon Jacobs, *Naming-Day in Eden: The Creation and Recreation of Language*, 2nd ed. (Toronto: Collier-Macmillan, 1969), p. xvii.

32. Ernst Cassirer, *An Essay on Man: An Introduction to a Philosophy of Human Culture* (1944; reprint ed., New Haven: Yale University Press, 1948), p. 109.

33. Ibid., p. 81.

34. Ibid., p. 121.

35. Joshua Trachtenberg, *Jewish Magic and Superstition: A Study in Folk Religion* (New York: Behrman's Jewish Book House, 1939), p. 78.

36. *Sefer Hasidism*, Bologna version, p. 1452, cited in Trachtenberg, *Jewish Magic and Superstition*, p. 80.

37. Wayne Shumaker, *Literature and the Irrational: A Study in Anthropological Backgrounds* (New York: Washington Square, 1966), p. 108.

38. Otto Rank, *Art and Artist: Creative Urge and Personality Development* (New York: Tudor, 1932), p. 79.

39. Ibid., pp. 85–87.

40. Ibid., pp. 238–39.

41. Gerhard Ebeling, *God and Word*, trans. James W. Leitch (Philadelphia: Fortress, 1966), pp. 29–32.

42. Ibid., pp. 40–41.

43. Gerhard Ebeling, *Word and Faith*, trans. James W. Leitch (London: SCM, 1963), p. 318.

44. Ibid., p. 319.

45. Ibid., p. 327.

46. Roloff, *Perception and Evocation*, p. 273.

47. Ibid., p. 9.

48. Bacon, *Interpretation*, p. 9.

49. Ernst Cassirer, *The Philosophy of Symbolic Forms*, vol. I, *Language*, trans. Ralph Manheim (New Haven: Yale University Press, 1953), p. 188.

50. Ibid., p. 252.

51. Wm. Norman Pittinger, *Christ and Christian Faith: Some Presuppositions and Implications of the Incarnation* (New York: Round Table, 1941), p. 147.

52. J. Armitage Robinson, *Some Thoughts on the Incarnation* (London: Longmans, Green and Co., 1903), p. 17.

53. Origen, *On First Principles*, trans. G. W. Butterworth (New York: Harper and Row, Torchbooks Edition, 1966), bk. 2, ch. 1, pp. 78–79.

54. Ibid., p. 81.

55. Ibid., p. 111.

56. Bacon and Breen, *Literature as Experience*, p. 276, quoting Alfred North

Whitehead, *The Aims of Education and Other Essays* (New York: Macmillan, 1929), p. 91.

57. From Thomas Merton, *The Asian Journal of Thomas Merton,* extracted in *Intellectual Digest,* 4, no. 3 (November, 1973), p. 60.

58. Burnshaw, *Seamless Web,* p. 1.

59. Ibid., pp. 7–13.

60. See Leicester Bradner, *Incarnation in Religion and Literature,* Faculty Papers, 4th series (New York: The National Council [of the Episcopal Church], 1957), pp. 8–9.

61. Ibid., p. 1.

62. Jacques Maritain, *Art and Poetry,* trans. E. de P. Matthews (New York: Philosophical Library, 1943), p. 88.

63. Sayers, *Mind of the Maker,* p. 137.

64. Ibid., p. 47.

65. Maritain, *Art and Poetry,* p. 61.

66. Constantin Stanislavski, *Building a Character,* trans. Elizabeth Reynolds Hapgood (New York: Theatre Arts Books, 1949), p. 242 and passim.

67. Ibid., p. 20.

68. See Whalley, *Poetic Process,* p. 41.

69. Ibid., p. 46.

70. Edward Caird, "The Evolution of Theology in the Greek Philosophers," quoted in John Kenneth Mozley, *Some Tendencies in British Theology: From the Publication of Lux Mundi to the Present Day* (London: SPCK, 1951), p. 122.

71. Martin Buber, *I and Thou,* 2nd ed., trans. Ronald Gregor Smith (New York: Scribner's, 1958), p. 13.

72. Ibid., pp. 14–15, 39.

73. *Martin Buber and the Theatre,* ed. and trans. Maurice Friedman (New York: Funk and Wagnalls, 1969), ch. 1.

74. Maurice Friedman, *Martin Buber: The Life of Dialogue* (Chicago: University of Chicago Press, 1955), p. 87.

75. Ibid., p. 49.

76. Ibid., p. 81.

77. Maurice Merleau-Ponty, *Signs,* trans. Richard C. McCleary (Evanston: Northwestern University Press, 1964), translator's preface, p. xv.

78. McCleary in Merleau-Ponty, *Signs,* p. xvii.

79. Merleau-Ponty, *Signs,* p. 19.

80. Ibid., p. 43.

81. Ibid., p. 54.

82. Barral, *Merleau-Ponty,* p. 49.

83. Sam Keen, *Gabriel Marcel* (London: Carey Kingsgate, 1966), p. 6.

84. Ibid., pp. 21–23.

85. Ibid., pp. 139, 161.

86. Gabriel Marcel, *Tragic Wisdom and Beyond: Including Conversations Between Paul Ricoeur and Gabriel Marcel* (Evanston: Northwestern University Press, 1973), p. 243.

87. Gabriel Marcel, *The Mystery of Being,* vol. II, *Faith and Reality,* trans. René Hague (London: Harvill, 1951), pp. 7–8.

88. Gabriel Marcel, *The Mystery of Being*, vol. I, *Reflection and Mystery*, trans. G. S. Fraser (Chicago: Regnery, 1950), p. 209.

89. Marcel, *Tragic Wisdom*, p. 11.

90. Ibid., p. xxviii.

91. Gabriel Marcel, *Presence and Immortality*, trans. Michael A. Machado (Pittsburgh: Duquesne University Press, 1967), pp. 239–40.

92. Marcel, *Mystery of Being*, I, pp. 119, 131–32.

93. Gabriel Marcel, *Creative Fidelity*, trans. Robert Rosthal (New York: Farrar, Straus, 1964), pp. 28–36.

94. Ibid., p. 34.

95. Ibid., p. xvii.

96. Gabriel Marcel, *Being and Having*, trans. Katharine Farrer (London: Dacre, 1949), p. 10.

97. Marcel, *Presence and Immortality*, p. 153.

98. Marcel, *Mystery of Being*, I, pp. 207–08.

99. Ong, *Barbarian Within*, p. 58.

100. Ibid., p. 59.

101. Ibid., pp. 58–60.

102. See James Hillman, *Insearch: Psychology and Religion* (London: Hodder and Stoughton, 1967), pp. 57–59.

103. Jacques Maritain, *The Responsibility of the Artist* (New York: Scribner's, 1960), p. 101.

104. Jacques Maritain, *On the Grace and Humanity of Jesus*, trans. Joseph W. Evans (London: Burns and Oates; New York: Herder and Herder, 1969), p. 121.

105. Macquarrie, *Principles of Christian Theology*, pp. 65–66.

106. Maritain, *Creative Intuition*, pp. 143–44.

107. David L. Miller, *George Herbert Mead: Self, Language, and the World* (Austin: University of Texas Press, 1973), see ch. 10, "Creativity."

108. Ibid., p. 166.

109. Nikolai Berdiaev, *The Meaning of the Creative Act*, trans. Donald A. Lowrie (New York: Harper and Brothers, 1955), p. 113.

110. Ibid., p. 135.

111. Ibid., pp. 308–09.

112. See Bacon, "Reverberation."

113. Vladimir Lossky, *The Mystical Theology of the Eastern Church*, trans. by members of the Fellowship of St. Alban and St. Sergius (Greenwood, S.C.: The Attic Press, 1968), p. 143.

114. Ibid., pp. 53–54.

115. Quoted in Schlitzer, *Redemptive Incarnation*, p. 122.

116. See Francis J. Hall, *The Incarnation* (1915; reprint ed., Pelham Manor, New York: The American Church Union, 1963), pp. 33, 102–04.

117. Schlitzer, *Redemptive Incarnation*, p. 123.

118. Bacon, *Interpretation*, p. 44.

119. Lossky, *Mystical Theology*, p. 39.

120. Ibid., p. 146.

121. *The Catechetical Lecture of S. Cyril Archbishop of Jerusalem*, vol. VII, *Nicene and Post-Nicene Fathers of the Christian Church*, ed. Philip Schaff and Henry Wace, 2nd series (Grand Rapids: Wm. B. Eerdmans, 1955), Orat. 7:23, p. 237.

122. Lossky, *Mystical Theology,* p. 136.

123. Werner Jaeger, *Two Rediscovered Works of Ancient Christian Literature: Gregory of Nyssa and Macarius* (Leiden, Netherlands: E. J. Brill, 1965), p. 103.

124. Ibid., p. 94.

125. A. H. Armstrong, ed., *The Cambridge History of Later Greek and Early Medieval Philosophy* (1967; reprint ed., Cambridge: Cambridge University Press, 1970), p. 431.

126. *Catechetical Lecture,* vol. VII, *Nicene and Post-Nicene Fathers,* Second Oration on Easter, Orat. 45:22, p. 431.

127. Armstrong, *Cambridge History,* Nazianzen, Orat. 28:28, p. 440.

128. Lossky, *Mystical Theology,* p. 103.

129. Raïssa Maritain, *Situation of Poetry,* pp. 9, 17–18.

130. Ibid., p. 21n.

131. Bacon, *Interpretation,* p. 47.

132. Ibid., p. 135.

133. Ibid., p. 136.

134. *Stanislavski's Legacy: A Collection of Comments on a Variety of Aspects of an Actor's Art and Life,* trans. Elizabeth Reynolds Hapgood (New York: Theatre Arts Books, 1968), p. 131.

135. Stanislavski, *Building a Character,* pp. 7–8, 19.

136. Don Geiger, "The Oral Interpreter as Creator," *The Speech Teacher,* 3 (1954), pp. 269–77.

137. See Sayers, *Mind of the Maker,* p. 121.

138. Roloff, *Perception and Evocation,* pp. 104–05.

139. Bacon, *Interpretation,* p. 35.

140. Stanislavski, *An Actor Prepares,* pp. 188–89.

141. Lossky, *Mystical Theology,* pp. 38–39.

142. Ibid., p. 71.

143. Otto, *Idea of the Holy,* p. 69.

144. Ibid., p. 70.

145. In Lionel de Fonseka, *On the Truth of Decorative Art: A Dialogue Between an Oriental and an Occidental* (London: Greening and Co., 1912); also see Maritain, *Creative Intuition,* p. 35.

146. Otto, *Idea of the Holy,* pp. 12–13.

147. From Rafael Lefort, *The Teachers of Gurdjieff,* quoted in Robert Ornstein, "Intuition," *Intellectual Digest,* 4, no. 3 (November, 1973), pp. 25–32.

148. Ibid., p. 29.

149. See Sam Keen, *Apology for Wonder* (New York: Harper and Row, 1969), pp. 193–94.

150. See Wheelright, *Metaphor and Reality,* p. 46.

151. Victor White, *God and the Unconscious* (1952; reprint ed., Cleveland: World Publishing Co., Meridian Books, 1965), pp. 126–52.

152. Ibid., pp. 144–45.

153. A. A. Milne, *The House at Pooh Corner* (1928; reprint ed., New York: Dell Publishing Co., 1956), pp. 147–49.

154. Hillman, *Insearch,* p. 16.

155. Paul Reps, comp., *Zen Flesh, Zen Bones: A Collection of Zen and Pre-Zen Writings* (New York: Doubleday, Anchor Books, 1961), pp. 171–73.

156. Ibid., p. 5.

157. From *Buddhist Scriptures,* quoted in Dom Aelred Graham, *Zen Catholicism: A Suggestion* (New York: Harcourt, Brace and World, Harvest Books Edition, 1963), p. 47.

158. William Johnston, *The Still Point: Reflections on Zen and Christian Mysticism* (New York: Fordham University Press, 1970), p. xii.

159. T. S. Eliot, "Tradition and the Individual Talent," in *Selected Essays* (1932; reprint ed., New York: Harcourt, Brace and Co., 1950), p. 11.

160. See Johnston, *Still Point,* p. 22.

161. Maritain, *Creative Intuition,* p. 43.

162. Rollo May, *Love and Will* (New York: W. W. Norton and Co., 1969), p. 157.

163. Merton, *Asian Journal,* p. 63.

164. Donald G. Dawe, *The Form of a Servant: A Historical Analysis of the Kenotic Motif* (Philadelphia: Westminster, 1963).

165. Gerhard Kittel, ed., *Theological Dictionary of the New Testament,* vol. III, trans. and ed. Geoffrey W. Bromiley (Grand Rapids: Wm. B. Eerdmans, 1965), p. 661.

166. Thomasius, the Lutheran spokesman for *kenosis,* cited in Alexander Balmain Bruce, *The Humiliation of Christ: In Its Physical, Ethical, and Official Aspects,* 2nd ed. (New York: A. C. Armstrong and Son, 1901), p. 154.

167. Dawe, *Form of a Servant,* p. 153.

168. Lossky, *Mystical Theology,* pp. 144, 168.

169. Eric L. Mascall, *Christ, the Christian, and the Church: A Study of the Incarnation and Its Consequences* (London: Longmans, Green and Co., 1946), pp. 25–27.

170. Herbert A. Watson, *The Incarnation and Personality* (London: SPCK and New York: Macmillan, 1920), pp. 50–51.

171. Quoted in Nadejda Gorodetzky, *The Humiliated Christ in Modern Russian Thought* (London: SPCK and New York: Macmillan, 1938), p. 67.

172. John Keats, *Selected Poetry and Letters,* ed. Richard Harter Fogle (New York: Holt, Rinehart and Winston, 1969), pp. 324–25.

173. Maslow, *Farther Reaches of Human Nature,* p. 67.

174. Ibid., pp. 253–54.

175. Sam Keen, *To a Dancing God* (New York: Harper and Row, 1970), p. 45. See idem, *Apology for Wonder,* pp. 193–94.

176. Paul Evdokimov, *The Struggle with God,* trans. Sister Gertrude, S.P. (Glen Rock, N.J.: Paulist Press, 1966), pp. 98–100.

177. Ibid., p. 107.

178. *Meister Eckhart: A Modern Translation,* trans. Raymond Bernard Blakney (New York: Harper and Brothers, 1941), p. 88.

179. Leslie Gillian Abel and Robert M. Post, "Towards a Poor Readers Theatre," *Quarterly Journal of Speech,* 59, no. 4 (December, 1973), pp. 436–42.

180. Jerzy Growtowski, *Towards a Poor Theatre,* trans. T. K. Wiewiorowski (New York: Simon and Schuster, 1968), pp. 16–17; also Abel and Post, "Towards a Poor Readers Theatre," p. 440.

181. Bacon, *Interpretation,* pp. 15, 137.

182. See Roloff, *Perception and Evocation,* p. 69.

183. Ibid., p. 19.

184. See Bacon, *Interpretation,* p. 11.

185. P. T. Forsyth, *The Person and Place of Jesus Christ* (Boston: Pilgrim Press, 1909), pp. 349–50, 352.

186. See Charles Hanna, *The Face of the Deep: The Religious Ideas of C. G. Jung* (Philadelphia: Westminster, 1967), p. 76.

187. June K. Singer, *Boundaries of the Soul: The Practice of Jung's Psychology* (New York: Doubleday, 1972), pp. 357–58.

188. Ornstein, "Intuition," p. 26.

189. C. G. Jung, *Modern Man in Search of a Soul*, trans. W. S. Dell and Cary F. Baynes (New York: Harcourt, Brace and Co., 1933), pp. 196–97.

190. See C. G. Jung, *The Letters of C. G. Jung*, vol. I, *1906–1950*, ed. Gerhard Adler et al. (Princeton: Princeton University Press, 1973), pp. 108–09.

191. C. G. Jung, "The Transcendent Function," in *The Portable Jung*, ed. Joseph Campbell, trans. R. F. C. Hull (New York: Viking, 1971), pp. 273–300.

192. Bacon, *Interpretation*, p. 136. Bracketed insertions are mine.

193. Jung, "Transcendent Function," p. 293.

194. Maslow, *Farther Reaches of Human Nature*, pp. 82–83, 89.

195. Ibid., p. 66.

196. Ibid., p. 89.

197. Ibid., pp. 251ff.

198. Hillman, *Insearch*, pp. 59–60.

199. Ibid., p. 79.

200. Johnston, *Still Point*, p. 13.

201. Stanislavski, *Building a Character*, p. 266.

202. Sonia Moore, *The Stanislavski Method: The Professional Training of an Actor Digested from the Teaching of Konstantin S. Stanislavski* (New York: Viking, 1960), p. 9.

203. Johnston, *Still Point*, p. 51.

204. Bacon, *Interpretation*, p. 175.

205. Johnston, *Still Point*, p. 46 and passim.

206. Erich Fromm, *Psychoanalysis and Religion*, p. 79, cited in Johnston, *Still Point*, p. 99.

207. C. G. Jung, *Psychology and Religion: West and East*, p. 546, quoted in Johnston, *Still Point*, p. 49.

208. Pierre Teilhard de Chardin, *The Divine Milieu: An Essay on the Interior Life*, trans. Alex Dru et al. (New York: Harper and Row, Torchbooks Edition, 1960), p. 129.

209. Roloff, *Perception and Evocation*, p. 158.

210. In Nicholas Arseniev, *Russian Piety*, trans. Asheleigh Moorhouse (London: Faith Press, 1964), p. 39.

211. Ibid., p. 41.

212. Marcel, *Presence and Immortality*, p. 82.

213. Roloff, "Critical Study," p. 409.

214. Maurice Merleau-Ponty, "L'oeil et l'esprit," *Les temps modernes*, 27, nos. 184–85 (July–August, 1960), p. 197; and Barral, *Merleau-Ponty*, p. 53.

215. Barral, *Merleau-Ponty*, p. 54.

216. Bacon, *Interpretation*, p. 37.

217. Ibid., p. 38.

218. Merleau-Ponty, *Signs*, p. 91.

219. See Norman Hepburn Baynes, *Byzantine Studies: And Other Essays* (London: University of London, Athlone Press, 1960), especially "Idolatry and the Early Church."

220. Armstrong, *Cambridge History,* p. 509.

221. Ibid., pp. 506–07.

222. Ibid., pp. 515–16.

223. Evdokimov, *Struggle with God,* p. 98.

224. Susan Miller, *Icons* (New York: St. Martin's Press, 1972), introduction.

225. John Walstead, "Window Open into Heaven: Iconography Related to God's Creative Nature," *The Oregon Episcopal Churchman* (April, 1973), p. 5.

226. Cassirer, *Essay on Man,* p. 148.

227. Walstead, "Window Open into Heaven."

228. Ibid.

229. See Baynes, "Idolatry and the Early Church."

230. Walstead, "Window Open into Heaven."

231. Ibid.

232. See Fuchs in Robinson, *New Hermeneutic,* p. 54.

233. Lossky, *Mystical Theology,* p. 189.

234. "Work in Progress: Voznesensky Magic," an interview with Herbert R. Lottman in *Intellectual Digest,* 4, no. 3 (November, 1973), p. 8.

235. *The Jerusalem Bible,* ed. Alexander Jones et al. (London: Darton, Longman and Todd, 1966), N. T., p. 147.

236. Roloff, *Perception and Evocation,* p. 188.

237. Ibid., p. 17.

238. Paul Schilder, *The Image and Appearance of the Human Body: Studies in the Constructive Energies of the Psyche* (New York: International Universities Press, 1950), pp. 201–02.

239. Ibid., pp. 208, 247.

240. See Bacon, *Interpretation,* p. 135.

241. Moore, *Stanislavski Method,* p. 45.

242. See Bacon, *Interpretation,* p. 180.

243. See Ralph J. Hallman, "Aesthetic Motivation in the Creative Arts," *Journal of Aesthetics and Art Criticism,* 23 (summer, 1965), pp. 453–59.

244. See Karl Rahner, "The Unity of Spirit and Matter," in *Man Before God: Toward a Theology of Man,* Juna Alfaro et al. (New York: P. J. Kenedy and Sons, 1966), p. 44.

245. J. R. Illingworth, *Divine Immanence: An Essay on the Spiritual Significance of Matter* (New York: Macmillan, 1898), p. 13.

246. Bacon, *Interpretation,* p. 33.

247. Illingworth, *Divine Immanence,* pp. 63–64.

248. "Offices of Instruction," *The Book of Common Prayer: And Administration of the Sacraments and Other Rites and Ceremonies of the Church,* 1928 version (New York: The Church Pension Fund, 1945), p. 292.

249. R. P. Blackmur, *Language as Gesture: Essays in Poetry* (London: Allen and Unwin, 1954), p. 6.

250. Paraphrased in Miller, *George Herbert Mead,* p. 46.

251. Vogel, *Body Theology,* p. 104.

252. For a detailed discussion of divergent viewpoints on aesthetic distance in interpretation theory, see Leland H. Roloff, "Critical Study," pp. 286ff.

253. See ibid., and Schilder, *Image and Appearance,* p. 248.

254. *Stanislavski's Legacy,* p. 185.

255. Ibid., p. 7.

256. Bacon, *Interpretation,* p. 7.

257. See Keen, *Gabriel Marcel,* pp. 21–22.

258. Vladimir Solovyov, "The Meaning of Love," in *Russian Philosophy,* vol. III, *Pre-Revolutionary Philosophy and Theology,* ed. James M. Edie et al. (1965; reprint ed., Chicago: Quadrangle Books, 1969), pp. 88–89.

259. Ibid., p. 90.

260. Charles Williams, "The Way of Exchange," in *Selected Writings,* ed. Anne Ridler (London: Oxford University Press, 1961).

261. Ibid., p. 129. For a detailed exposition of substitution see Charles Williams, *Descent into Hell* (London: Faber and Faber, 1949), ch. 6, "The Doctrine of Substituted Love."

262. Roloff, *Perception and Evocation,* p. 305.

263. Ibid., p. 320.

264. See Paul Tillich, *The Courage to Be* (New Haven: Yale University Press, 1952), p. 46.

265. Ibid., p. 88.

266. Bacon, *Interpretation,* p. 9.

267. Tillich, *Courage to Be,* p. 124.

268. Whalley, *Poetic Process,* pp. 27–28.

269. *Stanislavski's Legacy,* p. 6.

Chapter Four

1. Stanislavski, *An Actor Prepares,* p. 151.

2. Bacon, *Interpretation,* passim.

3. Lev Semenovich Vygotsky, *The Psychology of Art,* trans. Scripta Technica (Cambridge, Mass.: Massachusetts Institute of Technology Press, 1971).

4. Ibid., A. N. Leontiev, introduction, p. vii.

5. Ibid., pp. 210–14.

6. Wolfhart Pannenberg, *The Idea of God and Human Freedom,* trans. R. A. Wilson (Philadelphia: Westminster, 1973), p. 133.

7. Günther Müller, "Morphological Poetics," in *Reflections on Art: A Source Book of Writings by Artists, Critics, and Philosophers,* ed. Suzanne K. Langer (1958; reprint ed., Baltimore: Johns Hopkins Press, 1960), pp. 214–15.

8. Iredell Jenkins, *Art and the Human Enterprise* (Cambridge, Mass.: Harvard University Press, 1958), p. 114.

9. Roloff, *Perception and Evocation,* p. 8.

10. Barral, *Merleau-Ponty,* p. 154.

11. Quoted in ibid., p. 154.

12. See ibid., pp. 154–58.

13. See Maslow, *The Farther Reaches of Human Nature,* "A Holistic Approach to Creativity," p. 74.

14. May, *Love and Will*, p. 156.

15. Bacon, *Interpretation*, p. v.

16. May, *Love and Will*, p. 157.

17. Sidney M. Jourard, *The Transparent Self* (New York: Van Nostrand Reinhold, 1971), pp. 60–61.

18. See Vygotsky, *Psychology of Art*, p. 250.

19. See Roloff, *Perception and Evocation*, p. 185.

20. Ibid., p. 4.

21. Tillich, *Eternal Now*, p. 86.

22. *Interpreter's Dictionary of the Bible* [R-Z], p. 643.

23. Ibid.

24. Ibid., p. 645.

25. Ibid., p. 646.

26. Oscar Cullman, *Christ and Time: The Primitive Christian Conception of Time and History*, trans. Floyd V. Filson (Philadelphia: Westminster, 1950).

27. Ibid., pp. 39–42, 67.

28. Paul Minear, *Eyes of Faith: A Study in the Biblical Point of View* (London: Lutterworth Press, 1948), p. 98.

29. Ibid., pp. 100, 112.

30. Ibid., p. 99.

31. Ibid., p. 101.

32. See Arthur Koestler, *Dialogue with Death* (New York: Macmillan, 1942), pp. 120–21; also Minear, *Eyes of Faith*, p. 101.

33. Minear, *Eyes of Faith*, p. 106.

34. *Theological Dictionary of the New Testament*, vol. III, p. 458.

35. Minear, *Eyes of Faith*, p. 108.

36. Keen, *Apology for Wonder*, p. 198.

37. Keen, *To a Dancing God*, p. 52.

38. Ibid., p. 54.

39. See Elizabeth Drew, *T. S. Eliot: The Design of His Poetry* (New York: Scribner's, 1949), p. 187.

40. St. Augustine of Hippo, *The Confessions*, trans. Edward Bouverie Pusey, Great Books of the Western World, 18, ed. Robert Maynard Hutchins (Chicago: William Benton, Encylopaedia Britannica, 1952), book 11.

41. Merleau-Ponty, *Signs;* also McCleary in preface, p. xv.

42. See Marcel, *Mystery of Being*, I, p. 202.

43. Ibid., pp. 194–97.

44. Ibid., p. 138. Cf. Hebrew time as *mô'ēd*, or "place of meeting," p. 244.

45. Ibid., p. 123.

46. Merton, *Asian Journal*, p. 62.

47. See Marcel, *Mystery of Being*, I, p. 138.

48. Cassirer, *Essay on Man*, p. 146. (Cassirer borrows and elaborates this concept of Goethe's.)

49. Ibid., pp. 145–46.

50. Roloff, *Perception and Evocation*, p. 113.

51. See Henri Bergson, *Time and Free Will: An Essay on the Immediate Data of Consciousness*, trans. F. L. Pogson (London: Allen and Unwin, 1959), pp. 127–32.

52. Roloff, *Perception and Evocation*, pp. 112, 114.

53. Ibid., pp. 114–15.

54. Ibid., p. 118.

55. Ibid., p. 120.

56. Ibid., pp. 121–22.

57. Sayers, *Mind of the Maker*, p. 116.

58. Ibid., pp. 116–17.

59. Mattingly and Grimes, *Interpretation: Writer, Reader, Audience*, p. 282.

60. Siirala, *Divine Humanness*, p. 54.

61. See Frederick H. Lund and Anna Anastasi, "An Interpretation of Aesthetic Experience," *The American Journal of Psychology*, 40 (July, 1928), pp. 434–48.

62. Roloff, *Perception and Evocation*, p. 15.

63. Moore, *Stanislavski Method*, p. 18.

64. Roloff, *Perception and Evocation*, p. 117.

65. Ibid., p. 121.

66. Bacon, *Interpretation*, p. 365.

67. George Herbert Mead, *Selected Writings*, ed. Andrew J. Reck (New York: Bobbs-Merrill, 1964), editor's introduction, pp. xlvii–l.

68. Ibid., pp. xlix–l.

69. Roloff, *Perception and Evocation*, p. 18.

70. Maslow, *Farther Reaches of Human Nature*, p. 61.

71. Bacon, *Interpretation*, p. 47.

72. Roloff, *Perception and Evocation*, p. 21.

73. Bacon and Breen, *Literature as Experience*, p. 106.

74. Nelson, *Incarnate Word*, p. 51.

75. Bacon, *Interpretation*, p. 46.

76. In T. S. Eliot, *The Complete Poems and Plays* (New York: Harcourt, Brace and Co., 1952), pp. 106–08. Quoted with permission of the publishers.

77. Bacon, *Interpretation*, p. 134.

78. Cf. Merton, *Asian Journal*, p. 57.

79. Maud Bodkin, *Archetypal Patterns in Poetry: Psychological Studies of Imagination* (1934; reprint ed., London: Oxford University Press, 1968), p. 5.

80. See Bacon, *Interpretation*, p. 33.

81. Bodkin, *Archetypal Patterns*, pp. 321–22.

82. Bacon, *Interpretation*, p. 62.

83. Nelson, *Incarnate Word*, p. 6.

84. Barral, *Merleau-Ponty*, p. 144.

85. Hillman, *Insearch*, p. 32.

86. Ibid.

87. Ibid., pp. 32–33.

88. Ong, *Barbarian Within*, pp. 27–28.

89. See Kenneth Burke, *Language as Symbolic Action: Essays on Life, Literature, and Method* (Berkeley: University of California Press, 1966), pp. 298–99.

90. See Kenneth Burke, *A Rhetoric of Motives* (New York: Prentice-Hall, 1950), p. 21.

91. Bacon, *Interpretation*, p. 165.

bibliography

Primary Sources

Books

Abbey, Merrill R. *The Word Interprets Us.* Nashville: Abingdon, 1967.

Alfaro, Juna, et al. *Man Before God: Toward a Theology of Man.* Readings in Theology Series. New York: P. J. Kenedy and Sons, 1966.

Allport, Gordon W. *The Individual and His Religion: A Psychological Interpretation.* New York: Macmillan, 1950.

Ante-Nicene Christian Library: Irenaeus. Vol. L. Trans. Alexander Roberts. London: Hamilton and Co., 1868.

Aquinas, Thomas. *A Digest of S. Thomas on the Incarnation.* Ed. anon. London: J. T. Hayes, 1868.

Aristotle. *On Poetics.* Trans. Ingram Bywater. *Aristotle.* Vol. I. Great Books of the Western World, 9. Ed. Robert Maynard Hutchins. Chicago: William Benton, Encyclopaedia Britannica, 1952.

Armstrong, A. H., ed. *The Cambridge History of Later Greek and Early Medieval Philosophy.* 1967. Reprint. Cambridge: Cambridge University Press, 1970.

Arseniev, Nicholas. *Russian Piety.* Trans. Asheleigh Moorhouse. London: Faith Press, 1964.

Athanasius, St. *The Incarnation of the Word of God: Being the Treatise of St. Athanasius, De Incarnatione Verbi Dei.* Trans. by a Religious of C.S.M.V., S.Th. New York: Macmillan, 1947.

Augustine of Hippo, St. *The Confessions.* Trans. Edward Bouverie Pusey. Great Books of the Western World, 18. Ed. Robert Maynard Hutchins. Chicago: William Benton, Encyclopaedia Britannica, 1952.

————. *On Christian Doctrine.* Trans. J. F. Shaw. Great Books of the Western World, 18. Ed. Robert Maynard Hutchins. Chicago: William Benton, Encyclopaedia Britannica, 1952.

Bacon, Wallace A. *The Art of Interpretation.* 2nd ed. New York: Holt, Rinehart and Winston, 1972.

Bacon, Wallace A., and Breen, Robert S. *Literature as Experience.* New York: McGraw-Hill, 1959.

Balthazar, Hans Urs von. *Martin Buber and Christianity: A Dialogue Between Israel and the Church.* Trans. Alex Dru. London: Harvill, 1961.

Barral, Mary Rose. *Merleau-Ponty: The Role of the Body-Subject in Interpersonal Relations.* Pittsburgh: Duquesne University Press, 1965.

Barrett, William. *Irrational Man: A Study in Existential Philosophy.* New York: Doubleday, 1958; Anchor Books, 1962.

Barth, Karl. *The Humanity of God.* Richmond: John Knox Press, 1960.

Baynes, Norman Hepburn. *Byzantine Studies: And Other Essays.* London: University of London, Athlone Press, 1960.

Beloof, Robert. *The Performing Voice in Literature.* Boston: Little, Brown and Co., 1966.

Berdiaev, Nikolai Aleksandrovich. *The Meaning of the Creative Act.* Trans. Donald A. Lowrie. New York: Harper and Brothers, 1955.

———. *Slavery and Freedom.* New York: Scribner's, 1944.

Bergson, Henri Louis. *The Creative Mind.* Trans. Mabelle L. Andison. New York: Philosophical Library, 1946.

———. *Mind-Energy: Lectures and Essays.* Trans. H. Wildon Carr. New York: H. Holt and Co., 1920.

———. *The Philosophy of Poetry: The Genius of Lucretius.* Ed., trans. Wade Baskin. New York: Philosophical Library, 1959.

———. *Time and Free Will: An Essay on the Immediate Data of Consciousness.* Trans. F. L. Pogson. London: Allen and Unwin, 1959.

———. *The Two Sources of Morality and Religion.* Trans. Ashley Audra and Cloudesley Brereton. 1935. Reprint. Notre Dame: University of Notre Dame Press, 1977.

Blackmur, Richard Palmer. *Language as Gesture: Essays in Poetry.* London: Allen and Unwin, 1954.

Blamires, Harry. *The Offering of Man.* New York: Morehouse-Barlow, 1960.

Bodkin, Maud. *Archetypal Patterns in Poetry: Psychological Studies of Imagination.* 1934. Reprint. London: Oxford University Press, 1968.

The Book of Common Prayer: And Administration of the Sacraments and Other Rites and Ceremonies of the Church. 1928 version. New York: The Church Pension Fund, 1945.

Bradner, Leicester. *Incarnation in Religion and Literature.* Faculty Papers, 4th series. New York: The National Council [of the Episcopal Church], 1957.

Bruce, Alexander Balmain. *The Humiliation of Christ: In Its Physical, Ethical, and Official Aspects.* 2nd ed. New York: A. C. Armstrong and Son, 1901.

Brunner, Emil. *Truth as Encounter.* 2nd ed. Trans. David Cairns. Philadelphia: Westminster, 1964.

Buber, Martin. *I and Thou.* 2nd ed. Trans. Robert Gregor Smith. New York: Scribner's, 1958.

———. *Martin Buber and the Theatre.* Ed. and trans. with three introductory essays by Maurice Friedman. New York: Funk and Wagnalls, 1969.

Burke, Kenneth. *Language as Symbolic Action: Essays on Life, Literature, and Method.* Berkeley: University of California Press, 1966.

———. *Permanence and Change: An Anatomy of Purpose.* 2nd ed. New York: Bobbs-Merrill, 1965.

———. *The Philosophy of Literary Form: Studies in Symbolic Action.* 2nd ed. Baton Rouge: Louisiana State University Press, 1967.

———. *A Rhetoric of Motives.* New York: Prentice-Hall, 1950.

Burnshaw, Stanley, *The Seamless Web: Language-Thinking, Creature-Knowledge, Art-Experience.* New York: Braziller, 1970.

Campbell, Joseph. *Flight of the Wild Gander: Explorations in the Mythological Dimension.* Zurich: Rhein-Verlag, AG, 1960; Chicago: Regnery Gateway Edition, 1972.

Campbell, Paul. *The Speaking and the Speakers of Literature.* Belmont, California: Dickenson Publishing Co., 1967.

Cassirer, Ernst. *An Essay on Man: An Introduction to a Philosophy of Human Culture.* 1944. Reprint. New Haven: Yale University Press, 1948.

————. *The Philosophy of Symbolic Forms.* Vol. I. *Language.* Trans. Ralph Manheim. New Haven: Yale University Press, 1953.

————. *The Philosophy of Symbolic Forms.* Vol. III. *The Phenomenology of Knowledge.* Trans. Ralph Manheim. New Haven: Yale University Press, 1957.

The Catechetical Lecture of S. Cyril Archbishop of Jerusalem. Vol. VII. *Nicene and Post-Nicene Fathers of the Christian Church.* Ed. Philip Schaff and Henry Wace. 2nd series. Grand Rapids: Wm. B. Eerdmans, 1955.

Chiari, Joseph. *Realism and Imagination.* London: Barrie and Rockliff, 1960.

Ciardi, John. *Dialogue with an Audience.* Philadelphia: Lippincott, 1963.

Claudel, Paul. *The Eye Listens.* Trans. Elsie Pell. New York: Philosophical Library, 1950.

Coleridge, Samuel Taylor. *Selected Poetry and Prose of Coleridge.* Comp. Donald A. Stauffer. New York: Random House, Modern Library College Edition, 1951.

Collingwood, R. G. *The Principles of Art.* 1938. Reprint. Oxford: Clarendon Press, 1955.

Cox, David. *Jung and St. Paul: A Study of the Doctrine of Justification by Faith and Its Relation to the Concept of Individuation.* New York: Associated Press, 1959.

Cullman, Oscar. *Christ and Time: The Primitive Christian Conception of Time and History.* Trans. Floyd V. Filson. Philadelphia: Westminster, 1950.

Dawe, Donald G. *The Form of a Servant: A Historical Analysis of the Kenotic Motif.* Philadelphia: Westminster, 1963.

Dewey, John. *Art as Experience.* New York: Minton, Balch and Co., 1934.

Dodds, E. R. *The Greeks and the Irrational.* Boston: Beacon, 1957.

Drown, Edward Staples. *The Creative Christ: A Study of the Incarnation in Terms of Modern Thought.* New York: Macmillan, 1922.

Ducasse, Curt John. *The Philosophy of Art.* London: Allen and Unwin, 1929.

Ebeling, Gerhard. *God and Word.* Trans. James W. Leitch. Philadelphia: Fortress, 1966.

————. *Word and Faith.* Trans. James W. Leitch. London: SCM, 1963.

Ebersole, Frank. "Saying and Meaning." In *Ludwig Wittgenstein: Philosophy and Language,* ed. Alice Ambrose and Morris Lazerowitz. London: Allen and Unwin, 1972, pp. 186–221.

Eckhart, Meister. *Meister Eckhart: A Modern Translation.* Trans. Raymond Bernard Blakney. New York: Harper and Brothers, 1941.

Ehrenzweig, Anton. *The Psycho-Analysis of Artistic Vision and Hearing: An Introduction to a Theory of Unconscious Perception.* London: Routledge and Kegan Paul, 1953.

Eliade, Mircea. *Myths, Dreams and Mysteries: The Encounter Between Contemporary Faiths and Archaic Realities.* Trans. Philip Mairet. New York: Harper and Brothers, 1960.

Eliot, T. S. *The Complete Poems and Plays.* New York: Harcourt, Brace and Co., 1952.

————. *Selected Essays.* 1932. Reprint. New York: Harcourt, Brace and Co., 1950.

Elliott-Binns, L. E. *The Development of English Theology in the Later Nineteenth Century.* London: Longmans, Green and Co., 1952.

Erskine, Thomas [of Linlathan]. *The Unconditional Freeness of the Gospel: In Three Essays.* From 2nd Edinburgh Edition. Boston: Crocker and Brewster, 1828.

Evdokimov, Paul. *The Struggle with God.* Trans. Sister Gertrude, S.P. Glen Rock, New Jersey: Paulist Press, 1966.

Fedotov, G. P., ed. *A Treasury of Russian Spirituality.* New York: Harper and Row, Torchbooks Edition, 1965.

Forsyth, Peter Taylor. *The Person and Place of Jesus Christ.* Boston: Pilgrim Press, 1909.

Frank, Erich. *Philosophical Understanding and Religious Truth.* New York: Oxford University Press, 1945.

Franks, R. S. *The Work of Christ: A Historical Study of Christian Doctrine.* London: T. Nelson, 1962.

Friedman, Maurice. *Martin Buber: The Life of Dialogue.* Chicago: University of Chicago Press, 1955.

Gardiner, Alan H. *The Theory of Speech and Language.* New York: Oxford University Press, 1932.

Garrett, Alexander Charles. *The Philosophy of the Incarnation.* New York: James Pott and Co., 1891.

Geiger, Don. *The Dramatic Impulse in Modern Poetics.* Baton Rouge: Louisiana State University Press, 1967.

———. *The Sound, Sense, and Performance of Literature.* Chicago: Scott, Foresman and Co., 1963.

Ghiselin, Brewster, ed. *The Creative Process.* New York: Mentor Books, 1955.

Gifford, Edwin H. *The Incarnation: A Study of Philippians II, 5–11.* New York: Dodd, Mead, 1897.

Gore, Charles. *Dissertations on Subjects Connected with the Incarnation.* London: John Murray, 1907.

Gorodetzky, Nadejda. *The Humilated Christ in Modern Russian Thought.* New York: Macmillan, 1938.

Graham, Dom Aelred. *Zen Catholicism: A Suggestion.* New York: Harcourt, Brace and World, Harvest Books Edition, 1963.

Gregory of Nyssa, St. *St. Gregory of Nyssa: Ascetical Works.* Trans. Virginia Woods Callahan. The Fathers of the Church, vol. 58. Washington, D.C.: Catholic University of America Press, 1966.

Guardini, Romano. *The Humanity of Christ: Contributions to a Psychology of Jesus.* Trans. Ronald Walls. New York: Random House, Pantheon Books, 1964.

Gusdorf, Georges. *Speaking. (La parole).* Trans. Paul T. Brockelman. Evanston: Northwestern University Press, 1965.

Hall, Francis J. *The Incarnation.* 1915. Reprint. Pelham Manor, New York: The American Church Union, 1963.

Hanna, Charles Bartruff. *The Face of the Deep: The Religious Ideas of C. G. Jung.* Philadelphia: Westminster, 1967.

Harding, M. Esther. *Woman's Mysteries: Ancient and Modern: A Psychological Interpretation of the Feminine Principles as Portrayed in Myth, Story, and Dreams.* London: Longmans, Green and Co., 1935.

Heidegger, Martin. *Being and Time.* 7th ed. Trans. John Macquarrie and Edward Robinson. New York: Harper and Brothers, 1962.

Heller, Erich. *The Artist's Journey into the Interior: And Other Essays.* New York: Random House, 1965.

High, Dallas M. *Language, Persons, and Belief: Studies in Wittgenstein's Philosophical Investigations and Religious Uses of Language.* New York: Oxford University Press, 1967.

Hillman, James. *Emotion: A Comprehensive Phenomenology of Theories and Their Meanings for Therapy.* London: Routledge and Kegan Paul, 1960.

———. *Insearch: Psychology and Religion.* London: Hodder and Stoughton, 1967.

———. *The Myth of Analysis: Three Essays in Archetypal Psychology.* Evanston: Northwestern University Press, 1972.

Hirsch, Eric Donald, Jr. *Validity in Interpretation.* New Haven: Yale University Press, 1967.

Hopper, Stanley Romaine, and Miller, David L. *Interpretation: The Poetry of Meaning.* New York: Harcourt, Brace and World, 1967.

Hopper, Stanley Romaine, ed. *Spiritual Problems in Contemporary Literature.* 1957. Reprint. New York: Harper and Row, Torchbook Edition, 1965.

Horatius Flaccus, Quintus. *Ars Poetica.* Ed. and trans. Charles O. Brink. Cambridge: Cambridge University Press, 1963.

Hospers, John. *Meaning and Truth in the Arts.* Chapel Hill: University of North Carolina Press, 1946.

Illingworth, John Richardson, *Divine Immanence: An Essay on the Spiritual Significance of Matter.* New York: Macmillan, 1898.

———. "The Incarnation in Relation to Development." In *Lux Mundi,* ed. Charles Gore, 4th ed. London: John Murray, 1890.

———. *Personality, Human and Divine.* London: Macmillan, 1907.

The Interpreter's Dictionary of the Bible [R-Z]. Ed. George Arthur Buttrick et al. Nashville: Abingdon, 1962.

Jacobs, Noah Jonathon. *Naming-Day in Eden: The Creation and Recreation of Language.* 2nd ed. Toronto: Collier-Macmillan, 1969.

Jaeger, Werner. *Two Rediscovered Works of Ancient Christian Literature: Gregory of Nyssa and Macarius.* Leiden, Netherlands: E. J. Brill, 1965.

James, William. *The Varieties of Religious Experience: A Study in Human Nature.* New York: Longmans, Green and Co., 1902.

The Jerusalem Bible. Ed. Alexander Jones et al. London: Darton, Longman and Todd, 1966.

Johnston, J. S. *The Philosophy of the Fourth Gospel: A Study of the Logos Doctrine: Its Sources and Its Significance.* London: SPCK: 1910.

Johnston, William. *The Still Point: Reflections on Zen and Christian Mysticism.* New York: Fordham University Press, 1970.

Jourard, Sidney M. *The Transparent Self.* New York: Van Nostrand Reinhold, 1971.

Jung, C. G. *Collected Papers on Analytical Psychology.* Trans. Constance E. Long. London: Bailliere, Tindall and Cox, 1916.

———. *Memories, Dreams, Reflections.* Ed. Aniela Jaffe. Trans. Richard and Clara Winston. New York: Random House, Vintage Books, 1963.

———. *Modern Man in Search of a Soul.* Trans. W. S. Dell and Cary F. Baynes. New York: Harcourt, Brace and Co., 1933.

———. *The Portable Jung.* Ed. Joseph Campbell. Trans. R. F. C. Hull. New York: Viking, 1971.

———. *Psychology and Religion.* 1938. Reprint. New Haven: Yale University Press, 1969.

Kant, Immanuel. "Critique of Aesthetic Judgement." Trans. James Creed Meredity. *The Critique of Judgement.* Great Books of the Western World, 42. Ed. Robert Maynard Hutchins, Chicago: William Benton, Encyclopaedia Britannica, 1952.

Keats, John. *Selected Poetry and Letters.* Ed. Richard Harter Fogle. New York: Holt, Rinehart and Winston, 1969.

Keen, Sam. *Apology for Wonder.* New York: Harper and Row, 1969.

————. *Gabriel Marcel.* London: Carey Kingsgate, 1966.

————. *To a Dancing God.* New York: Harper and Row, 1970.

Kelsey, Morton. *Encounter with God: A Theology of Christian Experience.* Minneapolis: Bethany Fellowship, 1972.

Kendall, E. Lorna. *The Humanity of Christ.* New York: Morehouse-Barlow, 1964.

Kittel, Gerhard, ed. *Theological Dictionary of the New Testament.* Vol. III. Trans. and ed. Geoffrey W. Bromiley. Grand Rapids: Wm. B. Eerdmans, 1965.

Knox, John. *The Humanity and Divinity of Christ: A Study of Pattern in Christology.* Cambridge: Cambridge University Press, 1967.

Koestler, Arthur. *The Act of Creation.* London: Hutchinson, Danube Edition, 1969.

Kubler, George. *The Shape of Time.* New Haven: Yale University Press, 1962.

Langer, Suzanne K. *Feeling and Form: A Theory of Art.* New York: Scribner's, 1953.

————. *Philosophy in a New Key: A Study in the Symbolism of Reason, Rite, and Art.* Cambridge, Massachusetts: Harvard University Press, 1951.

————. *Problems of Art: Ten Philosophical Lectures.* New York: Scribner's, 1957.

Langer, Suzanne K., ed. *Reflections on Art: A Source Book of Writings by Artists, Critics, and Philosophers.* 1958. Reprint. Baltimore: Johns Hopkins Press, 1960.

Lee, Charlotte I. *Oral Interpretation.* 4th ed. Boston: Houghton Mifflin, 1971.

Lewis, Richard Warrington Baldwin. *Trials of the Word: Essays in American Literature and the Humanistic Tradition.* New Haven: Yale University Press, 1965.

Lewis, Wyndham. *Time and Western Man.* London: Chatto and Windus, 1927.

Longinus, Cassius. *"Longinus" On the Sublime.* Trans. Benedict Einarson. Chicago: University of Chicago Press, 1945.

Lossky, Vladimir. *The Mystical Theology of the Eastern Church.* Trans. by members of the Fellowship of St. Alban and St. Sergius. Greenwood, South Carolina: Attic Press, 1968.

Lynch, William F. *Christ and Apollo: The Dimensions of the Literary Imagination.* 1960. Reprint. Notre Dame: University of Notre Dame Press, 1975.

————. *Images of Hope: Imagination as Healer of the Hopeless.* 1965. Reprint. Notre Dame: University of Notre Dame Press, 1974.

McGraw, Charles J. *Acting Is Believing.* 2nd ed. New York: Holt, Rinehart and Winston, 1966.

McLuhan, Marshall. *The Gutenberg Galaxy: The Making of Typographic Man.* Toronto: University of Toronto Press, 1962.

————. *Understanding Media: The Extensions of Man.* New York: McGraw-Hill, 1964.

Macquarrie, John. *Principles of Christian Theology.* New York: Scribner's, 1966.

Marcel, Gabriel. *Being and Having.* Trans. Katharine Farrer. London: Dacre Press, 1949.

————. *Creative Fidelity.* Trans. Robert Rosthal. New York: Farrar, Straus, 1964.

————. *Homo Viator: Introduction to a Metaphysic of Hope.* Trans. Emma Crawford. Chicago: Regnery, 1951.

_____. *The Influence of Psychic Phenomena on My Philosophy*. Glasgow: The University Press, Robert MacLehose and Co., 1956.

———. *The Mystery of Being*. Vol. I. *Reflection and Mystery*. Trans. G. S. Fraser. Chicago: Regnery, 1950.

———. *The Mystery of Being*. Vol. II. *Faith and Reality*. Trans. René Hague. London: Harvill, 1951.

———. *Presence and Immortality*. Trans. Michael A. Machado. Pittsburgh: Duquesne University Press, 1967.

———. *Tragic Wisdom and Beyond: Including Conversations Between Paul Ricoeur and Gabriel Marcel*. Evanston: Northwestern University Press, 1973.

Maritain, Jacques. *Art and Faith: Letters Between Jacques Maritain and Jean Cocteau*. Trans. John Coleman. New York: Philosophical Library, 1948.

———. *Art and Poetry*. Trans. E. de P. Matthews. New York: Philosophical Library, 1943.

———. *Art and Scholasticism: With Other Essays*. Trans. J. F. Scanlan. New York: Scribner's, 1947.

———. *Bergsonian Philosophy and Thomism*. Trans. Mabelle L. Andison. New York: Philosophical Library, 1955.

———. *Creative Intuition in Art and Poetry*. New York: Pantheon Books, 1953.

———. *On the Grace and Humanity of Jesus*. Trans. Joseph W. Evans. London: Burns and Oates; New York: Herder and Herder, 1969.

———. *The Responsibility of the Artist*. New York: Scribner's, 1960.

Maritain, Jacques and Raïssa. *The Situation of Poetry: Four Essays on the Relations Between Poetry, Mysticism, Magic, and Knowledge*. Trans. Marshall Suther. New York: Philosophical Library, 1955.

Mascall, Eric L. *Christ, the Christian, and the Church: A Study of the Incarnation and Its Consequences*. London: Longmans, Green and Co., 1946.

Maslow, Abraham H. *The Farther Reaches of Human Nature*. New York: Viking, 1971.

Mattingly, Alethea Smith, and Grimes, Wilma H. *Interpretation: Writer, Reader, Audience*. 2nd ed. Belmont, California: Wadsworth Publishing Co., 1970.

May, Rollo. *Love and Will*. New York: W. W. Norton and Co., 1969.

Mead, George Herbert. *Selected Writings*. Ed. Andrew J. Reck. New York: Bobbs-Merrill, 1964.

Merleau-Ponty, Maurice. *Signs*. Trans. Richard C. McCleary. Evanston: Northwestern University Press, 1964.

Michalson, Carl, ed. *Christianity and the Existentialists*. New York: Scribner's, 1956.

Miller, David L. *George Herbert Mead: Self, Language, and the World*. Austin: University of Texas Press, 1973.

Miller, Susan. *Icons*. New York: St. Martin's Press, 1972.

Milne, A. A. *The House at Pooh Corner*. 1928. Reprint. New York: Dell Publishing Co., 1956.

Minear, Paul. *Eyes of Faith: A Study in the Biblical Point of View*. London: Lutterworth Press, 1948.

Moore, Sonia. *The Stanislavski Method: The Professional Training of an Actor Digested from the Teaching of Konstantin S. Stanislavski*. New York: Viking, 1960.

Morgan, R. C. *God's Self-Emptied Servant: Also a Key to the Philippian Epistle*. 2nd ed. London: Morgan and Scott, 1907.

Mozley, John Kenneth. *The Doctrine of the Incarnation*. London: Geoffrey Bles, 1949.

————. *Some Tendencies in British Theology: From the Publication of Lux Mundi to the Present Day*. London: SPCK, 1951.

Nelson, Cary. *The Incarnate Word: Literature as Verbal Space*. Chicago: University of Illinois Press, 1973.

Ong, Walter J. *The Barbarian Within: And Other Fugitive Essays and Studies*. New York: Macmillan, 1962.

————. *The Presence of the Word: Some Prolegomena for Cultural and Religious History*. New Haven: Yale University Press, 1967.

Origen. *On First Principles*. Trans. G. W. Butterworth. New York: Harper and Row, Torchbooks Edition, 1966.

Orr, James. *The Christian View of God and the World as Centered in the Incarnation*. 8th ed. New York: Scribner's, 1907.

Otto, Rudolf. *The Idea of the Holy: An Inquiry into the Non-Rational Factor in the Idea of the Divine and Its Relation to the Rational*. 2nd ed. Trans. John W. Harvey. 1950. Reprint. New York: Oxford University Press, 1968.

The Oxford Dictionary of the Christian Church. Ed. F. L. Cross. 1958. Reprint. London: Oxford University Press, 1966.

Palmer, Richard E. *Hermeneutics: Interpretation Theory in Schleiermacher, Dilthey, Heidegger, and Gadamer*. Evanston: Northwestern University Press, 1969.

Pannenberg, Wolfhart. *The Idea of God and Human Freedom*. Trans. R. A. Wilson. Philadelphia: Westminster, 1973.

Pelikan, Jaroslav. *Fools for Christ: Essays on the True, the Good, and the Beautiful*. Philadelphia: Muhlenberg, 1955.

Pittinger, Wm. Norman. *Christ and Christian Faith: Some Presuppositions and Implications of the Incarnation*. New York: Round Table, 1941.

Plato. *The Dialogues of Plato*. Trans. Benjamin Jowett. Great Books of the Western World, 7. Ed. Robert Maynard Hutchins. Chicago: William Benton, Encyclopaedia Britannica, 1952.

Pole, David. *The Later Philosophy of Wittgenstein: A Short Introduction with an Epilogue on John Wisdom*. London: University of London, Athlone Press, 1958.

Rank, Otto. *Art and Artist: Creative Urge and Personality Development*. New York: Tudor Publishing Co., 1932.

Robinson, James M., and Cobb, John B., Jr., eds. *The New Hermeneutic*. New York: Harper and Row, 1964.

Robinson, J. Armitage. *Some Thoughts on the Incarnation with a Prefatory Letter to the Archbishop of Canterbury*. London: Longmans, Green and Co., 1903.

Roloff, Leland H. *The Perception and Evocation of Literature*. Glenview, Illinois: Scott, Foresman and Co., 1973.

Santayana, George. *The Sense of Beauty: Being the Outlines of Aesthetic Theory*. New York: Scribner's, 1898.

Sayers, Dorothy Leigh. *The Mind of the Maker*. New York: Harcourt, Brace and Co., 1941.

Schaer, Hans. *Religion and the Cure of Souls in Jung's Psychology*. Trans. R. F. C. Hull. New York: Pantheon Books, 1950.

Schilder, Paul. *The Image and Appearance of the Human Body: Studies in the Constructive Energies of the Psyche*. New York: International Universities Press, 1950.

Schleiermacher, Friedrich. *The Christian Faith: In Outline.* Trans. D. M. Baillie. Edinburgh: W. F. Henderson, 1922.

———. *Christmas Eve: Dialogue on the Incarnation.* Trans. Terrence N. Tice. Richmond: John Know, 1967.

Schlitzer, Albert. *Redemptive Incarnation: Sources and Their Theological Development in the Study of Christ.* 3rd ed. Notre Dame: University of Notre Dame Press, 1962.

Scott, Nathan A., Jr. *The Broken Center: Studies in the Theological Horizon of Modern Literature.* New Haven: Yale University Press, 1966.

———, ed. *The New Orpheus: Essays toward a Christian Poetic.* New York: Sheed and Ward, 1964.

Shumaker, Wayne. *Literature and the Irrational: A Study in Anthropological Backgrounds.* New York: Washington Square, 1966.

Siirala, Aarne. *Divine Humanness.* Trans. T. A. Kantonen. Philadelphia: Fortress, 1970.

Singer, June K. *Boundaries of the Soul: The Practice of Jung's Psychology.* New York: Doubleday, 1972.

Smyth, Frederic Hastings. *Manhood into God.* New York: Round Table, 1940.

Solovyov, Vladimir. "The Meaning of Love." *Russian Philosophy.* Vol. III. *Pre-Revolutionary Philosophy and Theology.* Ed. James M. Edie et al. 1965. Reprint. Chicago: Quadrangle Books, 1969.

Sontag, Susan. "Against Interpretation." In *Literary Criticism: An Introductory Reader,* ed. Lionel Trilling. New York: Holt, Rinehart and Winston, 1970.

Stanislavski, Constantin. *An Actor Prepares.* Trans. Elizabeth Reynolds Hapgood. New York: Theatre Arts Books, 1936.

———. *Building a Character.* Trans. Elizabeth Reynolds Hapgood. New York: Theatre Arts Books, 1949.

———. *Stanislavski's Legacy: A Collection of Comments on a Variety of Aspects of an Actor's Art and Life.* Trans. Elizabeth Reynolds Hapgood. New York: Theatre Arts Books, 1968.

Teilhard de Chardin, Pierre. *Activation of Energy.* Trans. René Hague. New York: Harcourt Brace Jovanovich, 1971.

———. *The Divine Milieu: An Essay on the Interior Life.* Trans. Alex Dru et al. New York: Harper and Row, Torchbooks Edition, 1960.

———. *Human Energy.* Trans. J. M. Cohen. New York: Harcourt Brace Jovanovich, 1969.

———. *Man's Place in Nature.* Trans. René Hague. New York: Harper and Row, 1966.

Thass-Thienemann, Theodore. *Symbolic Behavior.* New York: Washington Square, 1968.

Thomasius, Gottfried. "Christ's Person and Work." In *God and Incarnation: In Mid-Nineteenth Century German Theology,* ed. and trans. Claude Welch. New York: Oxford University Press, 1965.

Thornton, Lionel S. *The Incarnate Lord: An Essay Concerning the Doctrine of the Incarnation in Its Relation to Organic Conceptions.* London: Longmans, Green and Co., 1928.

Tillich, Paul. *The Courage to Be.* New Haven: Yale University Press, 1952.

———. *Dynamics of Faith.* New York: Harper and Brothers, 1956–1957.

———. *The Eternal Now.* New York: Scribner's, 1963.

————. *The New Being.* New York: Scribner's, 1955.

Trachtenberg, Joshua. *Jewish Magic and Superstition: A Study in Folk Religion.* New York: Behrman's Jewish Book House, 1939.

Trilling, Lionel. *The Liberal Imagination: Essays on Literature and Society.* New York: Doubleday, Anchor Books, 1957.

Ulanov, Ann Belford. *The Feminine: In Jungian Psychology and in Christian Theology.* Evanston: Northwestern University Press, 1971.

Underhill, Evelyn. *Jacapone da Todi: Poet and Mystic—1228–1306: A Spiritual Biography.* London: J. M. Dent and Sons, 1919.

Veilleux, Jeré. *Oral Interpretation: The Re-creation of Literature.* New York: Harper and Row, 1967.

Vivas, Eliseo. *The Artistic Transaction and Essays on Theory of Literature.* Columbus: Ohio State University Press, 1963.

————. *Creation and Discovery.* New York: Noonday, 1955.

Vogel, Arthur A. *Body Theology: God's Presence in Man's World.* New York: Harper and Row, 1973.

————. *The Christian Person.* New York: Seabury, 1963.

Vygotsky, Lev Semenovich. *The Psychology of Art.* Trans. Scripta Technica. Cambridge, Massachusetts: Massachusetts Institute of Technology Press, 1971.

Walker, James Lynwood. *Body and Soul: Gestalt Therapy and Religious Experience.* Nashville: Abingdon, 1971.

Watson, Herbert A. *The Incarnation and Personality.* New York: Macmillan, 1920.

Whalley, George. *Poetic Process.* Cleveland: World Publishing Co., Meridian Books, 1967.

Wheelwright, Philip. *The Burning Fountain: A Study in the Language of Symbolism.* 1954. Reprint. Bloomington: Indiana University Press, 1959.

————. *Metaphor and Reality.* 1962. Reprint. Bloomington: Indiana University Press, 1967.

White, Victor. *God and the Unconscious.* 1952. Reprint. Cleveland: World Publishing Co., Meridian Books, 1965.

Williams, Charles. *Descent into Hell.* London: Faber and Faber, 1949.

————. *Selected Writings.* Ed. Anne Ridler. London: Oxford University Press, 1961.

Wingren, Gustaf. *The Living Word: A Theological Study of Preaching and the Church.* Philadelphia: Muhlenberg, 1960.

————. *Man and the Incarnation: A Study in the Biblical Theology of Irenaeus.* Trans. Ross MacKenzie. London: Oliver and Boyd, 1954.

Wittgenstein, Ludwig. *Philosophical Investigations.* 3rd ed. Trans. G. E. M. Anscombe. Oxford: Basil Blackwell, 1968.

Wordsworth, William. "Preface to the Second Edition of Lyrical Ballads." In *The Norton Anthology of English Literature.* Vol. II. 2nd ed. Ed. M. H. Abrams et al. New York: W. W. Norton, 1968.

Articles

Abel, Leslie Gillian, and Post, Robert M. "Towards a Poor Readers Theatre." *Quarterly Journal of Speech,* 59, no. 4 (December, 1973), 436–442.

Bacon, Wallace A. "The Dangerous Shores: From Elocution to Interpretation."
    Quarterly Journal of Speech, 46, no. 2 (April, 1960), 148–152.
Dixon, John W., Jr. "Prolegomena to a Christian Erotics." *Christian Scholar,* 50, no.
    1 (spring, 1967), 53–65.
Geiger, Don. "The Oral Interpreter as Creator." *The Speech Teacher,* 3 (1954),
    269–277.
————. "Poetic Realizing as Knowing." *Quarterly Journal of Speech,* 59, no. 3 (Octo-
    ber, 1973), 311–318.
Hallman, Ralph J. "Aesthetic Motivation in the Creative Arts." *The Journal of
    Aesthetics and Art Criticism,* 23 (summer, 1965), 453–459.
Harder, Helmut G., and Stevenson, W. Taylor. "The Continuity of History and
    Faith in the Theology of Wolfhart Pannenberg: Toward an Erotics of History."
    Reprinted for private circulation from *Journal of Religion,* 51, no. 1 (January,
    1971), 34–56.
Harrell, Maila; Bowers, John Waite; and Bacal, Jeffrey P. "Another Stab at
    'Meaning': Concreteness, Iconicity, and Conventionality." *Speech Monographs,*
    40, no. 5 (August, 1973), 199–207.
Jung, C. G. "From The Letters of C. G. Jung . . . ." *Transformation: The Bulletin of
    the Analytical Psychology Club of Chicago,* 4, no. 1 (September, 1973), 5.
Lottman, Herbert R. "Work in Progress: Voznesensky Magic." *Intellectual Digest,* 4,
    no. 3 (November, 1973), 8–12.
Merton, Thomas. *The Asian Journal of Thomas Merton. Intellectual Digest,* 4, no. 3
    (November, 1973), 57–64.
Ornstein, Robert E. "Intuition." *Intellectual Digest,* 4, no. 3 (November, 1973),
    25–32.
Sittler, Joseph, Jr. "A Theology for Earth." *The Christian Scholar,* 37 (1954),
    367–374.
Tillich, Paul. "Psychoanalysis, Existentialism, and Theology." *Pastoral Psychology*
    (October, 1958), 9–17.
Vernon, John. "Poetry and the Body." *American Review,* 16 (February, 1973),
    145–172.
Walstead, John. "Window Open into Heaven: Iconography Related to God's
    Creative Nature." *The Oregon Episcopal Churchman* (April, 1973), 5.

Unpublished Works

Bacon, Wallace A. "Reverberation: An Ontological View of Interpretation." An
    unpublished typescript circulated for teaching purposes in the Department of
    Interpretation, Northwestern University, Evanston, Illinois.
Henning, W. Keith. "A Semantic for Oral Interpretation: A Wheelwrightean
    Perspective." Ph.D. dissertation, University of Southern California, Los
    Angeles, California, 1973.
Jonas, Hans. "Heidegger and Theology." Opening address for the Consultation
    of the Problem of Non-Objectifying Thinking and Speaking in Contemporary
    Theology, n.d.
Roloff, Leland H. "A Critical Study of Contemporary Aesthetic Theories and
    Precepts Contributing to an Aesthetic for Oral Interpretation." Ph.D. disserta-
    tion, University of Southern California, Los Angeles, California, 1968.

Salper, Donald. "A Study of an Oral Approach to the Appreciation of Poetry."
Ph.D. dissertation, University of Minnesota, 1964.

Secondary Sources

Books

Alexander, Hubert. *Meaning in Language.* Palo Alto: Scott, Foresman and Co.,
1969.

Allport, Gordon W., and Vernon, Philip E. *Studies in Expressive Movement.* New
York: Macmillan, 1933.

Aristotle. *Nichomachean Ethics.* Trans. W. D. Ross. New York: Random House,
1941.

Armstrong, Chloe, and Brandes, Paul S. *The Oral Interpretation of Literature.* New
York: McGraw-Hill, 1963.

Beardsley, Monroe. *Aesthetics from Classical Greece to the Present.* New York: Macmillan, 1966.

Beckerman, Barnard. *Dynamics of Drama.* New York: Alfred A. Knopf, 1970.

Betti, Emilio. *Teoria generale della interpretazione.* 2 vols. Milan: Giuffré, 1955.

Blake, R. R., and Ramsey, G. V., eds. *Perception: An Approach to Personality.* New
York: Ronald, 1951.

Dawson, Christopher. *Progress and Religion.* London: Murray, 1921.

Drew, Elizabeth. *T. S. Eliot: The Design of His Poetry.* New York: Scribner's, 1949.

Ehrenzweig, Anton. *The Hidden Order of Art.* Berkeley: University of California
Press, 1967.

Eliot, T. S. *From Poe to Valéry.* New York: Harcourt, Brace and Co., 1948.

Fiedler, Konrad. *Von Wesen der Kunst: Auswahl ans seiner Schriften.* Munich: R.
Piper, 1942.

Fonseka, Lionel de. *On the Truth of Decorative Art: A Dialogue Between an Oriental and
an Occidental.* London: Greening and Co., 1912.

Gadamer, Hans-Georg. *Wahrheit und Methode: Grundzuge einer philosophischen Hermeneutik.* 2nd ed. Tübingen: J. C. B. Mohr, 1965.

Gill, Eric. "The Priesthood of Craftsmanship." In *Artists on Art,* ed. and trans.
Robert J. Goldwater. New York: Pantheon Books, 1945.

Gotshalk, D. W. *Art and the Social Order.* Chicago: University of Chicago Press,
1947.

Growtowski, Jerzy. *Towards a Poor Theatre.* Trans. T. K. Wiewiorowski. New York:
Simon and Schuster, 1968.

Havelka, Jaroslav. *The Nature of the Creative Process in Art: A Psychological Study.* The
Hague: Martinus Nijhoff, 1968.

Heard, Gerald. *Social Substance of Religion.* London: Allen and Unwin, 1931.

Hester, Marcus B. *The Meaning of Poetic Metaphor.* New York: Humanities Press,
1967.

Jenkins, Iredell. *Art and the Human Enterprise.* Cambridge, Massachusetts: Harvard
University Press, 1958.

Jung, C. G. *Mysterium Coniunctionis.* Collected Works 14. Trans. R. F. C. Hull.
London: Routledge and Kegan Paul, 1963.

———. *Psychology and Religion: West and East.* Trans. R. F. C. Hull. London: n.c.,
1958.

Koestler, Arthur. *Dialogue with Death.* New York: Macmillan, 1942.

Krieger, Murray. *The Tragic Vision.* New York: Holt, Rinehart and Winston, 1960.

Mai-Mai Sze. *The Tao of Painting with "The Mustard Seed Garden Manual."* New York: Pantheon Books, 1956.

Mead, Hunter. *An Introduction to Aesthetics.* New York: Ronald, 1952.

Ogden, Robert M. *The Psychology of Art.* New York: Scribner's, 1938.

Pepper, Stephen C. *Aesthetic Quality: A Contextualistic Theory of Beauty.* New York: Scribner's, 1937.

Polanyi, Michael. *The Tacit Dimension.* London: Routledge and Kegan Paul, 1967.

Rader, Melvin. *A Modern Book of Esthetics.* 3rd ed. New York: Holt, Rinehart and Winston, 1940.

Reid, Louis A. *A Study in Aesthetics.* New York: Macmillan, 1931.

Reps, Paul, comp. *Zen Flesh, Zen Bones: A Collection of Zen and Pre-Zen Writings.* New York: Doubleday, Anchor Books, 1961.

Rosenblatt, Louise M. *Literature as Exploration.* New York: Noble and Noble, 1968.

Rowley, George. "Simplicity, Emptiness, and Suggestion." In *Principles of Chinese Painting.* Princeton: Princeton University Press, 1947.

Sapir, Edward. *Language.* New York: Harcourt, Brace and Co., 1921.

Schleiermacher, Friedrich. *Hermeneutik.* Ed. Heinz Kimmerle. Heidelberg: Carl Winter, Universitatsverlag, 1959.

Silone, Ignacio. *The Seed Beneath the Snow.* Trans. F. Frenaye. New York: Harper and Brothers, 1942.

Sloan, Thomas O. "An Overview: Philosophy, Objectives, Content." In *The Communicative Arts and Sciences of Speech,* ed. Keith Brooks. Columbus: Charles Merrill, 1967.

Tejera, Victorino. *Art and Human Intelligence.* New York: Appleton-Century-Crofts, 1965.

Tresmontant, Claude. *Essai sur la pensée biblique.* Paris: Les éditions du Cerg, 1953.

Walsh, Dorothy. *Literature and Knowledge.* Middletown, Connecticut: Wesleyan University Press, 1969.

Weiss, Paul. *Nine Basic Arts.* Carbondale: Southern Illinois University Press, 1961.

————. *The World of Art.* Carbondale: Southern Illinois University Press, 1961.

Werfel, Franz. *Between Heaven and Earth.* New York: Philosophical Library, 1944.

Werner, Heinz. *On Expression in Language.* Worcester, Massachusetts: Clark University Press, 1955.

Whitehead, Alfred North. *The Aims of Education and Other Essays.* New York: Macmillan, 1929.

Wolff, Charlotte. *A Psychology of Gesture.* 2nd ed. London: Methuen and Co., 1948.

Articles

Barbara, Dominick A. "Listening to the Essence of Things." *The Southern Speech Journal,* 25 (Winter, 1959), 134–137.

Kondo, Akihisa. "Zen in Psychotherapy: The Virtue of Sitting." *The Chicago Review,* 12, no. 2 (1958).

Lund, Frederick H., and Anastasi, Anna. "An Interpretation of Aesthetic Experience." *The American Journal of Psychology,* 40 (July, 1928), 434–448.

Merleau-Ponty, Maurice. "L'oeil et l'esprit." *Les temps moderne,* 27, nos. 184–185 (July–August, 1960).

Pannenberg, Wolfhart. "The God of Hope." *Cross Currents,* 18, no. 3 (Summer, 1968), 284–295.

Sloan, Thomas O. "Oral Interpretation in the Ages Before Sheridan and Walker." *Western Speech,* 35 (Summer, 1961).

Stallknecht, Newton P. "Awareness of Actuality in the Esthetic Experience." *Journal of Psychology,* 32 (June 6, 1935), 323–324.

index